Advance Praise for *Behavioral Health*

"Dr. Len Sperry describes the future of health care in his groundbreaking *Behavioral Health*. As a physician and major contributor to counselor education, Dr. Sperry has the breadth of professional experience to offer a highly integrative model for emerging health care practice, which takes into account individual personality factors, family dynamics, multicultural influences, and spiritual dimensions. Len masterfully weaves together perspectives from different systemic levels to construct meaningful case conceptualization, a domain in which he is widely recognized as an expert. He offers rich case studies and treatment recommendations for chronic illnesses affecting many family lives including arthritis, asthma, cardiac disease, and diabetes. Extending the basic approach of combined medication and psychotherapy, Dr. Sperry attends to issues such as illness perspectives and motivational interviewing to improve treatment compliance and quality of family life. This book will be an excellent resource for clinicians from counseling, marriage, and family therapy, psychology, and other behavioral health care disciplines. *Behavioral Health* will become a standard reference for practitioners in an emerging 21st century specialization."

—**Stephen Southern**, PhD, Professor and Chair, Psychology and
Counseling Department, Mississippi College

"What makes reading a Len Sperry book so enjoyable is that you are in the hands of a master teacher who can show you exactly what to do to be a more effective mental health practitioner. In *Behavioral Health: Integrating Individual and Family Interventions in the Treatment of Medical Conditions*, Sperry brings together his years of experience in medicine, psychology, family therapy, and counselor education to produce the most practical, 'how to,' biopsychosocial approach to behavioral health available."

—**Brian A. Gerrard**, PhD, Associate Professor, Counseling
Psychology Department, and Executive Director, Center for Child
and Family Development, University of San Francisco, California

"Integrated behavioral health has its roots in the interdisciplinary field of behavioral medicine, which applies behavioral and other psychological principles in the treatment of medical conditions and the prevention of chronic illness. Dr. Sperry's approach adds the biopsychosocial model and family therapy interventions to individual psychological interventions. The approach he describes, advocates, and illustrates is supported by documented evidence proving its effectiveness and efficacy while at the same time reducing cost. Just look at the table of contents and you will want to read this book!"

—**S. Richard Sauber**, PhD, Forensic Family
and Clinical Psychologist, and Editor-in-Chief,
American Journal of Family Therapy

"The more individual, couple, and family therapists enter in the real world of primary health care, the more they will need to practice with emotionally and physically impaired individuals and their families. Furthermore, they will need to interact continually with other practitioners whose major concerns for their patients may be physical. However, these professionals will need mental health professionals to deal with the inevitable emotional and relational aspects of any physical disorder. Hence, the days of solo practice for both primary care physicians and mental health professionals are slowly giving way to integrated group and team work. No single professional in physical and mental health can continue to practice on her or his own. In this ground-breaking volume, Len Sperry has achieved the apex of his productive and original publishing career. No physical or mental health professional can continue to practice without this important, pioneering contribution in this century."

—**Luciano L'Abate**, PhD, ABPP, Professor Emeritus of
Psychology, Georgia State University

With healthcare reform taking center stage, our nation is increasingly focusing on integrating behavioral and physical health care endeavors and on collaborative family health care. Thus, Sperry's book *Behavioral Health: Integrating Individual and Family Interventions in the Treatment of Medical Conditions* is extremely timely and much needed. This volume offers valuable, up-to-date commentaries related to conceptualizing integrated behavioral health, utilizing this framework to guide the treatment of common medical problems, and incorporating this approach in the training of competent behavioral health care professionals. Sperry skillfully utilizes current scholarship to guide his recommendations for practical application. This is a must-read for anyone providing integrative behavioral health care services."

—**Nadine J. Kaslow**, PhD, ABPP, Emory University School of Medicine, Georgia, and 2014 President, American Psychological Association

"Our healthcare system is plagued by symptom-based models of care that rely on ineffective applications of medications or manualized treatments. Dr. Sperry's new book is a welcome antidote in recognizing the causal psychopathology underlying patient physical symptoms in primary care. He guides the reader through integrated care approaches that address individual personality, defenses and coping styles, illness perceptions, and couple and family dynamics that are essential for effective and efficient treatment. Dr. Sperry outlines a model that is systematic and fits the new model of brief interventions designed to improve outcome and reduce cost of care, including many examples of common medical conditions and related psychopathology. These elements are sorely lacking in most integrated treatment models and this [book] should be required reading for novice and expert alike."

—**Ronald R. O'Donnell**, PhD, Director, The Nicholas A. Cummings Doctor of Behavioral Health program, Arizona State University

"As a psychologist and physician, Dr. Sperry has a unique perspective on integrative health care. This book will be a valuable resource for those wanting to know more about these changes and how to implement them into practice."

—**James H. Bray**, PhD, 2009 President, American Psychological Association, and Editor, Primary Care Psychology

"Health care in the U.S. is in crisis, in large part due to the failure to integrate care for medical and psychological problems, and to offer healthcare for the whole person. Hence, Dr. Sperry's newest book is very timely, as it provides an excellent guide to providing integrated care for common chronic illnesses. This book is essential reading for both for both graduate students and professionals in mental health."

—**Ronald F. Levant**, EdD, ABPP, Co-Editor, *A New Psychology of Men;* 2005 President, American Psychological Association, and Professor, The University of Akron, Ohio

"Len Sperry's newest book, *Behavioral Health: Integrating Individual and Family Interventions in the Treatment of Medical Conditions*, is a roadmap for the paradigm shift that must occur in the health professions. For too long, the disciplines associated with medicine and the helping professions have remained separated in applied knowledge, practice, and training. Sperry's integrative approach fulfills the promise of a biopsychosocial approach to medicine by connecting the various disciplines in a collaborative/cooperative process that reduces costs while still improving the overall health of clients. Sperry's book is a complete operation manual for the implementation of integrated behavioral health from a multi-perspective conceptualization to applications for specified medical conditions to competency-based training. It is all here: the roadmap to a very necessary future is perfectly laid out."

—**James Robert Bitter**, EdD, NCC, MFC, Professor of
Counseling and Human Services, East Tennessee State University

"Dr. Sperry has done it again. In this insightful and practical book, he has provided behavioral health clinicians and trainees with the conceptual frameworks, competencies, and interventions to guide their work with individuals, couples, and families coping with acute and chronic illness. This book provides a wealth of clinical tools, supported by a solid conceptual and theoretical foundation. The numerous case examples bring into bold relief the principles and concepts discussed in this valuable book, which belongs in the library of all systemically-oriented behavioral health clinicians."

—**Mark B. White**, PhD, Associate Professor of Medical Family
Therapy & Marriage and Family Therapy, East Carolina University

"Dr. Sperry has once again produced an essential tool which should be on the active bookshelf of every health care provider. His integrative treatment model is the answer to what many have asked for as an integrated approach to health care. This model will allow any health care provider to greatly expand his or her diagnostic and treatment abilities and options."

—**Richard H. Cox**, MD, PhD, Adjunct Professor, Department of
Psychiatry & Behavioral Science, Duke University Medical School

BEHAVIORAL HEALTH

The emergence of behavioral health, how it is practiced, and how it will be practiced is at the heart of this book. Len Sperry, a prominent clinician and author, is one of the first to describe and advocate for an approach to health care that can significantly increase its efficacy and efficiency and reduce costs for patients with chronic medical conditions. He does so by addressing both core theoretical constructs and core practice competencies to help readers comfortably provide effective integrated psychosocial treatment to individuals and families.

His book is split into three parts. The first provides an overview of the key family and personality dynamics and how medical conditions impact individual and family members throughout the family life cycle. Important considerations in this part include ethical and clinical issues, spiritual considerations, treatment non-compliance, motivational interviewing, and case conceptualization. Of particular importance is Dr. Sperry's description of four illness stages, which reflect patients' psychosocial adjustment to their chronic illnesses. The second part consists of seven chapters dedicated to common medical conditions, followed by the last part that addresses integrated behavioral health competency and competency-based training.

Behavioral health clinicians and trainees in various behavioral health specialties, including individual psychotherapists and family therapists, will find this practical book of interest and value to their work. No matter their experience, all readers will walk away from this book with the knowledge necessary to increase motivation, deal with non-compliance issues, and tailor therapeutic change, while increasing treatment efficacy and efficiency with their patients.

Len Sperry, MD, PhD, is Professor of Mental Health Counseling at Florida Atlantic University, and Clinical Professor of Psychiatry and Behavioral Medicine at the Medical College of Wisconsin where, for several years, he held appointments as a tenured full professor in the Departments of Psychiatry, Preventive Medicine, and Family and Community Medicine, and is board certified in Psychiatry and in Preventive Medicine. He has more than 600 publications, including 60 professional books. He is also a member of 13 book and journal editorial boards.

THE FAMILY THERAPY AND COUNSELING SERIES

SERIES EDITOR
JON CARLSON, Psy.D., Ed.D.

Kit S. Ng
*Global Perspectives in Family Therapy:
Development, Practice, Trends*

Phyllis Erdman and Tom Caffery
*Attachment and Family Systems: Conceptual,
Empirical, and Therapeutic Relatedness*

Wes Crenshaw
*Treating Families and Children in the Child
Protective System*

Len Sperry
*Assessment of Couples and Families:
Contemporary and Cutting-Edge Strategies*

Robert L. Smith and R. Esteban Montilla
*Counseling and Family Therapy with Latino
Populations: Strategies that Work*

Catherine Ford Sori
*Engaging Children in Family Therapy:
Creative Approaches to Integrating Theory
and Research in Clinical Practice*

Paul R. Peluso
*Infidelity: A Practitioner's Guide to Working
with Couples in Crisis*

Jill D. Onedera
*The Role of Religion in Marriage and Family
Counseling*

Christine Kerr, Janice Hoshino, Judith
Sutherland, Sharyl Parashak,
and Linda McCarley
Family Art Therapy

Debra D. Castaldo
*Divorced Without Children: Solution
Focused Therapy With Women at Midlife*

Phyllis Erdman and Kok-Mun Ng
*Attachment: Expanding the Cultural
Connections*

Jon Carlson and Len Sperry
*Recovering Intimacy in Love Relationships: A
Clinician's Guide*

Adam Zagelbaum and Jon Carlson
*Working with Immigrant Families: A
Practical Guide for Counselors*

Shea M. Dunham, Shannon B. Dermer,
and Jon Carlson
*Poisonous Parenting: Toxic Relationships
Between Parents and Their Adult Children*

David K. Carson and Montserrat Casado-
Kehoe
*Case Studies in Couples Therapy: Theory-
Based Approaches*

Bret A. Moore
Handbook of Counseling Military Couples

THE FAMILY THERAPY AND COUNSELING SERIES

SERIES EDITOR
JON CARLSON, Psy.D., Ed.D.

Len Sperry
Family Assessment: Contemporary and Cutting-Edge Strategies, 2nd ed.

Patricia A. Robey, Robert E. Wubbolding, and Jon Carlson
Contemporary Issues in Couples Counseling: A Choice Theory and Reality Therapy Approach

Paul R. Peluso, Richard E. Watts, and Mindy Parsons
Changing Aging, Changing Family Therapy: Practicing With 21st Century Realities

Dennis A. Bagarozzi
Couples in Collusion: Short-Term, Assessment-Based Strategies for Helping Couples Disarm Their Defenses

Katherine M. Helm and Jon Carlson
Love, Intimacy, and the African American Couple

Judith V. Jordan and Jon Carlson
Creating Connection: A Relational-Cultural Approach with Couples

Len Sperry
Behavioral Health: Integrating Individual and Family Interventions in the Treatment of Medical Conditions

BEHAVIORAL HEALTH

Integrating Individual and Family Interventions
in the Treatment of Medical Conditions

Len Sperry

NEW YORK AND LONDON

First published 2014
by Routledge
711 Third Avenue, New York, NY 10017

Simultaneously published in the UK
by Routledge
27 Church Road, Hove, East Sussex BN3 2FA

Routledge is an imprint of the Taylor & Francis Group, an informa business

© 2014 Taylor & Francis

The right of Len Sperry to be identified as author of this work has been asserted by him in accordance with sections 77 and 78 of the Copyright, Designs and Patents Act 1988.

Library of Congress Cataloging in Publication Data
Behavioral health : integrating individual and family interventions in the treatment
  of medical conditions / authored by Len Sperry
  p.cm.
  Includes bibliographical references and index.
  1. Mental health services. 2. Family psychotherapy. 3. Integrated delivery of health care
  I. Sperry, Len.
  RA790.5 .S66 2013
  616.89/156
  2013005093

ISBN: 978-0-415-63735-0 (hbk)
ISBN: 978-0-415-63736-7 (pbk)
ISBN: 978-0-203-08463-2 (ebk)

Typeset in Garamond
by EvS Communication Networx, Inc.

Printed and bound in the United States of America by Sheridan Books, Inc. (a Sheridan Group Compa

CONTENTS

SERIES EDITOR'S FOREWORD

It is more important to know what sort of person has a disease than to know what sort of disease a person has.

(Hippocrates)

Over the past 2 years I have been dealing with several chronic illnesses including heart disease and cancer. These illnesses have changed our family lifestyle necessitating long hospital stays and at times daily visits to labs for medical testing or appointments with the various specialists providing my care. I would not be writing this Preface if it were not for family, friends, and an understanding employer.

I have recently noticed that most (over half) of my present clients are involved with major medical issues as well as diagnosable mental illness and relationship issues. The changing demographics of today's treatment population require different conceptualizations and interventions. However, few clinicians have had any training in treating the various problems that accompany health issues.

Len Sperry has created an important book that clearly shows how to integrate behavioral and medical treatment. Sperry's training as a medical doctor and as a clinical psychologist/family therapist makes him the ideal resource for designing a model for providing treatment in the new health care landscape. We will no longer be able to treat problems such as depression or anxiety without working closely with other health care personnel who are treating other aspects of the patient's life and lifestyle. Therapists will need to work closely with all of the various medical personnel currently treating the client. Therapists will need to go to where health care is being provided, such as primary care and integrative care facilities, tertiary care hospitals, rehabilitation centers, nursing homes, outpatient surgery centers, and substance abuse treatment centers.

In addition to working in venues that differ significantly from the private practice suite, the therapist will need to provide care and treatment to a wide variety of client populations including pediatric, geriatric, acute and chronically ill, those being treating for medical or mental health conditions, as well as those from diverse cultures and socioeconomic groups. Therapists will be sought for their special expertise in communication, behavioral issues, patient decision making, and a wide spectrum of problems and treatment settings. This is a world where therapists have limited experience and have not had formal training.

It because of these conditions and changes in the health care climate that Len Sperry's new book *Behavioral Health: Integrating Individual and Family Interventions in the Treatment of Medical Conditions* will be mandatory reading for practicing therapists and those in training. This volume provides the necessary ingredients for a therapist to be successful in an integrated health practice. Dr. Sperry provides material on the core theoretical constructs as well as necessary practice competencies for both individual and family work. In addition to various medical and psychological problems he covers areas such as family dynamics, personality dynamics, illness perceptions, and the stages of chronic illness. He elaborates on the various ethical and spiritual considerations at issue when working in an integrated behavioral health fashion. Sperry also includes many practical examples as well as entire chapters on how to work with the treatment of some of the more common medical conditions. His ideas on compliance, case conceptualization, and cultural sensitivity offer the insight needed to effectively operate in a climate of growing accountability. I was most impressed with his chapter on combining treatment when both medication and psychotherapy are necessitated.

When reading this book I was reminded of the World Health Organization's long-standing definition: "Health is a state of complete physical, mental and social well-being, and not merely the absence of disease or infirmity." Future professionals will finally be providing integrated medical and mental care facilitating healthy lives.

Jon Carlson, PsyD, EdD, ABPP
Series Editor

FOREWORD

It is well known to everyone who has had even the most superficial contact with any media in the past decade that the United States is in a health care crisis. This is not a crisis of just one dimension—for example, cost—but rather it is a crisis involving several problematic aspects of the way care is being delivered. Cost is certainly one of the problems; in 1960 health care consumed only 5% of GDP and currently it takes about 17% of a much larger GDP and the rate of increase is still escalating (Cummings & O'Donohue, 2011). But there are other documented problems: current service delivery is not consumer centric, it is not very transparent; it is not safe; it does not focus on health and prevention but rather on illness; access to it is problematic; it does not capture and use information efficiently; it is oriented toward acute care and not chronic care; it is really not prepared to deal with demographic shifts like the growing preponderance of the elderly; it is not evidence based and so on. Thus, we have a knotty, complex problem that is of fundamental importance—a lack of affordable, high quality health care can be deadly or at a minimum cause much unnecessary pain. It is even responsible for the majority of bankruptcies as well as a lack of international competitiveness for our products. And who would think there is reason for optimism because the political class is on the front lines of trying to solve the problem?

Thus, clearly we need sound innovations—often fairly radical and what are known as disruptive innovations. Clearly we do not need innovation for innovation's sake. If we are to make progress on this problem we need innovations that are well thought out, tested, and shown to have a beneficial effect on health care delivery. And part of the bottom line is that these innovations have to be clinically astute—for that is where the proverbial rubber meets the road. We can fall in love with solutions from technology such as Electronic Health Records (EHRs)—and these certainly have a role to play—but these technology solutions are not the entire answer, and as anyone who has experienced a tech implementation can tell you, they are a wonderful laboratory for someone who wants to study Murphy's Law.

Integrated care has been proposed as a partial solution to these problems (O'Donohue, Cummings, Cucciarre, Cummings, & Runyan, 2006). The theory is that integrated care can reduce overall medical costs by intervening in the behavioral health pathways to medical presentations (Cummings & O'Donohue, 2011). Integrated care can also improve patient safety by more comprehensively and accurately diagnosing the full range of the patient's problems. It can increase access by one stop shopping, in which patients have access to both physical and behavioral health care in their primary care physician's office. It can use integrated EHRs that even contain decision support tools that help clinicians on the integrated team see and treat patients holistically. It can better address chronic conditions such as diabetes as well as treatment compliance with these conditions. It is not a panacea, but studies have shown that it has effectively addressed some of the key dimensions of the health care crisis (Cummings & O'Donohue, 2011; James & O'Donohue, 2008).

Dr. Len Sperry has a very distinguished career of high quality scholarly work related to key aspects of this problem. He has published seminal works on chronic illness, personality disorders, treatment outcomes, health promotion, disability management, cognitive behavior therapy, clinical competence and proficiency, as well as integrated care. He is in a unique position as both a physician and a psychologist to provide an integrative perspective, and that is exactly what he does in this important book.

Others have made the general case for integrated care at the system level. However, there has been a relative paucity of books providing high quality information to clinicians on how to perform well *clinically* in an integrated setting. This book admirably fills this gap. And, as mentioned previously, enhancing these clinical contacts is certainly a bottom line. If we redesign the delivery system but have little impact on how providers and patients interact—we will see only small improvements at best. Dr. Sperry realizes this and offers a number of important insights and clinical pathways that will result in improved care. After quickly reviewing the historical case for integrated care as well as placing it in the context of modern health care reform, Dr. Sperry moves to present a number of helpful paradigms for the integrated care clinician. Typically if one reads a case presented by a clinician there is much information about physical conditions such as results from blood panels, physical diagnoses such as diabetes, and treatments that intervene on this level such as medications, but there is little to no information about the person as a psychological being. The reverse is true if one reads a case description written by a psychologist: there is much information about mental status and psychological history, as well as DSM diagnoses, but there is little medical information about the person. Dr. Sperry corrects these imbalances in case after case and depicts a patient in a holistic, balanced, biopsychosocial manner. This is a new paradigm and one that Dr. Sperry instantiates very well.

He covers topics that have had too little attention in the integrated care literature. How does this patient's past and current family life affect her or his presentation? How do the individual's personality and illness perceptions affect her or his presentation? How do we understand the patient in terms of critical dimensions such as stages of chronic illness, spiritual life, and treatment compliance? Finally, he offers very valuable and much needed insights into the roles of motivational interviewing, case conceptualization, combined treatments, and overall dimensions of therapeutic competence. These topics have not received the attention they deserve and Dr. Sperry's book and his unique clinical acumen fill this gap. He presents many hypotheses that ought also to be noted by researchers so their research can be clinically relevant. As if this is not enough, he achieves this in an engaging writing style that is practical and illustrates his points with numerous case studies of integrated care. This is an important book and a necessary one for an accomplished therapist who wishes to function in integrated care.

William O'Donohue, Ph.D.
University of Nevada, Reno

References

Cummings, N., & O'Donohue, W. (Eds.). (2011). *Understanding the behavioral health care crisis.* New York: Routledge.

Cummings, N. A., O'Donohue, W., & Ferguson, K. (Eds.). (2002). *The impact of medical cost offset on practice and research: Making it work for you.* Reno, NV: Context Press.

James, L., & O'Donohue, W. (Eds.). (2008). *The primary care toolkit: Tools for behavioral medicine.* New York: Springer.

O'Donohue, W., Cummings, N., Cucciarre, M., Cummings, J., & Runyan, C. N. (2006). *Integrated behavioral health care: A guide for effective action.* New York: Prometheus.

PREFACE

Imagine that you are asked to evaluate and plan treatment for these individuals:

> Allison is a 45-year-old teacher who has been treated for chronic recurrent bouts of depression from which she achieved only partial relief. Despite medication and 4 years of biweekly therapy sessions, her therapist has convinced her that she has reached her best level of "adjustment." But her symptoms have worsened in the past month and she is looking for another therapist.

> Jesse is a 28-year-old married Haitian American with a 3-year history of untreated depression that has worsened in the past two months. His employee assistance program refers him for evaluation and treatment because of increased absences and decreased job performance.

How would you conceptualize these cases? Later in this Preface, integrated behavioral health case conceptualizations are provided for both of these cases.

This is a book about integrated behavioral health and integrated behavioral health practice. It is one of the first books to both describe and advocate for an approach to health care that can significantly increase the effectiveness and efficacy of health care and reduce health care costs with patients experiencing chronic medical conditions. These outcomes are particularly important today because chronic medical conditions are threatening to overwhelm and undermine our current health care system.

Statistics on chronic medical conditions are daunting: 75% of adults over age 65 have one or more chronic illnesses, 70% of all deaths are attributed to these conditions, and 50% of Americans constantly experience chronic medical symptoms. Even more surprising to most Americans is that prevalence rates of chronic medical conditions are more than *three times higher* than mental illness. It is even more daunting for clinicians and policy makers to hear that the majority of clients and families presenting for psychological treatment, experience one or more chronic medical conditions. This means that most psychotherapists and other clinicians will or should be dealing with comorbid chronic medical conditions whether they want to or not, and whether or not they have the requisite training to do so.

In this age of accountability, and irrespective of whether they work in health care settings or conventional mental health settings, all clinicians will be increasingly expected to provide effective psychosocial treatment to individuals and families who face morbid medical conditions. While it can be helpful to conceptualize treatment of these patients in terms of individual dynamics and utilize cognitive behavioral strategies, it can be much more effective to formulate individual *and* family dynamics in an integrated case conceptualization, and then utilize systemic interventions as indicated. For most therapists, this means additional training.

Many therapists and therapists-in-training unfortunately have little or no training in dealing with health issues that affect individuals and their families. For example, few know that:

- The risk for divorce is very high when one partner succumbs to a debilitating chronic medical condition, and when a child has a life-threatening chronic illness. That is, unless the risk can be lowered considerably by therapists who are skilled in fostering protective factors in the relationships.
- Many with chronic medical conditions like asthma, diabetes, and lupus cycle from crisis to crisis and overly utilize emergency medical services. That is, unless clinicians can assist these patients in accepting their illness and integrating it into their self-identity which allows them to break this cyclical pattern and reduce strain on their families.
- Families attempting to deal with the chronic medical conditions of a family member regularly get stuck in unhealthy roles and patterns resulting in increased distress, stunted development, depression, or other psychiatric or medical conditions. That is, unless clinicians can foster their movement through the family life cycle.
- Illness perceptions, what anthropologists call explanatory models, reflect family and cultural values and beliefs patients have about the causes and effects of their medical condition, and their involvement in its treatment. Unless, clinicians can educate and negotiate even slight modifications in these perceptions, treatment noncompliance may be inevitable.

The prospect of upgrading graduate training programs and retraining clinicians is also being prompted by anticipated changes in the health care system itself. A concerted effort is currently underway to change the health care system in America to systematically reduce cost and increase the effectiveness and efficiency of health and mental health care. The goal is to create an integrated system of health care in which psychological or behavioral health personnel and interventions are "integrated" with medical personnel and interventions. This system is radically different from the present approach in which psychological services are currently "carved out" and separate from medical care. Integrated medical care will require more than just "integrating" mental health or behavioral health clinicians into the existing health care team of physician, nurse practitioner, nurse, physical therapist, and nutritionist. It will require that behavioral health will become "integrated behavioral health." Integrated behavioral health, in this book, refers to "integrated" service delivery, meaning that behavioral health clinicians will combine and integrate individual *and* family dynamics and individual *and* family or systemic interventions in their practice. Here are integrated behavioral health case conceptualizations of the cases of Allison and Jesse.

Allison. A biopsychosocial assessment provided this additional information: Allison, with a histrionic personality disorder, is married to Jeremy, with an obsessive-compulsive personality style. He had been diagnosed with irritable bowel syndrome (IBS) which has worsened in the past few months. Complicating matters is their emotionally needy 22-year-old son who had just moved back home after losing his job. An integrated conceptualization is: The interlocking of Allison's histrionic personality with Jeremy's obsessive-compulsive pattern is relatively complementary when stress is minimal but exacerbates situations as stress increases. Thus, Jeremy's increased work and travel demands are significant stressors that trigger his biological vulnerability with the expression of IBS symptoms. These stressors have also resulted in an increase in Allison's depression as she receives even less attention from Jeremy. To the extent to which she reacts negatively to this loss, their already strained relationship further complicates Jeremy's response to his medical treatment. This case is elaborated in chapter 3.

Jesse. A biopsychosocial assessment provided this additional information: Jesse was diagnosed with Type 2 diabetes while hospitalized for "blacking out" on the job 8 months ago. He did not respond as expected to diet and exercise interventions and stated that the diet plan excluded most of his "native foods" and he disliked doing blood sugar checks. Recently, he was hospitalized for a second time; both his depression and diabetes have worsened, and his medical providers consider him a noncomplier. While his wife and family are distraught, they have not been included in his treatment plan. Not surprisingly, his depression has also worsened. An integrated conceptualization is: Because of his denial of both depression and diabetes, Jesse is stuck "looping" or cycling between the crisis and stabilization phases of chronic illness. Such denial is common among many with chronic medical conditions and frustrating to health care providers because of noncompliance. Such looping serves to reinforce his sense of hopelessness and confirms his family and culturally based illness perceptions. Unless Jesse is helped by a knowledgeable clinician to break this cycle, both depression and diabetes will likely worsen.

This is a book about the emergence of integrated behavioral health and how it is and will be practiced. It describes and advocates for the integration of individual and family interventions in behavioral health practice. What follows is a brief overview of the book, which is arranged in three parts.

Part I introduces the necessary components of integrated behavioral health practice. It includes chapters on both core theoretical constructs and core practice competencies. Chapter 1 provides an introduction and overview of this section. It highlights the need for integrated behavioral health care and training of providers who can incorporate family dynamics, the biopsychosocial model, and family or systemic interventions along with individual dynamics and interventions. Chapter 2 provides an overview of the key family dynamics and how chronic medical conditions impact individual and family members throughout the family life cycle. In this book, the term *individual dynamics* refers to personality, illness perceptions and illness stages, and other topics covered in chapters 3 through 7. Chapter 3 describes personality dynamics and how they influence the experience of a chronic medical condition. Six personality styles and disorders common in medical settings are described and illustrated: obsessive-compulsive, histrionic, dependent, avoidant, narcissistic, and borderline personality. Chapter 4 describes how patients' illness perceptions or explanations of their medical conditions reflect how they will respond to treatment, while chapter 5 describes four illness stages which reflect patients' psychosocial adjustment to their chronic illness. Too many patients get stuck and repeatedly cycle between the first two stages and are nonresponsive or noncompliant with treatment because they have not been helped to integrate their chronic illness into their self-identity. Chapter 6 suggests that the ethical perspective of clinicians either facilitates or impedes their capacity to anticipate and address ethical as well as clinical issues in behavioral health practice. Similarly, chapter 7 describes various spiritual considerations in clinical practice. Chapter 8 addresses compliance considerations which are commonplace in health care and challenge the expertise of behavioral health clinicians. Chapter 9 describes motivational interviewing, a powerful intervention for engaging patients in the treatment process, increasing their readiness and motivation for change, and decreasing noncompliance with their treatment regimens. It describes and illustrates the use of motivational interviewing in a family context. Chapter 10 describes and illustrates the core competency of case conceptualization, which is the clinician's capacity to quickly and accurately conceptualize or formulate cases and develop effective and tailored treatment interventions. Chapter 11 focuses on the process of making treatment decisions when culturally sensitive treatments are indicated. The capacity to develop culturally sensitive case conceptualizations and treatment interventions is a core competency of integrated behavioral health. Chapter 12 describes and illustrates an evidence-based therapeutic strategy for effecting change in integrated medical settings. Finally, chapter 13 describes and illustrates how medication and psychotherapy can be combined to increase treatment effectiveness.

Part II consists of seven chapters on effective treatment of common medical conditions in integrated health settings. Chapter 14 addresses arthritis in a systematic way: it begins with medical factors as well as individual and family dynamics. It describes individual and systemic treatment considerations and provides a clinical illustration. The same format is followed in chapter 15 on asthma, chapter 16 on breast cancer, chapter 17 on cardiac disease, chapter 18 on chronic fatigue syndrome, chapter 19 on diabetes, and chapter 20 on systemic lupus erythematosus, commonly called lupus.

Part III consists of two chapters that address integrated behavioral health competency and competency-based training. Chapter 21 describes competency in terms of the clinical, ethical, and cultural competencies. Chapter 22 begins a discussion on the need to shift from input-based training to competency-based training in preparing professionals to meet the challenges of a changing health care system.

The book will be of interest and value to three audiences. The first is behavioral health clinicians who practice in primary care or other health care settings that provide direct care or consultation to individuals and families facing medical conditions. The second is trainees in the different behavioral health specialties, whether counseling or clinical psychology, psychiatry, psychiatric nursing, family therapy, or medical family therapy. The third is individual psychotherapists and family therapists who work with individuals or families presenting with medical conditions.

ACKNOWLEDGMENTS

It is most fitting that I begin this Acknowledgment section by recognizing Jon Carlson, EdD, PsyD, editor of the Family Therapy and Counseling Series. From the outset, he recognized the value of the idea for this book and encouraged its development throughout the contracting and writing process. Thanks again, Jon. Much appreciation is extended to Richard Sauber, PhD, editor of the *American Journal of Family Therapy*. Dr. Sauber had the foresight over 20 years ago to establish a department of Family Behavioral Medicine and Health for the journal and invited me to be its first editor. Stephen Southern, EdD, is the editor of *The Family Journal: Counseling and Therapy for Couples and Families*. I wish to express my gratitude to him for his continued support over the years, and for providing a forum for my articles about behavioral health and health counseling. Since much of this book is adapted from articles published in that journal, a special thanks is extended to Adele Hutchison, senior permissions editor at Sage Publications, for assistance in preparing the appropriate citations.

It is most fitting that I recognize my mentors in behavioral health over the years. First is the late Kenneth I. Howard, PhD, who introduced me to psychotherapy outcomes research when I was a graduate student at Northwestern and then invited me to collaborate with him in developing various outcomes instruments including one for primary care practice. Another is Richard H. Cox, MD, PhD, who supervised me as a postdoctoral intern in learning the interface between medical and psychological practice. Richard has been a model of clinical excellence and compassion as mentor, colleague, and friend. Next, is Barry Blackwell, MD, my primary supervisor during my Fellowship in Behavioral Medicine at the University of Wisconsin. In both inpatient and clinic settings, I learned the art and science of dealing with the complexity of compliance issues from the acknowledged expert in the field. Other colleagues whom I want to acknowledge are James Bray, PhD, Ronald Levant, EdD, Ron Chenail, PhD, William Doherty, PhD, Peter Brill, MD, Edwin Edgehill, William T. O'Donohue, PhD, Grant R. Grissom, PhD, and Ronald O'Donnell,

PhD. Above all, the vision and pioneering spirit of Nicholas Cummings, PhD, the father of behavioral health care, has continued to inspire me.

Finally, a special thanks to my colleagues at Routledge who have made this book a reality. Thanks, to George Zimmar, PhD, publisher, the editorial leadership of Anna Moore and Marta Moldvai, and to Emily Pickett, production editor.

Part I

INTEGRATED BEHAVIORAL HEALTH

Basic Considerations

1

INTEGRATED BEHAVIORAL HEALTH

An Overview[1]

Traditionally, most health care has been provided in primary care settings by physicians trained in the biomedical model. Not surprisingly, the treatment they provide consists largely of medications, medical procedures, and advice. Since more than half of medical patients have comorbid psychological issues, it is quite common for their psychological issues to exacerbate, complicate, or masquerade as physical symptoms. Sometimes, these patients have been referred for psychological treatment by psychologists and mental health counselors. Occasionally, this psychological help has been effective. Often, however, that treatment has not been effective or patients have refused it. The result was and is overutilization of medical services and rising health care costs. Initiatives like the Affordable Care Act—also called Obamacare—are efforts to reduce cost and increase the effectiveness and efficiency of health and mental health care. Implementing the Affordable Care Act will require a gradual shift from the traditional to a more integrative form of health. In broad designs, psychological or behavioral health interventions would be integrated with medical interventions. This is quite different from from the way in which psychological services or behavioral health is currently "carved out" and separate from medical care. Instead, integrated behavioral health is colocated—provided in the same location as primary care—and collaborative, with the behavioral health provider working as an integral member of the treatment team.

Integrated medical care will require more than just "integrating" mental health or behavioral health clinicians into the existing health care team of physician, nurse practitioner, nurse, physical therapist, and nutritionist. It will require "integrated behavioral health," meaning that behavioral health clinicians will provide "integrated" services that combine and

---

1. Adapted from Sperry, L. (2013). Integrated behavioral health: Implications for mental health and family counseling practice. *The Family Journal: Counseling and Therapy for Couples and Families, 21*(3), 347–350. DOI:10.1177/1066480713478375

integrate individual and family dynamics and individual and family or systemic interventions.

This chapter begins with a description of the need and justification for integrated behavioral health services, including the "medical offset effect." Next, models and their anticipated role in health care settings and the importance of cultural competence in behavioral health care are described. Then, emerging trends in mental health practice are noted. Finally, implications of integrated behavioral health for the practice of individual and family therapy are discussed.

Integrated Behavioral Health: Need, Models, Roles, Culture, and Clinical Trends

Need

The need for behavioral health is important because about 50% of all patients in primary care present with psychological comorbidities, and 60% of psychological or psychiatric disorders are treated in primary care settings (Pirl, Beck, Safren, & Kim, 2001). Furthermore, the need for integrating behavioral health care has been obvious to many for some time. Simply stated, most physicians cannot provide the psychological care needed by the increasing numbers of medical patients. However, it was not until the financial justification for integrating it was made that behavioral health care became a reality. There have been several efforts to integrate behavioral health into medical practice since the 1960s. These include Kaiser Permanente, Health Care Partners, Group Health Cooperative of the Puget Sound, Kaiser Group Health of Minnesota, Duke University Medical Center, and more recently, the Veterans Administration (Cummings, O'Donohue, Hays, & Follette, 2001). All of these efforts have consistently demonstrated significant cost savings, which are referred to as medical cost offset.

A major meta-analysis of 91 studies published between 1967 and 1997 provided evidence for what the researchers called the "medical cost-offset effect." Behavioral health interventions that included various forms of psychotherapy were provided to medical patients with a history of overutilization as well as to patients being treated only for psychological disorders such as substance abuse. Average savings resulting from implementing psychological interventions were estimated to be about 20% (Chiles, Lambert, & Hatch, 1999). In short, the medical cost offset effect occurs when emotionally distressed medical patients receive appropriate behavioral health treatment. As a result of this treatment they tend to reduce their utilization of all forms of medical care. Even though there is a cost associated with behavioral health treatment, the overall cost savings is considerable.

A second area of medical cost savings is workplace wellness programs. A meta-analysis of the literature on costs and savings associated with such programs found that medical costs fall by about $3.27 for every $1 spent on wellness programs. It also found that costs attributed to absenteeism fall by about $2.73 for every $1 spent (Baicker, Cutler, & Song, 2010). Since more than 130 million Americans are in the workforce, wellness programs are increasingly important in containing health care costs. Presumably, mental health and family counselors can have a central role in both medical settings and wellness program settings.

Models

As already noted, most physicians operate from the biomedical model in which they were trained. The biopsychosocial model is an extension of the biomedical model (Sperry, 2006a) that incorporates the psychological and sociocultural dimensions with the biomedical dimension. The biopsychosocial model fosters integrative care and is the operative model in the practice of behavioral health.

Roles

Currently, behavioral health providers are most likely to be trained as psychologists, social workers, mental health counselors, or family counselors. They work side-by-side with the rest of the health care team—physicians, nurses, and other allied health providers—to enhance preventive and clinical care for psychological problems that typically were treated solely by physicians. The role of behavioral health providers is to collaborate with the health care team to develop integrative treatment plans, monitor patient progress, and provide direct behavioral health care to patients.

Cultural Competence

Rapidly changing demographics in the United States will increasingly require that cultural competence be incorporated into the delivery of behavioral health services. Hunter, Goodie, Oordt, and Dobmeyer (2009) propose a patient-centered, culturally competent approach to behavioral health care that is sensitive to the patient's explanatory model of health and illness, various social and environmental factors affecting treatment adherence, as well as fears and concerns about medication and side effects. With such an approach, behavioral health counselors can effectively assist primary care providers in meeting the medical, psychological, and cultural needs of patients and their families.

Trends in Clinical Practice

The following are some predictions about trends in clinical and psychotherapy practice. First, assuming current reimbursement trends, psychotherapy will be less frequently carried out by psychologists and more often by social workers and mental health counselors. It is predicted that most psychotherapy will occur in integrative medical settings. In contrast, only a small number of clients will pay out-of-pocket to the few therapists who will be able to make a living serving only self-pay clients. Currently only 5 to 7% of patients with insurance benefits will forgo those benefits and pay out-of-pocket for psychotherapy (Cummings & O'Donohue, 2008).

Second, the mode of psychotherapy practice is predicted to change: "Only 25% of the psychotherapy of the future will be individual. Another 25% will be group psychotherapy, while at least 50% will be psychoeducational programs" (Thomas & Cummings, 2000, p. 399). Third, mental health and substance abuse treatment currently constitutes a mere 5% of the health care budget in the United States. In the future, mental health providers will increasingly provide psychologically oriented services to the other 95% because "that's where the money is" (Cummings & O'Donohue, 2008, p. 83). Presumably, this will occur in integrated primary care settings by behavioral health providers or behavioral care professionals (BCP), the designation coined by Nick Cummings (Cummings & Cummings, 2013). Instead of practicing in a location different from the primary care site, BCPs are able to work more effectively when they are colocated within the primary care site. The rationale for colocation is clear: when the behavioral health provider is off-site about 10% of patients follow through with a physician referral for outpatient mental health treatment. This contrasts with a 90% follow-up rate when the BCP is colocated (Cummings & Cummings, 2013).

Fourth, it is predicted that psychotherapy will become briefer and more focused. Third-party payers will increasingly require that psychotherapy be as brief as possible, and not scheduled simply based on tradition or the convenience of the therapist. Reimbursed treatment will increasingly require that therapy be "medically necessary," rather than being aimed at problems of living, improving self-esteem, pursuing self-actualization, or other nonspecific goals. This emphasis on treating only specific and at least moderately severe disorders means that psychotherapy in the future will look more medical or clinical than it does today. The 50-minute hour will be replaced by the 15-minute hour wherein the therapist will diagnose patients and begin treatment in 15 minutes, just as physicians do (Cummings & O'Donohue, 2008).

Fifth, in addition to becoming briefer, it is predicted that psychotherapy will become more standardized, with sessions being spaced further apart rather than occurring weekly. Psychotherapy and other behavioral health services will be provided on an as needed basis, rather than on a continuing basis as is currently the case (Cummings et al., 2001). Evidence-based and focused interventions will become the expected standard of practice, in sharp contrast to the way psychotherapy is practiced today (Thomason, 2010). Inevitably, psychotherapy will become a behavioral health intervention rather than a stand-alone profession.

While some of these predictions may seem extreme and far-fetched, mental health and family counselors cannot afford to be complacent, given the economic challenges facing Americans (Thomason, 2010). In the next few years the plausibility of these predictions will become evident as the Affordable Care Act, with its integrative health care vision, is further implemented.

Clinical Implications of Integrated Behavioral Health

The emerging integrated health care philosophy is that integrated behavioral health care will utilize behavioral interventions for a wide range of health and mental health concerns. The primary focus will be on resolving problems within the primary care setting, as well as on engaging in health promotion and compliance enhancement for "at risk" patients. The goal of health care integration is to position the behavioral health counselor to support the physician or other primary care provider and bring more specialized knowledge to problems that require additional help.

Accordingly, the behavioral health counselor's role will be to identify the problem, target treatment, and manage medical patients with psychological problems using a behavioral approach. They will help patients to replace maladaptive behaviors with more adaptive ones. In addition, they will use psychoeducation and client education strategies to provide skill training.

More specifically, the behavioral health counselor will be expected to provide expertise in dealing with undermotivated, noncompliant, or otherwise resistant patients. They will utilize motivational interviewing with individual patients (Rollnick, Miller, & Butler, 2008) and with patients' families (Sperry, 2012) to increase readiness for change. They will also utilize focused cognitive behavioral strategies to increase compliance with treatment regimens, reduce symptoms, and increase their acceptance of chronic and life-threatening illnesses (Sperry, 2006a; Sperry, 2009).

Increasing Readiness for Change and Treatment Compliance with Family Interventions

Failure to follow treatment regimens or advice is called treatment noncompliance or nonadherence. It is a significant problem. Research indicates that 40 to 50% of patients in the United States do not comply with the health care plan for treatment, such as taking medication as directed, while nearly double that number fail to comply with dietary restrictions, exercise, or other health-compromising behaviors (DiMatteo, Giordani, Lepper, & Croghan, 2002). Typically, health education was the approach or strategy most commonly used to increase treatment adherence.

Unfortunately, this approach is insufficient in changing patients' behavior, probably because it is persuasive, prescriptive, and focused on providing general advice. In contrast, a more collaborative, family-centered approach, which focuses on the family's beliefs, values, and health behaviors, and enhances the family's self-efficacy and skills, is more likely to increase treatment adherence. Research that compared these two approaches showed a 64% success rate with knowledge or general advice alone and an 85% success rate for the more collaborative, family approach (Burke & Fair, 2003).

Family-Focused Motivational Interviewing. Because it is a collaborative approach that empowers patients, motivational interviewing (MI) has become the intervention of choice in increasing treatment adherence to medical regimens (Rollnick et al., 2008). Furthermore, using MI with the patient's family is noted to be superior to using MI with individual patients (Gance-Cleveland, 2007). Chapter 9 provides an overview and case illustration of family-based motivational interviewing that includes an extended session transcription.

Family Compliance Counseling. Family compliance counseling (Doherty & Baird, 1983) endeavors to educate patients and their families about their treatment regimen, provide a forum for patients and family members to share their emotional reactions and concerns about the disease and regimen, and achieve an agreement among the family members as to how the client will be supported in adhering to the treatment program. They offer a six-step process for conducting family-oriented compliance counseling: (a) assemble the family for a family interview, (b) begin with a discussion of the medical or lifestyle problem, (c) seek family feedback, (d) assist the family and client in making a contract about compliance with the prescribed regimen, (e) give them patient information material to read, and (f) schedule a follow-up meeting to monitor progress (Sperry, 2006b). Essentially, this approach is psychoeducational.

Brief Family Psychotherapeutic Strategy. A focused, psychotherapeutic strategy called cognitive behavior analysis system of psychotherapy (CBASP) can be utilized in about 15 minutes to process a problematic situation, such as treatment noncompliance, and come up with alternatives ways of achieving the expected health outcomes. Unlike clients who present themselves for conventional individual, couples, or family therapy, medical clients are not as likely to be receptive to more conventional therapeutic treatment strategies that are longer in duration and less focused than the treatment strategy described and illustrated here. Typically, these issues involve treatment compliance, denial of illness, difficulty with a physician, and even symptom remission. Chapter 12 provides an overview and a detailed case example with session transcription that illustrates this family-based intervention to increase treatment compliance.

Concluding Note

Given the changes already noted, it appears that integrated behavioral health practice will become a dominant force in health care while transforming the traditional practice of individual and family therapy. To the extent that integrated health care becomes the norm, the practice of individual and family therapy within an integrated behavioral health context will be notably different. Shorter and more focused interventions will replace the 50-minute hour and conventional methods and strategies for intervening with individuals and families. As reimbursement shifts to favor integrated health care, increasing numbers of therapists will work in primary care settings, with smaller numbers in clinics, agencies, or private practice.

Those trained in health counseling and clinical health psychology programs to utilize individual psychological interventions with patients increasingly will be expected to broaden their focus and incorporate family dynamics and systemic interventions. Those who take jobs in integrated behavioral health settings will be expected to deal with undermotivated, noncompliant, or otherwise resistant patients and utilize focused interventions like family motivational interviewing and family compliance interventions to increase the patient's readiness for change and enhance treatment compliance (Sperry, 2006b, 2012). Developing and providing such expertise will greatly increase the credibility and clinical value of the psychologists, counselors, and other clinicians practicing in integrated behavioral health settings. Finally, it should be noted that much of the vision, training, clinical practice, and research on behavioral health and medical offset originated with Nicholas Cummings, PhD, the pioneer and father of behavioral health care practice.

References

Baicker, K., Cutler, D., & Song, Z. (2010). Workplace wellness programs can generate savings. *Health Affairs, 29*, 304–311.

Burke, L., & Fair, J. (2003). Promoting prevention: Skill sets and attributes of health care providers who deliver behavioral interventions. *Journal of Cardiovascular Nursing, 18* (4), 256–266.

Chiles, J., Lambert, M., & Hatch, A. (1999). The impact of psychological interventions on medical cost offset: A meta-analytic review. *Clinical Psychology: Science and Practice, 6*(2), 204–220.

Cummings, N., & Cummings, J. (2013). *Refocused psychotherapy as the first line intervention in behavioral health.* New York, NY: Routledge.

Cummings, N., & O'Donohue, W. (2008). *Eleven blunders that cripple psychotherapy in America.* New York, NY: Routledge.

Cummings, N., O'Donohue, W., Hays, S., & Follette, V. (2001). *Integrated behavioral healthcare: Positioning mental health practice with medical/surgical practice.* San Diego, CA: Academic Press.

DiMatteo, M., Giordani, P., Lepper, H., & Croghan, T. (2002). Patient adherence and medical treatment outcomes: A meta-analysis. *Medical Care, 40*(9), 794–811.

Doherty, W., & Baird, M. (1983). *Family therapy and family medicine.* New York, NY: Guilford.

Gance-Cleveland, B. (2007). Changing the way we teach: Motivational interviewing in primary care. *Journal of Pediatric Health Care, 21,* 81–88.

Hunter, C. L., Goodie, J. L., Oordt, M. S., & Dobmeyer A. C. (2009). *Integrated behavioral health in primary care: Step-by-step guidance for assessment and intervention.* Washington, DC: American Psychological Association.

Pirl, W., Beck, B. J., Safren, S., & Kim, H. (2001). A descriptive study of psychiatric consultations in a community primary care center. *Primary Care Companion to the Journal of Clinical Psychiatry, 3*(5), 190–194.

Rollnick, S., Miller, W. R., & Butler, C. (2008). *Motivational interviewing in health care: Helping patients change behavior.* New York, NY: Guilford.

Sperry, L. (2006a). *Psychological treatment of chronic illness: The biopsychosocial therapy approach.* Washington, DC: APA Books.

Sperry, L. (2006b). Family-oriented compliance counseling: A therapeutic strategy for enhancing health status and lifestyle change. *The Family Journal, 14,* 412–416.

Sperry, L. (2009). *Treatment of chronic medical conditions: Cognitive-behavioral therapy strategies and integrative treatment protocols.* Washington, DC: APA Books.

Sperry, L. (2012). Motivational interviewing, non-adherence with medical treatment, and families. *The Family Journal, 20,* 306–308.

Thomas, J., & Cummings, J. (2000). *The value of psychological treatment.* Phoenix, AZ: Zeig, Tucker.

Thomason, T. C. (2010). The trend toward evidence-based practice and the future of psychotherapy. *American Journal of Psychotherapy, 64*(1), 29–38.

2

FAMILY DYNAMICS[1]

Generally speaking, behavioral health professionals primarily focus their efforts on individual dynamics. This can be short sighted because family dynamics can significantly impact health in both positive and negative ways. For example, family life that is characterized by caring and concern tends to positively affect the health and well-being of family members, whereas family life that is characterized by stress and conflict tends to negatively affect health and well-being, often doing so at the expense of family dynamics.

The term *family dynamics* refers to the forces within a family that produce particular behaviors or symptoms. Behavioral health professionals will find helpful the considerable research on the influence of family dynamics on health. Family dynamics are essential in conceptualizing and intervening with patients, especially when other family members exert a positive or negative influence. Two types of family dynamics are particularly useful in working with patients and their families in integrative care settings: family style and family life cycle. The first part of this chapter reviews the influence of family dynamics on health; family style and the family life cycle are then described.

Family Dynamics and Health

A family's social support is one of the main ways that a family positively impacts health. Supportive relationships have been demonstrated to decrease the likelihood of the onset of chronic disease, disability, mental illness, and death (Ross, Mirowsky, & Goldsteen, 1990).

Stinnet and DeFrain (1985) have identified the qualities of strong families. Their research indicates that strong families with healthy relationships

---

1. Adapted from Sperry, L. (2011). Recognizing family dynamics in the treatment of chronic fatigue syndrome. *The Family Journal: Counseling and Therapy for Couples and Families, 20,* 79–85.

have commitment, appreciation for one another, and good communication. They also spend time together, are spiritually well, and have good coping abilities.

A national survey described the communication style, conflict, and relational commitment of married, divorced, and cohabiting partners (Stanley, Markman, & Whitton, 2002). The survey found that partners who did not withdraw from conflict but instead solved their problems constructively, and had positive communications and interactions with one another tended to have a better quality of life, greater satisfaction with their relationship, and better health. In addition, partners who reported higher levels of commitment spent less time thinking about alternate partners or ending the relationship, nor did they feel trapped by their relationship. These findings are consistent with more recent research on couples' health and well-being (Sperry, Carlson, & Peluso, 2006).

Marriage protects health and enhances well-being by providing companionship, emotional support, and economic security. It is associated with physical health, psychological well-being, and low mortality. Married individuals are more likely to avoid risky behavior, such as heavy drinking and high fat diets, and have checkups and health screenings. In contrast, problematic and nonsupportive familial interactions tend to have a negative impact on physical and mental health. Individuals in unhappy marriages experience worse physical and mental health than unmarried persons. Research suggests that growing up in an unsupportive, neglectful, or abusive family is associated with poor physical health and development (Ross et al., 1990; Seeman, 2000).

One does not have to be married to obtain these health benefits as there are other sources of social support. Studies have also confirmed that social support from parents, friends, and relatives has positive effects, especially on mental health. Research confirms the direct beneficial effects of social support on overall mental health, incidence of depressive symptoms, recovery from a unipolar depressive episode, psychological distress, psychological strain, physical symptoms, and other causes of mortality. Social integration and social support, like marriage, have protective effects on reducing mortality risks. For example, "those reporting higher levels of support from close friends and family exhibit lower heart rate and systolic blood pressure, lower serum cholesterol, and higher immune function" (Seeman, 1996, p. 449).

This conclusion is supported by an extensive analysis of research studies on the influence of family and friends on health status. A critical review of studies published between 1970 and 1998 found that these relationships can have a protective effect, meaning that they lower the risk of developing mental and physical health conditions and increase the likelihood for better recovery after the onset of a medical or psychiatric condition. Though such positive relationships and social support serve as protective factors against mortality risks and improve overall health, other studies have shown that some relational behaviors can negatively impact health. The review also identified the negative health effects of relational interactions marked by criticalness and demandingness. Such interactions were associated with elevated stress hormones, increased cardiovascular activity, and depressed immune function. This contrasted with more positive, supportive interactions that were associated with the health enhancing effects (Seeman, 2000).

In short, research supports the view that an individual's family and social environment "does get under the skin to affect important physiologic parameters, including neuroendocrine, immune, and cardiovascular functioning" (Ross et al., 1990, p. 1075). It is essential that behavioral health professionals are not only aware of the protective effects of family and friends but also include family and social dynamics in their assessment and treatment planning.

Family Style and Family Life Cycle

Family Style

Family style is defined as the degree of centripetal and centrifugal qualities in the family (Beavers & Hampson, 1990; Beavers & Voeller, 1983), both of which contribute to the health or impairment of family relationships. Centripetal refers to a force of energy drawn inwards toward its center. It is analogous to petals on a flower, tightly formed and organized around a center. Centrifugal refers to a force of energy that drifts away from the center. Healthy family styles blend characteristics of both of these polarities at differing points on the life cycle. Generally speaking, young families with small children are naturally centripetal, while families with adolescents start exhibiting centrifugal forces as the teenagers become more independent, and this continues as adolescents and young adults individuate as they leave home for college or work. A flexible balance between centrifugal and centripetal is considered necessary for healthy adjustment over time.

Here is an illustration of family style involving chronic fatigue syndrome (CFS). Because of the relapsing course for CFS, families need sufficient resources to reorganize themselves regularly because it will be necessary to manage periods of stability, of variable duration, with mild symptoms, that alternate with periods of exacerbation, called flares. To accomplish this, two kinds of family organization are needed, one for periods of stability/improvement and others for exacerbations. Although a number of chronic medical conditions, such as CSF have an episodic course but are not life threatening, they can be very demanding for families in psychosocial terms. The unpredictable nature of these diseases can

13

lead to overprotection on the part of the family, as well as certain secondary benefits for the patient, particularly if they are childhood diseases.

Generally, the appearance of a disease such as CFS leads to a centripetal attraction, pushing the processes of individual and family development toward a transition with increased cohesion. However, if the onset of CSF coincides with a centrifugal period in the family (e.g., in stage 1, leaving home), the disease can be disruptive. The inherently greater demands for cohesion in CFS will be in conflict with the naturally lower demands of a centripetal phase in the family life cycle. It may mean that a young adult with CFS returns to the family home to receive support and care related to the medical condition. Or, it may mean that an individuating young adult with CSF may not achieve a fuller level of independence because that individual assumes some or much responsibility for the care of a parent who is also experiencing a chronic medical condition.

Case Example.   Joan, age 30, is attempting to cope with her father's Parkinson disease as well as her own CFS. Because a stroke has left her mother partially paralyzed, the mother is only able to provide limited caregiving for Joan's father. While Joan endeavors to be independent and live alone without outside help, increasingly she has borne the brunt of responsibility for her father's care. She can provide adequate care for him when she is less stressed and fatigued, but at other times she cannot do so and then feels guilty. During a behavioral health consultation, the focus was on what she could continue doing rather than what she was unable to do. She was also encouraged to ask for help and to step back from caregiving and take care of herself when fatigued, and to do so without feeling guilty. These were changes she could not previously allow herself.

Family Life Cycle

From a family life cycle perspective, the family is viewed as developing in progressive stages that include periods of imbalance related to the persons involved and their environment. The resulting instability provokes a shift to a new state, in which the family will have to develop new tasks and aptitudes. While there are various family life cycle models, the family systems-illness model (Rolland, 1984, 1987, 1994) provides a clinically useful framework for assessment and intervention with families that are facing chronic medical and life-threatening conditions. This model is most useful in conceptualizing the psychosocial demands of a medical condition on patients and their families over time. The ability to recognize and differentiate between periods of greater and lesser psychosocial demand can lead to improved care for patients with chronic disabling disease. In addition, the model is helpful in predicting a family's response when facing medical conditions that have differing onsets and courses.

For example, many families can more effectively respond to diseases with an acute onset and limited course and full recovery, such as a viral infection, than families faced with a chronic medical condition like juvenile diabetes or cancer.

The life cycle of a family with a chronic medical condition passes through the following stages: leaving home; commitment to a couple relationship; parenting the first child; living with an adolescent; launching the children; and retirement and old age (Haley, 1973). Needless to say, each of these stages provides unique challenges to family members; however, the challenge is heightened when a chronic medical condition is present.

1. Leaving Home

The challenge facing young adults in this stage is simultaneous involvement with both their parents and their peers. Adaptation to family challenges may impede their normal development with persons their own age. A level of independence is not completely achieved until the young adult begins to live away from home and establish intimate relationships outside the family. In the current economic downturn, difficulties in attaining economic independence often delay this process as young adults often continue living at home instead of preparing themselves for a separate life. Parents can let their offspring go or perpetually retain them within the family organization. A diagnosis of a chronic medical condition in this phase could lead to several behavioral shifts. The young adult's development and independence from the family might be delayed because of a lack of initiative with others, such as when a girl friend or boyfriend leaves them because of the illness, parental overprotection, or because of difficulties finding a job.

2. Forming a Stable Couple Relationship

In this phase in which a committed couple relationship is established, the partners must establish several pacts. These include defining boundaries with their respective families and other social systems, such as friends and coworkers, and clarifying rules, including those that relate to communications patterns. The diagnosis of a chronic medical condition in this phase can be devastating for a couple that is not fully consolidated. When the illness has an episodic course, the more the fluctuations or symptom changes, the greater is the need for adaptation in the family system. By committing themselves to the relationship, partners accept the necessity to respond to the needs of the other when necessary. In any chronic medical condition, the normal roles can change, with one partner becoming the caregiver, and the other the patient. When the patient expresses vulnerability in emotions such as fear, sadness, or anxiety, the caregiver is likely to interpret these as indicators of need and to feel compelled to offer help (Graham, Huang, Clark, & Helgeson, 2008). When the roles become too rigid, they can trap the two partners: one strong-solicitous-healthy and the other weak-demanding-ill.

Effective therapy can foster the necessary adaptability needed by these couples. It is essential that efforts are made to keep both partners as active participants in the relationship so that one partner is not viewed primarily as a caregiver and the other as a passive recipient of care. Furthermore, effective couple counseling encourages reasonable involvement of the families of each partner. When one or both families become excessively involved, it becomes more difficult for the couple to achieve the independence required of the next stage, bearing children.

3. Birth of Children

In this stage, when the committed couple bears children they must find new ways to relate to each other. Not only do the rules change, a new family subsystem is formed: the parental subsystem. Childbirth necessitates more distancing of the couple from their families of origin, while at the same time involving proximity because the two families are joined by this event, as grandparents, aunts, and uncles are created.

The couple must take care that the members of their respective family systems of origin do not interfere with their functions as parents or undermine their family organization. For instance, it is not uncommon following childbirth that symptoms of the chronic medical condition intensify and the new mother becomes frustrated because she cannot care for her newborn child alone. She may feel increasingly tired and exasperated with the task of child rearing, which can be complicated by a father who is unavailable because of job demands or possibly, to escape from the tension at home (Kagel, White, & Coyne, 1978).

If the medical condition affecting a parent is particularly debilitating, its impact on the childrearing family is twofold. First, the ill parent becomes for the family like another child with "special needs," and competes with the other children for scarce family resources. Second, a parent is "lost," and for all practical purposes a single-parent family is created. It is not uncommon to find that while this situation is somewhat challenging for higher functioning families, it can have devastating consequences on less functional families wherein there is increased reliance on community services and separation and divorce (Kagel et al., 1978).

Sometimes the child is the symptomatic family member, and in this case, considerable alterations in family activities may result. Family life may become focused exclusively on the needs of the ill child. These children can grow to be apprehensive and overly dependent on their parents, whereas the mothers become highly solicitous and emotionally implicated.

In fact, high levels of family stress and exaggerated dedication can place undue attention on the physical symptoms and unintentionally prolong their duration.

4. Living with Adolescents

In the fourth stage, the children have become adolescents, the couple's initial difficulties have resolved with time, their vision of life has matured, and stable relationships have been forged with their families of origin and with each other.

Sometimes, a couple at this stage achieves some degree of stability by adopting rigid, repetitive patterns of interaction to resolve or to avoid creating problems. However, when the children are grown and the family changes, these patterns may be inappropriate and are likely to create crises that oblige the couple to decide whether they will continue together or separate. Unfortunately, such rigid patterns of interaction established with the passing of time make it difficult to adapt the system to the new needs of this stage of the life cycle.

Growing children are increasingly less dependent on the parental subsystem, and a parent with a chronic medical condition must begin to seek other activities to fill his or her life. Often "hierarchal" problems arise because the children are going through adolescence. The patient may not be able to cope with the burden of this stage and the boundaries of the parent–child subsystem may break down. As couples approach midlife, the high levels of stress associated with multiple obligations related to the family roles and changes can have a negative impact on marital satisfaction (Gagnon, Hersen, Kabacoff, & Van Hasselt, 1999; Kovacs, 1988). Couples are likely to experience increased marital satisfaction and remain together into old age if they are able to successfully negotiate these transitions in the postparenting years (Christensen & Jacobson, 2000).

5. Launching Children

Families can experience a crisis when their children leave home. Couples can face a turbulent period that progressively abates after their children have gone and the couple creates a new relationship with corresponding new rules and boundaries. They can resolve remaining conflicts and allow their grown children to have partners and professions, while as a couple they prepare for the transition to the role of grandparents. This entails learning how to be good grandparents and create new rules so that they can participate in the life of their children and be able to function on their own at home. Typically, they will have to face the loss of their own parents in this period, and the sorrow this implies.

A common challenge in this stage is that the couple finds that they have little to share with each other. For years their conversation has been centered on the children. They may begin to argue about the same things that were issues before they had children. These issues were not resolved at that time and were put aside with the arrival of the first baby. The presence of a chronic medical condition only exacerbates these unresolved issues. Couples counseling is particularly useful for the couple to help it continue coping with the adaptations of daily life this syndrome requires.

6. Retirement and Old Age

Withdrawal from active life can mean that the couple is face-to-face, 24 hours a day, a fact that can create friction. One problem that may arise in this stage is excessive protection of one member over the other, thereby enhancing a debilitating chronic medical condition.

One positive alternative to somatization in retired couples is to increase the activities they carry out together (Vinick & Eckerdt, 1990). Solitude can be a risk factor for physical inactivity in persons of advanced age and predicts discontinuing physical activity over time, which may worsen the symptoms of the chronic medical condition. Being married is associated with a higher probability of being linked to behavior patterns such as exercise, that enhance health, perhaps because partners exert a certain influence on this behavior (Pettee et al., 2006).

It should be remembered that this classification is only an approximation and cannot be applied to all the emergent family models, which are becoming increasingly more prevalent, such as reconstituted families, single-parent families (single women with children), couples without children, and couples of the same sex, in which a chronic medical condition can also appear. Cultural and gender-related aspects should also be taken into account when the family as a group is being evaluated.

Concluding Note

Often, a patient's chronic medical condition is influenced by family members or their social support system. Accordingly, it is imperative that operative family system dynamics be identified. This chapter has reviewed research on the impact of family dynamics on health. It has also emphasized how family style and stage of the family life cycle can provide a useful lens with which to assess specific family dynamics and provide a focus for treatment. Behavioral health professionals with a working knowledge of family dynamics can assist patients and their families in achieving a reasonable degree of adjustment to that stage so that a chronic medical condition does not unduly influence the personal development of individual family members, or the family itself.

References

Beavers, W., & Hampson, R. (1990). *Successful families: Assessment and intervention.* New York, NY: Norton.

Beavers, W., & Voeller, M. (1983). Family models: Comparing and contrasting the Olson circumplex model with the Beavers systems model. *Family Process, 22,* 85–99.

Christensen, A., & Jacobson, N. (2000). *Reconcilable differences.* New York, NY: Guilford.

Combrinck-Graham, L. (1985). A developmental model for family systems. *Family Process, 24,* 139–150.

Gagnon, M., Hersen, M., Kabacoff, R., & Van Hasselt, V. (1999). Interpersonal and psychological correlates of marital dissatisfaction in late life: A review. *Clinical Psychology Review, 19,* 359–378.

Graham, S., Huang, J. Y., Clark, M., & Helgeson, V. (2008). The positives of negative emotions: Willingness to express negative emotions promotes relationships. *Personality and Social Psychology Bulletin, 34,* 394–406.

Haley, J. (1973). *Uncommon therapy.* New York, NY: Grune & Stratton.

Kagel, S., White, R., & Coyne, J. C. (1978). Father-absent and father-present families of disturbed and nondisturbed adolescents. *American Journal Orthopsychiatry, 48,* 342–352.

Kovacs, L. (1988). Couple therapy: An integrated developmental and family system model. *Family Therapy, 15,* 133–155.

Pettee, K., Brach, J., Kriska, A., Boudreau, R., Richardson, C., Colbert, L., … Newman, A. (2006). Influence of marital status on physical activity levels among older adults. *Medicine and Science in Sports and Exercise, 38,* 541–546.

Rolland, J. (1984). Toward a psychosocial typology of chronic and life-threatening illness. *Family Systems Medicine, 2,* 245–263.

Rolland, J. (1987). Chronic illness and the life cycle: A conceptual framework. *Family Process, 26,* 203–221.

Rolland, J. (1994). In sickness and in health: The impact of illness on couples' relationships. *Journal of Marital and Family Therapy, 20,* 327–349.

Ross, C., Mirowsky, J., & Goldsteen, K. (1990). The impact of the family on health: The decade in review. *Journal of Marriage and the Family, 52,* 1059–1078.

Seeman, T. (1996). Social ties and health: The benefits of social integration. *Annals of Epidemiology, 6,* 442–451.

Seeman, T. (2000). Health promoting effects of friends and family on health outcomes in older adults. *American Journal of Health Promotion, 14,* 362–370.

Sperry, L., Carlson, J., & Peluso, P. (2006). *Couples therapy: Integrating theory and technique* (2nd ed.). Denver, CO: Love.

Stanley, S., Markman, H., & Whitton, S. (2002). Communication, conflict and commitment: Insights on the foundations of relationship success from a national survey. *Family Process, 41,* 659–675.

Stinnet, N., & DeFrain, J. (1985). *Secrets of strong families.* Boston, MA: Little, Brown.

Vinick, B. H., & Eckerdt, D. J. (1990). Retirement: What happens to husband-wife relationships? *Journal of Geriatric Psychiatry, 24,* 23–40.

3

PERSONALITY DYNAMICS[1]

Personality is commonly understood as the characteristic and predictable manner in which an individual thinks, feels, and behaves. It includes conscious attitudes, beliefs, and values, as well as personal strivings, unconscious conflicts, and defense mechanisms. The term *personality dynamics* refers to how an individual's personality interacts or functions within his or her environment, particularly interpersonal relationships. Personality dynamics are operative in every patient in every health care setting and encounter. To the extent that therapists and other clinicians are aware of these dynamics, they can more effectively relate to and achieve treatment goals with patients and their families. This chapter provides a brief overview of personality dynamics and specifies how personality styles (and personality disorders) can and do influence health and chronic medical conditions. Six personality styles/disorders are common in medical and mental health settings. They are: obsessive-compulsive, histrionic, dependent, avoidant, narcissistic, and borderline. The personality dynamics of each are briefly described. The ways in which each style characteristically experiences and responds to the same chronic medical condition, Type 2 diabetes, is then described. Because patients and family members often have different personality styles/disorders, a description and illustration of how two different personality styles/disorders interact in a health care setting rounds out this chapter.

Personality Dynamics, Personality Styles, and Personality Disorders

A useful way of conceptualizing personality dynamics is in terms of personality styles which is an individual's distinctive pattern of understanding one's self and others and of functioning in the world. Personality styles

---

1. Adapted from Sperry, L., & Carlson, J. (2000). Couples therapy with a personality-disordered couple. *The Family Journal: Counseling and Therapy for Couples and Families, 8,* 118–123.

reflect an individual's unique self-view, worldview, and resulting life strategy (Sperry, 2003). In short, personality style is the distinctive pattern of one's manner of thinking, feeling, and behaving and one's characteristic level of functioning.

There is a normal range of personality functioning but there is also a pathological range of functioning. An individual's functioning can be conceptualized on a continuum, with one end being more adaptive and healthy and the other end being more maladaptive and less healthy. Personality styles are usually associated with more adaptive functioning while personality disorders are associated with more maladaptive functioning (Sperry, 2003). Personality disorders are personality styles that become sufficiently inflexible and maladaptive so as to cause impaired functioning or distress or both. Predictably, individuals with a personality disorder have difficulty taking responsibility for their behavior and cooperating with others (Sperry, 2006a). This includes complying with treatment regimens and cooperating with medical personnel. Effective psychotherapeutic interventions can and do shift the individual's functioning in the adaptive direction, from the personality disorder end to personality styles end of the continuum.

Knowing a patient's personality style or disorder can be quite helpful in working with patients in formal psychotherapy or in consulting with patients and their families on any number of treatment issues, such as noncompliance, in a health care setting. Effective psychotherapeutic interventions can result in a goal that is less habit-driven, more open, and with increased awareness of rigidity and the limitations of one's operative personality dynamics, which can lead to a healthier shift in one's self-view, worldview, and life strategy. Following is a brief summary of the most common personality style/disorder patterns presenting in health care settings. An expanded discussion of personality dynamics in medical settings can be found in Harper (2003).

Obsessive-Compulsive Personality Dynamics

Obsessive-compulsive personality dynamics are recognizable by the following behavior and interpersonal styles, cognitive style, and emotional style. The individual's behavior is characterized by perfectionism. Individuals with this disorder are likely to be workaholics. In addition to dependability, obsessive-compulsive people tend to be stubborn and possessive. They, like passive-aggressive disordered individuals, can be indecisive and procrastinating. Interpersonally, these individuals are exquisitely conscious of social rank and status and modify their behavior accordingly. That is, they tend to be deferential and obsequious to superiors, and haughty and autocratic to subordinates and peers. They can be doggedly insistent that others do things their way without an appreciation or awareness of how others react to this insistence. At their best they are polite and loyal to the organizations and ideals they espouse (Sperry, 2003).

Of all the personality styles, the obsessive-compulsive personality seems to be best suited for dealing with a chronic illness like diabetes, an illness requiring lifelong self-monitoring, discipline, self-denial, and self-regulation. Provided that diabetic self-care measures can be integrated into the daily routines and health patterns of the compulsive patient, they will become part of his or her rigid mode of functioning. Difficulties that do arise in the treatment process are more likely to emerge early in the treatment course rather than later. Specifically, problems are noted in initially establishing health behavior changes. When the diabetic condition is diagnosed in older individuals their routines are already deeply ingrained and they may have a strong appetite that must be curbed, such as for sugar, alcohol, caffeine, and nicotine. Such health behavior changes pit unhealthy but automatic routine habits against the compulsive individual's good intentions to preserve his or her health and conform to medical recommendations.

Diabetes is a lifelong condition with serious consequences for nonadherence, so there are many incentives for these individuals to reduce their risk behaviors. It is important that clinicians recognize the unique dynamics of the compulsive personality and tailor their response to the patient's efforts to establish and maintain the requisite health behaviors. Thus, it can be counterproductive to be too harsh in evaluating early deviations from the treatment plan as these individuals struggle to conform to their regimen. Such harshness may actually intensify their preoccupation with punishment, leading to greater rigidity in their mode of coping. Furthermore, if their experience of shame is too intense, their determined efforts to change may be replaced with fear and avoidance behaviors, which are likely to result in them withholding or concealing evidence of nonadherence. Not surprisingly this will be accompanied by nonproductive guilt and self-recrimination, and such patients will distance themselves from their health care providers (Sperry, 2006b). For this reason it is essential to communicate an accepting, supportive attitude toward these patients that recognizes their struggles and conflicts, while conveying confidence that they are doing enough to manage their illness, despite occasional lapses.

Histrionic Personality Dynamics

Histrionic personality dynamics are recognizable in the following style characteristics. The behavioral style is characterized as charming, dramatic, and expressive, while also being demanding, self-indulgent, and inconsiderate. Persistent attention-seeking, mood lability, capriciousness, and superficiality further characterize their behavior. Interpersonally, these individuals tend to be exhibitionistic and flirtatious in their manner, with attention-seeking and manipulativeness being prominent (Sperry, 2003).

Childhood or adolescent Type 1 diabetes, although typically more severe and brittle than Type 2 diabetes, provides young individuals with the opportunity to develop critical self-management skills that utilize blood sugar monitoring and insulin injections. Self-management of early onset diabetes establishes habit patterns that are quite challenging for those with later life onset of this chronic disease. It is a challenge that is particularly difficult for histrionic individuals to meet successfully given their rather fragmented, undisciplined existence. Thus, for adults with histrionic personalities diagnosed with Type 2 diabetes, the challenge of developing appropriate health habits and a disciplined daily regimen of regulating their blood sugar levels, calculating calories, and evaluating food choices, especially when dining out, can be overwhelming. Thus, these patients inevitably require longer and more varied training to achieve sufficient proficiency in disease management applicable to their particular circumstances. Often it is useful to introduce a social dimension in the training for these competencies given the gregarious interpersonal nature of this personality type. Not surprisingly, skill training groups and dining out groups are popular and effective with these individuals.

Extreme blood sugar levels (i.e., hypoglycemia or hyperglycemia) can be a potentially serious weapon in the hands of individuals with a strong need for attention. Histrionic individuals have been known to demand attention and care taking by precipitating a diabetic crisis, particularly when they believe a valued relationship is being threatened. Furthermore, their natural excitability can also generate stress-related hormonal changes. In the aftermath of a crisis of this type, clinicians may conclude that this action involved deliberate nonadherence and justifies their censure or disapproval. Predictably, the histrionic individual will react with frenetic activity to seek social assurance, engaging in behavior that may ultimately undermine previous efforts to develop stable disease control routines (Sperry, 2006b). Clinicians may do better to help these patients process the situation and find alternative and less medically risky solutions.

Dependent Personality Dynamics

Dependent personality dynamics are recognizable in the following style characteristics. The behavioral and interpersonal styles of people with these dynamics are characterized by docility, passivity, and nonassertiveness. In interpersonal relations, they tend to be pleasing, self-sacrificing, clinging, and constantly requiring the assurance of others. Their compliance and reliance on others lead to a subtle demand that others assume responsibility for major areas of their lives (Sperry, 2003).

Since diabetes represents an ongoing demand for self-management, this chronic illness is a particularly difficult condition for patients with dependent personalities. Giving dependent patients' limited incentive to engage in disciplined behavior, the clinicians' expectations for them to engage in daily self-monitoring, self-denial, and self-regulation are likely to be ignored. Thus, from the onset of the diagnosis of diabetes, it is important that the notion of self-discipline as an essential element of illness management be discussed with these patients. It is also essential to elicit whatever apprehensions and concerns this idea may engender in them.

Demands and expectations placed on the dependent patient need to be manageable and achievable so that success is relatively assured both in the beginning and in the later stages of treatment. When difficulties arise, it is better to view these difficulties as opportunities for conjoint problem solving rather than as failures. This reframe can enhance the sense of closeness needed for a long-term medical relationship. In a sense, this strategy represents a reversal of what typically takes place in medical practice, wherein the absence of a symptom or health problem results in a reduction of contact (i.e., appointments, with the nurturing authority figure). For dependent individuals who are continually seeking security and care taking, such an attitude constitutes a negative model for illness management. Accordingly, ample opportunities for these patients to report success and effective regulation of blood sugar levels are needed, especially in the early stages of promoting this important health behavior. This means that a fixed, ongoing schedule of appointments is recommended.

Treating diabetes in dependent patients is best conceptualized as a shared concern and conjoint undertaking that reinforces the dependent individual's need to feel a part of the treatment process, a secure and attention providing atmosphere. Emphasizing periodic follow-ups wherein enthusiastic recognition is provided for their health maintenance efforts in the face of a potentially serious disease can help reinforce the dependent patient's positive attitude for maintaining a disciplined approach to illness management. It is also useful in engendering an increased sense of self-efficacy wherein their security needs are assured and even enhanced by their active participation in the treatment process (Sperry, 2006b).

Avoidant Personality Dynamics

Avoidant personality dynamics are recognizable by the following characteristics. These individuals are shy, lonely, hypersensitive individuals with low self-esteem. Although they are desperate for interpersonal involvement, they avoid personal contact with others because of their heightened fear of social disapproval and rejection sensitivity. In this regard, they are quite different from the schizoid personality who has little if any interest in personal contact. The avoidant personality is characterized by the following behavioral and interpersonal styles, thinking or cognitive styles, and emotional or affective styles. The behavioral style of avoidant personalities is characterized by social withdrawal, shyness, distrustfulness, and aloofness. Their behavior and speech is both controlled and inactive, and they appear apprehensive and awkward. Interpersonally, they are rejection-sensitive. Even though they desire acceptance by others, they keep at a distance from others and require unconditional approval before being willing to "open up." They gradually "test" others to determine who can be trusted to like them (Sperry, 2003).

Because they are anxiety prone, stressful situations can significantly alter the glucose metabolism in those with avoidant personalities. Dealing with such glucose fluctuations that are not diet related can be a source of interpersonal tension and recrimination with the health care providers, who are unlikely to consider alternative causes and instead attribute difficulty to patient misbehavior or nonadherence. Such a misunderstanding can result in a sense of rejection potentially strong enough that troubled, avoidant patients might exit the health care system entirely. Once rejected, these patients may remain fearful about seeking alternative care which they would anticipate as being ultimately rejecting. Therefore, health care providers need to manifest a patient, patient-centered orientation in relating to such patients as well as engaging in discussion and monitoring of all stressful factors that contribute to problematic blood sugar regulation (Sperry, 2006b).

Narcissistic Personality Dynamics

Narcissistic personality dynamics are recognizable by the following style characteristics. Behaviorally, narcissistic individuals are seen as conceited, boastful, and snobbish. They appear self-assured and self-centered, and they tend to dominate a conversation, seek admiration, and act in a pompous and exhibitionistic fashion. They are also impatient, arrogant, and thin-skinned or hypersensitive. Interpersonally, they are exploitive and use others to indulge themselves and their desires. Their behavior is socially facile, pleasant, and endearing. However, they are unable to respond with true empathy to others. When stressed, they can be disdainful, exploitive, and generally irresponsible in their behavior (Sperry, 2003).

Diabetes requires ongoing vigilance, self-monitoring, and a willingness to engage in self-denial from foods and other activities that can adversely affect blood sugar levels. Individuals preoccupied with lofty fantasies about their own self-importance are not well suited to the humbling task of self-discipline that diabetes requires. The presence of a spouse who is responsible for meal preparation can be invaluable in establishing and maintaining limits to the narcissistic personality's tendency toward self-indulgent excesses. However, the spouse may also bear the brunt of the narcissistic partner's frustration in the form of displaced anger over such constraints. Cavalier and dismissive behavior should be expected from these patients who may perceive and treat their condition as the medical team's responsibility. If this category of patient pays limited lip service to health care directives, even small deviations from full compliance can have long-range health consequences.

An overall strategy for working with these patients is to emphasize simple, straightforward, and easy-to-use directives. This approach is in contrast to the typical medical care counseling directive which emphasizes the importance of long-range adherence and future risk of complications if adherence is ignored. Such directives tend to have little impact on the narcissistic personality because of the absence of a dramatic immediate consequence (e.g., they will continue to smoke). Narcissistic patients tend to react in a condescending manner to physicians and other health personnel who might recommend something like smoking cessation. Their condescending and provocative behavior in the face of medical knowledge about their condition and long-range risk can be infuriating and test the resolve of many physicians who might be tempted to "fire" such individuals from their practice. The more burdensome the routines required to control diabetes, the more likely these patients will be unlikely to make and keep such a commitment. On the other hand, devices such as insulin pumps that require minimal patient involvement represent a highly cost-effective investment. Maintaining sufficient rapport so that the patient keeps appointments is essential to insure early identification and treatment of complications associated with progression of the debilitating disease, such as retinal changes, peripheral neuropathy, or renal changes and dysfunction (Sperry, 2006b).

Borderline Personality Dynamics

Borderline personality dynamics are recognizable by the following style characteristics. Behaviorally, borderline patients are characterized by physically self-damaging acts such as suicide gestures, self-mutilation, or provoking fights. Their social and occupational accomplishments are often less than their intelligence and ability warrant. Of all the personality disorders, those patients with borderline disorder are more likely to have irregularities of circadian rhythms, especially of the sleep-wake cycle. Thus, chronic insomnia is a common complaint. Interpersonally, people with borderline disorder are characterized by their paradoxical instability. That is, they fluctuate quickly between idealizing and clinging to another individual to devaluing and opposing that individual. They are exquisitely rejection-sensitive and experience abandonment depression following the slightest of stressors. Separation anxiety is a primary motivator of this personality disorder. Interpersonal relationships develop rather quickly and intensely, yet their social adaptiveness is rather superficial. They are extraordinarily intolerant of being alone and they go to great lengths to seek out the company of others whether in indiscriminate sexual affairs, late night phone calls to relatives and recent acquaintances, or late night visits to hospital emergency rooms with a host of vague medical or psychiatric complaints (Sperry, 2003).

Like other chronic illnesses that require self-monitoring, self-discipline, and consistency, borderline patients, as well as their health providers, face a constant challenge in dealing with diabetes. Mood lability and over-modulated affects are reflected in endocrine surges, and thus maintaining stable blood sugar levels is a major challenge for these patients. This instability is complicated by impulsive dietary indiscretion, substance abuse, and nicotine and caffeine use—which greatly constricts small blood vessels—as well as inattention to or neglect of insulin regulation due to emotional interpersonal conflicts. Being accountable for health behaviors, such as stable blood sugar, requires psychological requisites lacking in most borderline personalities. These include a cohesive sense of self and the capacity to modulate affects. Even in psychologically mature diabetics, maintaining a resolve to resist temptation is a difficult and significant accomplishment, often taken for granted by physicians and other health care providers.

Even though borderline patients may intellectually accept the responsibility to be accountable for maintaining stable blood sugar levels in order to prevent long-range complications, emotionally they find actualizing this promise extraordinarily difficult. Usually, the planning phase for chronic illness management is not necessarily problematic for these patients, unless they are smokers or obesity is a primary contributor to their illness. It is the action or implementation phase of the treatment plan that is problematic in terms of predictability. Even if they are initially successful in implementing a diet and blood sugar monitoring plan, maintaining it without relapse or departing from the schedule tends to be very difficult. While adverse physical consequences of poor control may have a transient sobering effect on these individuals at the time the indiscretions occur, these are not likely to serve as effective determinants of future health-related behaviors. Since the borderline's mood lability and instability are usually triggered by interpersonal issues, monitoring the relational aspect of their lives clearly must become an essential component of their treatment management. Self-neglect during a relationship conflict can precipitate a diabetic crisis, such as a coma. This usually occurs because the borderline patient transiently decompensates and forgets to take his or her insulin or deliberately stops taking insulin to elicit guilt or remorse from partner or family. Similarly, if these patients binge eat or drink excessively, their sugar levels can become unstable and result in a crisis. Knowing that these scenarios are possible and predicting the likelihood that they will occur should prompt an action plan. For example, if the diabetic patient's relationships are typically tumultuous and fragile, psychotherapy probably should be regarded as an essential component of their medical management (Sperry, 2006b).

Personality Dynamics in Histrionic and Obsessive-Compulsive Couples

Thus far, this chapter has focused on individual personality styles/disorders. In this section, the focus shifts to how two different personality styles interact. The two styles described are the obsessive-compulsive style and the histrionic style, which are common and complementary personality styles. There was a time when most couples who sought couples therapy were involved in a relational pattern of an obsessive-compulsive partner and a histrionic partner. While other relational patterns are seen in couples therapy today, this obsessive-compulsive/histrionic pattern is still quite common; and it is commonly encountered in the health care setting today.

Early descriptions of the histrionic-obsessive couple emphasized personality structure and dynamics rather than systemic factors. Thus, the histrionic—then called hysterical—partner was typically profiled as the only girl, only child, or youngest child in a family constellation in which her mother was cold, masochistic, and resentful of being a mother and woman and so overindulged her daughter as a compensation for not being able to love and nurture her. Her father was described as charming, indulgent, and seductive at times, while controlling and rejecting at other times. The end result was that the histrionic girl-in-training came to believe her father loved her more than he loved his wife. Thus, she learned to get her own way by playing each parent against the other by being coy, seductive, pretending she was ill, or having temper tantrums. Adulthood for the histrionic female became a search for a strong, idealized father-husband who would take care of her (Sperry & Maniacci, 1998).

Relational Conflicts among Histrionic-Obsessive Couples

The histrionic partner comes to recognize some of the costs of her obsessive-compulsive partner's refusal to take authentic personal stands. She does things she realizes he will find provocative and objectionable.

Yet, seldom does he protest or react emotionally. Rather than voicing any strong personal wants or desires, he insists that "anything is fine" with him. In time, this predictable response leads the histrionic partner to draw a number of conclusions. She comes to view him as indecisive, ineffectual, and emasculated. She thinks that he must be angry or have some objections to her behavior, but because he says nothing she concludes that

28

he must be dishonest and untrustworthy in his dealings with her. And she wonders if his failure to show anger means he no longer cares for her. She feels increasingly unloved, emotionally abandoned, and unable to make intimate contact with her husband. Furthermore, she experiences an increasing sense of rage.

The realization that her obsessive partner can only superficially respond to her need is devastating for her. Although her obsessive partner displays an endless willingness to listen to her troubles, to provide reassurance, and to present logical solutions to her difficulties, he offers little else. Consequently, she feels overburdened and overwhelmed. This state of affairs provides even more reason for the histrionic partner to experience an increasing sense of abandonment and rage as the months and years go by. In her anger and her desire to gain revenge, she resorts to predictable behaviors. Initially, she verbally attacks her partner. Rather than being informative and so potentially constructive, these attacks are often marked by scathing, global indictments of her husband's character. She assaults him simultaneously on numerous fronts. Next, she becomes provocative: She overspends, has affairs with other men, or resorts to hypochondriacal preoccupations. And, when her partner seems substantially unmoved by all of these, she may pull out her ultimate weapon, the suicidal gesture. All too frequently, she is left with the painful notion that her husband is really a "great guy" who deserves better, that she is the helpless victim of overpowering and irrational emotions and actions, and that she is doomed by external forces to be a "dysfunctional bitch."

Like his partner, the obsessive individual believes he has made the ideal mate choice. He has chosen a woman who makes him feel like a man, without requiring him to be authentic and assertive—both of which he finds so difficult. Nevertheless, the enormous emotional consequences of this choice soon become increasingly evident. He begins to realize that he is being exploited, that their relationship is a one-way street in which his partner does all the taking and he all the giving. Her wants and desires always seem to take priority in the relationship. Furthermore, he has great difficulty expressing the growing anger he feels toward his partner or taking a stand against her behavior. On those rare occasions when he was forthright, his assertiveness is met with dire consequences—she becomes rageful. Ultimately, he concludes that it is not worth fighting or taking a stand. Instead, he settles into other ways of expressing his anger and preserving his sense of autonomy. Typically, he employs passive-aggressive tactics learned in his family of origin. He withdraws more and more from his partner, often into his job, citing as his justification the requirements of the job and the increasing expenses of the family. He makes ever greater use of the tactic of stonewalling or emotional detachment. Finally, he gets even by abdicating his relational responsibilities outside those of breadwinner, resulting in his partner becoming overburdened with responsibilities and enormously harried in her attempts to fulfill them.

As the relationship progressively deteriorates and his partner engages in ever more extreme behavior, the obsessive becomes ever angrier. He becomes furious at the seemingly unprovoked verbal attacks, her over-spending, her affairs, her hypochondriasis, and her suicidal threats and gestures. At the height of the relational crisis, he feels thoroughly exploited. Even more devastating is the mounting conviction that he is neither loved nor respected and is only kept around because of his paycheck and because she is afraid to leave.

The Treatment Process

There are three treatment phases, with specific treatment goals, for effec-tively treating the histrionic-obsessive couple in couples therapy. The phases are (a) establishing a working therapeutic alliance, (b) rebalancing the couple's relationship, and (c) modifying individual dynamics in the partners. Sometimes, an additional phase of skill training may be neces-sary. If so, skill training interventions are used concurrent with or follow-ing the second phase.

The first phase of treatment involves establishing and maintaining a therapeutic alliance. Initial contact with the therapist frequently occurs during a period of extremes of emotionality and behavior and of severe marital maladjustment.

These couples can be helped to a state of greater calm, order, and opti-mism about their relationship. It is particularly valuable for the couple and the therapist to share certain assumptions. The first is that neither part-ner is "crazy" or mentally ill, but rather that each is an individual whose behavior makes sense and who is responsible for this behavior. The second is that neither partner is "the problem," but rather that each is in therapy in the role of client, because the behavior of each contributes to the shared marital difficulties. The third is that each partner's family-of-origin pat-tern can powerfully influence the couple's relationship.

These assumptions short-circuit some destructive and distressing con-ceptions typically held by the histrionic-obsessive couple at the outset of the treatment. Initially, the couple believes that the histrionic partner is insane because of her extreme behavior and emotionality in the apparent absence of any adequate reasons for these. The therapist's treatment of the histrionic partner as an individual whose behavior has rational anteced-ents, who is responsible for her behavior, and who is sane has a multiple impact. First, it reduces the distressing fear that the other partner will abandon her. Second, it deprives her of an excuse for being irresponsi-ble. Third, it deprives him of an excuse for not confronting her about her behavior. Similarly, each partner tends to believe that he or she alone is completely at fault for the relationship's problems. This phenomenon is most easily observed in the histrionic partner and accounts for vacillations in each between rage at the partner and severe self-condemnation. A consistent stance on the part of the therapist in which he or she repeatedly insists, demonstrates, and acts in accord with the view that each partner is contributing to the marital difficulties provides each with a more livable, realistic general view and, into the bargain, a better basis for responsible self-scrutiny and action. The achievement of such a therapeutic alliance usually results in a rapid and dramatic diminution of intense emotionality and extreme behavior. The end result is that the couple becomes amenable to viewing themselves and their relationship in a calmer and more orderly fashion. Furthermore, discussion of how family-of-origin patterns develop and affect the relationship can be quite useful in calming the couple by helping them understand the specific learned patterns that they have acquired. This is often beyond each partner's conscious awareness and helps them realize how much their relational problem is not of their making, although they can still take responsibility for it. After a working relationship between the couple and therapist is achieved, the second phase of treatment consists of establishing or restoring balance in the couple's relationship.

Rebalancing is typically needed in the areas of boundaries, power, and intimacy and represents the main systemic focus of change in couples therapy with histrionic-obsessive partners. Structural and strategic family techniques can be quite effective in accomplishing this rebalancing of boundaries and power. Issues of rebalancing the relationship of intimacy can be effectively addressed with communication or family-of-origin interventions.

The third phase of treatment involves modification of personality features in individual partners. This phase represents psychodynamic change in couples therapy. The primary individual goals for both the histrionic and her partner are relatively similar, though their starting points differ. There are two goals: First, that each of them comes to adopt more direct, honest, and fair modes of influence and assertion and, second, that each comes both to cooperate and communicate honestly in the face of control efforts on the part of the other partner.

As was previously noted, both the histrionic and the obsessive are often dishonest in their attempts to control each other. She may misrepresent facts, dishonestly seduce, or exaggerate her feelings, whereas he pretends he has no personal needs or desires or that he is not bothered by her behavior. In addition, she pretends utter helplessness, feigns illness, threatens suicide, and finds other unfair means of exerting enormous pressure on him. He may resort to passive-aggressive tactics such as physical and emotional withdrawal, feeling avoidance, procrastination, and indecisiveness. Through all of this, both partners remain remarkably uninfluenced by the rather extreme means taken by the other. By their actions, each person is saying to the other that he or she will not be controlled.

The goal of this phase of treatment is to get each partner to abandon such tactics and to employ more honest, forthright, and fair measures in relating to each other. This goal may be pursued therapeutically in any number of ways. An Adlerian or cognitive therapy treatment strategy that deals with these problems simultaneously and that modifies the mistaken lifestyle conviction or maladaptive schemes can be particularly valuable.

Case Illustration

Presenting Problem

Jeremy and Allison were married for nearly 24 years when Jeremy began treatment in a clinic specializing in irritable bowel syndrome (IBS). Allison was 45-year-old elementary school teacher who herself had suffered chronic, recurrent bouts of depression from which she seemed to have only temporary relief. She was prescribed antidepressants by her family physician and she was in individual psychotherapy where her therapist had convinced her that adjustment to her "condition" was the best that she could attain. They had a 22-year-old son, Teddy, who had moved back home after losing his job. Jeremy was upset with his son's "failure" but also felt guilty believing that he was responsible for this "because I was not a good role model for him." When he was not traveling, Jeremy spent almost all of his time with Teddy doing "guy stuff." This upset Allison who believed that Jeremy should focus his attention on her.

Jeremy was 47 years and moderately overweight and balding. He worked for a large management consulting firm and his job required considerable travel; in the past 2 years, travel demands had increased. Recently, he had been diagnosed with IBS, a chronic gastrointestinal condition with no known cause. His main symptoms were severe abdominal pain, bloating, and alternating diarrhea and constipation. He had experienced these symptoms on and off for the past 2 years, but lately they had worsened.

Initial Treatment and Referral

Consistent with the diagnosis of IBS, a treatment plan was devised that included medication and diet change which was planned by the clinic's nutritionist. After 2 months, Jeremy's condition had not responded to the prescribed treatment. Jeremy complained that his travel schedule made sticking to the prescribed diet nearly impossible and jet lag seemed to exacerbate his symptoms. His physician referred him to the clinic's psychologist for cognitive behavior therapy (CBT) as an adjunct to the medical regimen. It was hoped that CBT would provide him with better coping strategies as well as suppress thoughts and behaviors that increased his symptoms.

Assessment

Part of the clinic's behavioral health protocol included a family consultation which consisted of an extended meeting in which the couple was seen conjointly and each partner was interviewed separately. This extended assessment provided the following information.

Allison was the youngest born of four siblings and the prized child of the family. She was a very attractive child and received considerable attention for her brightness and vivaciousness. Shortly after her fifth birthday, her mother became ill and was diagnosed with bipolar disorder, which greatly impacted the family. Over the years she was hospitalized several times for long periods of time. Allison's father did his best to function as both parents. He worked two jobs and did what he could to take care of the children when he was at home. But he was gone much of the time, and when he was home, he was preoccupied. The end result was that he withheld much of his attention from Allison. Although she was still the favorite grandchild of her grandparents, she secretly envied her mother's privileged position. Everyone accommodated her every whim, and a common family motto was "Don't upset your mother!" Allison's first episode of depression manifested in middle adolescence after being heartbroken with the breakup of her first serious relationship and she felt devastated. She eventually decided to go into elementary school teaching and specialized in drama.

Jeremy had been the oldest of three and the only boy. His father was a marijuana user with occasional unpredictable mood swings. His mother was a depressive woman who had used Jeremy as her sole support. His sister had been disabled following a car accident at age 4, and Jeremy remembers the many times she was hospitalized and went for medical appointments. He recalls his guilt that somehow if he had only been a better brother and not gone to baseball practice the day that she was hit by a car she might he healthy like everyone else. As he became an adolescent, it became his mission to look out for her and he thereby became her surrogate parent, teacher, and friend. He got his first part-time job when he was 13, working as a busboy at a greasy spoon restaurant. He hated the work but because he was underage it was the only job he could find. He remembers making a promise that he would make life better for himself and his sister and that he would never lose his temper or use drugs as his father had done. Immediately after graduating from high school, he went on to college—which he paid for himself. After graduation, he worked his way up through various jobs, eventually into management and then consulting with others about how to run their businesses.

Case Conceptualization

In his conjoint joint meeting with the couple, the psychologist quickly identified the interlocking histrionic pattern of Allison and the obsessive-compulsive pattern in Jeremy. He came up with the following biopsychosocial case conceptualization: Jeremy's increasing work demands and travel and his biological vulnerability plus their interlocking personality dynamics led to the expression of IBS symptoms. This not only increased Allison's depression but also severely strained their relationship, which further complicated Jeremy's response to treatment.

Behavioral Health Interventions

The following interlocking dynamics were then explained to the couple. Allison grew up feeling special but also feeling cheated. Although she was aware that she could get attention for her specialness, she was also aware of how fleeting it could be. Getting attention was wonderful, but being able to hold on to it was another matter. She measured life and others as to how they could take care of her or notice her, and she became a master at playing roles to attract their attention. As she grew older, she felt her specialness, that is, her beauty, youth, and energy were fading. The empty nest syndrome was hitting her hard: her planned only child (so he would always feel special) was leaving home. She felt abandoned by her husband, who worked too many hours; soon to be abandoned by her son (he too had left her for college some 5 years earlier, as her first love had, and might eventually move out and go on his own); she was lonely and pessimistic. The onset of her current, chronic depression roughly coincided with her son's leaving for college. She seemed to be using depression as a coping device to deal with life, to draw others to her as she had seen modeled by her mother. Although it appeared that she was biologically vulnerable to clinical depression, there was no question that she had learned to use her symptoms to rally support for herself. Jeremy grew up believing that he had responsibility for everything. In many ways, this was an accurate assessment. His conscientiousness helped keep his family intact. Gradually, the line between conscientiousness and control began to blur, and unless he controlled his own and others' lives he sensed a somewhat uneasy, impending doom. His solution was to do more, to work harder, to control more, and to be busier. His only break from such a rigid, tense style was to be ill. Also, through his symptoms of fear of heights and insomnia, he could ask for a break and take time off for himself without having to admit that he was shirking responsibility.

Allison's depression was reframed as a way of asking to be cared for and her irritability as her strategy for keeping their relationship intact. She valued love, the marriage, and family, and she wanted the two of them to be happy. She was trying to keep them together and to look out for her husband and his health. Similarly, Jeremy was trying to keep his family together too, and his working so hard was reframed as being for the same motive that Allison had. In effect, they were told that their symptoms were serving the same purpose, just in different ways. Could they now communicate such desires in more prosocial, constrictive ways? Jeremy's controlling and Allison's emotionality were mutually complementary. She was encouraged to teach him to be more passionate, and he was urged to be her consultant on matters of organization. They grasped this formulation and reframing and found it useful in understanding Jeremy's IBS symptoms and nonresponse to treatment.

Subsequently, Jeremy met with the psychologist for eight individual sessions utilizing CBT to better cope with his IBS. For two of those sessions, Allison joined as a coach to incorporate recommended diet changes which previously she had been reluctant to make.

Outcomes

The CBT interventions along with medication and diet changes resulted in reduction and elimination of all his abdominal symptoms. Over the next 18 months, Jeremy and Allison met with the psychologists three more times to review their progress and get feedback. Both reported considerably more satisfaction with the marriage and little, if any, conflict. Jeremy learned to become less rigid and controlling. He was encouraged to start his own consulting firm and work with local clients. After some hesitancy, he made that change and began to work out of his home. His consulting business flourished. He gained greater control over his schedule, worked less hours more efficiently, and found more pleasure at home. Allison, although still somewhat dramatic, feels more connected and valued. Having her husband work out of the home and spend more time with her has helped her tremendously. It was evident that Jeremy had shifted from the maladaptive to the more adaptive end of the obsessive-compulsive continuum, and Allison made a similar shift on the histrionic continuum. Although they still had characteristic rough spots, they found they grew more affectionate with each other. Allison's depression gradually lifted, and although she could still be somewhat blue, she found more satisfaction with Jeremy.

Concluding Note

When a medical patient is not responding to treatment, the behavioral health professional would do well to undertake a biopsychosocial assessment. Assessing personality dynamics is often quite useful in dealing with treatment response issues. It may well be that personality style/disorder issues are operative, or, in the case of Jeremy, that personality style/disorder issues in a spouse or other family member are also operative.

Reference

Harper, R. (2003). *Personality-guided therapy in behavioral medicine.* Washington, DC: American Psychological Association.

Sperry, L. (2003). *Handbook of the diagnosis and treatment of DSM-IV-TR personality disorders* (2nd ed.). New York, NY: Brunner-Routledge.

Sperry, L. (2006a). *Cognitive behavior therapy of DSM-IV-TR personality disorders* (2nd ed.). New York, NY: Routledge.

Sperry, L. (2006b). *Psychological treatment of chronic illness.* Washington, DC: American Psychological Association.

Sperry, L., & Maniacci, M. (1998). The histrionic-obsessive couple. In J. Carlson & L. Sperry (Eds.), *The disordered couple* (pp. 187–206). New York, NY: Brunner/Mazel.

4

ILLNESS PERCEPTIONS[1]

What best predicts a client's or couple's receptivity and adherence to treatment? Is it the client's motivation for treatment, previous experience with treatment, level of readiness for change, or capacity to collaborate with treatment? This question and its answer are hardly academic considerations as the reality is that rates of nonadherence with treatment regimens and premature termination of psychotherapy are high (Sperry, 2006). Recent research indicates that a client's illness perceptions may be more predictive of treatment adherence and receptivity to treatment than other explanations (Broadbent, Petrie, Main, & Weinman, 2006).

So what exactly are illness perceptions and how can clinicians utilize them to improve receptivity to treatment? This chapter begins by defining illness and illness perceptions. It then describes how these perceptions develop and how they can be assessed. Next, it indicates how a clinician can incorporate knowledge of these perceptions into the counseling process. Finally, a case example and session transcription are used to illustrate these points.

Illness Perceptions

Illness is not the same as disease. While disease is the objective manifestation of a medical condition, illness is the subjective experience of a disease or medical condition. A key aspect of that subjective experience is one's illness perceptions. Clinical experience and research reveal that individuals cluster their ideas about an illness around five coherent themes (Leventhal, Diefenbach, & Leventhal, 1992; Leventhal, Leventhal, & Cameron, 2000). Together these five themes reflect an individual's perception of his or her illness. These themes provide individuals with a framework to make

---

1. Adapted from Sperry, L. (2007). Illness perceptions and receptivity to counseling: Implications for individual and couples therapy. *The Family Journal: Counseling and Therapy for Couples and Families, 15,* 298–302.

sense of their symptoms, assess their health status, and take corrective action and cope with their medical condition.

The five illness perception themes are: Identity, which involves the diagnostic label and the symptoms viewed as being part of the person's disease or condition; Cause, which involves personal ideas about causality whether it be a simple, single cause or a more complex, multiple causality; Timeline, which is how long the individual expects the illness will last. There are three time categories: acute, chronic, or periodic; Consequences, which involve the expected impact or effects and outcome of the illness; and, Cure/Control, which is how one anticipates recovery from, and control of, one's illness (Leventhal et al., 1992).

So how do illness perceptions develop? It seems that an individual's perceptions of illness develop over time from diverse sources ranging from first hand experiences with a family member who suffered from a particular medical condition, from information gleaned from written material or the media, as well as from relatives and friends. These perceptions tend to remain dormant until activated by one's own illness or that of someone close to that individual. Illness perceptions are essentially private theories or models. Thus, it shouldn't be too surprising that individuals can be reluctant to discuss their beliefs about their illness with health care providers for fear of being viewed as ignorant or misinformed. Assessment of illness perceptions is accomplished through direct questioning or by paper and pencil inventories (Broadbent et al., 2006; Moss-Morris et al., 2002; Weinman, Petrie, Moss-Morris, & Horne, 1996).

Why should clinicians be interested in illness perceptions? The answer is because such perceptions are related both to receptivity to counseling and counseling outcomes. First of all, educating and negotiating a more accurate and mutually agreeable illness perception has been suggested as critical for developing and maintaining an effective therapeutic alliance (Sperry, Carlson, & Kjos, 2003). Recall that besides achieving a bond of trust and caring, an effective therapeutic alliance requires an alignment of beliefs and goals as well as methods of treatment among both client and counselor (Bordin, 1994). An effective therapeutic alliance therefore increases a client's receptivity to treatment. Increasingly, research is demonstrating that such a therapeutic relationship is most predictive of effective treatment outcomes (Lambert & Barley, 2002). The obvious implication is that assessing clients' illness perceptions and modifying them when necessary, is essential for effective counseling.

Illness Perceptions and Treatment

Awareness of a client's illness perceptions is clinically useful in tailoring and implementing counseling interventions. The first step involves assessment. Clinicians, whether physicians or counselors, can assess an individual's illness perceptions by eliciting answers to the following questions:

How much do you experience symptoms from your illness? (Identity)
What do you think has caused your illness? (Cause)
How long do you think your illness will continue? (Timeline)
How much does your illness affect your life? (Consequences):
How much control do you feel you have over your illness? (Control)
How much do you think your treatment can help your illness? (Cure)

While eliciting these perceptions the clinician has the opportunity educate and then address those beliefs that are physiologically inaccurate or incompatible with realistic treatment methods. For example, a client with a long history of treatment for hypertension reports a new symptom: impotence. He says that the reason (cause) for it is "because of the impure thoughts I've been having about the new receptionist at my job. (pause) And, I think God is punishing me for having those bad thoughts." However, the clinician—whether physician or counselor—is more convinced that the client's impotence is due to a recent medication change for which impotence is a common drug side effect. Accordingly, the clinician can first educate the client about medication side effects of the new drug and then negotiate a more reasonable explanation or cause for the new symptom. Equally important, the clinician would then therapeutically process the client's conflicting feelings, including guilt, about being married and having sexual thoughts about another woman.

When the client's illness perceptions are reasonably accurate, the clinician's task is to consider how these perceptions influence other health beliefs and behaviors and then therapeutically process them accordingly. The following case study illustrates how a clinician assesses, modifies, and then therapeutically processes other beliefs and behaviors influenced by these illness perceptions.

Case Example

Sandra is a 29-year-old married female with a 16-year history of asthma. After graduating from college and working 2 years as an accountant she married Jim, an account executive for a mortgage corporation. Sandra had hoped to qualify as a CPA and work a couple more years before having children. Passing the CPA exam was the only hurdle left in that process. She complained of recently experiencing an "anxiety attack" which then triggered an asthma attack. Up until recently her asthma had been relatively well controlled on medication and an inhaler. She had asked Dr. Hamblin, her physician, for an antianxiety medication to curb her anxiety. But because of the high likelihood of negative drug interaction between that drug class and her asthma medications, he was reluctant to add such a medication. Instead, Dr. Hamblin suggested a referral for counseling. Sandra was hesitant to take the referral, indicating that she didn't think she had mental problems. Her thought was the medication would provide the short term relief she needed to pass the test. She seemed to think she could put up with any medication side effects for a couple of weeks.

Not sure how to proceed, the physician excused himself and talked briefly with Jerry Williams, PhD, a licensed mental health counselor with expertise in dealing with illness issues. Williams consulted at the clinic on three afternoons a week and typically saw patients with issues like Sandra's for all 15 of the clinic physicians. Williams agreed to talk with Sandra briefly. Dr. Hamblin introduced Dr. Williams to Sandra and told her that he had asked Williams to evaluate her anxiety symptoms and treatment options. She agreed. When Dr. Hamblin left the exam room, Dr. Williams proceeded to calm her down and then inquired her about her "anxiety attacks" and their triggers. Ruling out panic attacks, he learned more about Sandra's fear of failing the exam and her difficulty studying for it. It seemed that her difficulty concentrating appeared to be largely due to distractions since she and Jim lived in an apartment with "paper thin walls and noise travels." Jim's music listening in another part of the apartment appeared to be a prime source of distraction for her. The transcription picks up at this point.

CO: How much would you say your asthma affects your life?

CL: Until lately, not very much. I'm so thankful that Dr. Hamblin's been pretty good at controlling it with changing my medications as the allergy season comes and goes. But lately, I've become almost a basket case with all this anxiety and worry.

CO: So, using a 10 point scale, where 1 is very little and 10 is very high, how much control would you estimate you have had over your asthma before this anxiety started? And, how much control would you say you have now?

CL: I'd say about an 8 or 9 before, and about 3 or so now.

CO: Thanks, that's helpful. So, what do you think has caused your asthma?

CL: Well, it seems to run in the family. Heredity. My mother and sister have it. I've had it since I was 13. And, my doctor said that allergies to tree pollen and mold just make my asthma worse.

CO: Do you see a connection between your stress which you experience as anxiety and allergy symptoms?

CL: Definitely.

CO: How do you understand that connection?

CL: Well, I guess that stress aggravates it. The more stress and worry I have the worse my asthma gets and the harder to control it. That's why I asked for a new medication for it.

CO: So, psychological stress activates your asthma just as environmental stress like pollen and mold do. Psychological factors can affect your asthma in addition to environmental and hereditary factors. Is that what you're saying?
[Dr. Williams is attempting to expand Sandra's perception of causality to include both biological and psychological factors. A positive response to his question suggests she is more receptive to a multiple cause explanation; that is, biological and psychological as compared to a single causative, biological].

CL: Yes. (pause). I suppose I am.

CO: So, generally speaking biological treatments like your asthma medication and inhalers are the usual treatment for the biologically caused aspect of a medical condition like asthma. And, while medications can be a treatment for more psychologically caused aspects of it, psychological treatments like stress management and counseling are the usual treatments for it, particularly when medications are contraindicated, such as the potential for causing serious side effects. Does that make sense?

CL: (pause). It does. But, I'm not keen on therapy-stuff. That's why I'm willing to try the meds even though there may be problems.

CO: Even, though the new medication could inadvertently affect your ability to concentrate sufficiently enough to pass the exam when you take it?

CL: Well, if you put it that way … no, I guess that isn't what I want.

CO: I hear your concern about going into therapy. You seem to be viewing yourself more as someone with a medical problem that wants a biological treatment, than as someone with a psychological problem who wants a psychological treatment. Is that right?

CL: Yes, it is.

CO: Well, then I think I can be of some help to you. Right now. Today. (pause). You see it is possible to apply some very brief focused stress management and counseling techniques in this medical setting today that could make a big difference. Since medication seems out of question at the present time, I'm willing to work with you now for the next 15 to 20 minutes or so to deal with your stress, worry, and anxiety so that it doesn't trigger more asthma symptoms nor disrupt your concentration while you're studying. There may be a need for a follow-up session. But if there is, it would be short. Are you willing to give it a try?

CL: I am. I got to do something and now.

CO: Good. So why don't we begin by you telling me about a stressful situation that happened recently while you were attempting to study.

CL: This past weekend I planned to spend Saturday and Sunday after-noons taking an online CPA practice exam on the computer in my

41

study. It was one of those feedback exams tests that after you finish it tells you what areas you need to focus your study on. [uh-hum]. I am in my study about 15 minutes into the exam and Jim's music starts playing faintly at first and then a little louder. I put in my earplugs so I could concentrate better. You know it was one of those timed practice tests. I could still hear the music. Then I started getting mad at him. I was very upset, started feeling my heart flutter, and had a hard time breathing. I used my inhaler two more times than I should have. Of course, that started making my pulse go faster and my skin started flushing. It was like I was having a panic attack. By then I was too physically and emotionally upset and worn out to study, much less to finish that practice exam. All, I wanted to do was prepare for my exam in 3 weeks and it was a total waste.

CO: Okay. So, you were trying to study and take the CPA practice exam and you could hear Jim's music and you were getting so angry and stressed out that you not only couldn't concentrate but you started to have anxiety symptoms. Is that correct?

CL: Right, [okay] it was terrible.

CO: And just to clarify, you couldn't have really studied anyplace else, like the public library, that afternoon because you needed a specific online connection to take the practice exam.

CL: Yeah. I had to take the exam at home.

CO: Okay. What were your thoughts or interpretations of Jim playing his music loudly?

CL: I guess one was that he didn't care that his music was loud and he was only concerned about himself. He knew I was trying to study, but he didn't care what effect it had on me.

CO: Okay. So your first interpretations was that he knew you were studying but played his music anyway, and the second interpretation was that he didn't care what effect it was having on you. Is that accurate?

CL: Um-hum.

CO: Okay. Let's look at your behaviors in that situation. So what are some of the things you did?

CL: Well at first I tried to ignore it and that's when I put in my ear plugs. I got progressively more upset and I couldn't concentrate and I was getting anxious. Then I took extra puffs of my inhaler and I really went over the top and thought I was having a panic attack or something. I probably should have gone into his study—his inner sanctum as he calls it—but I know he just wants to be left undisturbed when he's in there.

CO: Okay. First, you put your ear plugs in and tried to ignore the music. Then you became more upset and your asthma started flaring. Next, you took extra puffs of your inhaler but it made things worse. The thing you said you didn't do was tell or signal Jim to turn down his music. Is that correct?

CL: Sure, um-hum.

CO: Okay. How did you want that situation to turn out? In other words, what did you want to happen?

CL: That's simple. I just wanted to finish the practice exam, get my practice score and feedback, and put in a couple hours of study.

CO: Fine. Now, what actually happened?

CL: What happened is that I never got to finish the practice test and study. All I got was aggravated asthma symptoms, an anxiety attack, and bad feelings about Jim. I really didn't feel good about myself either.

CO: So basically you didn't get any studying done, your asthma flared up, you felt bad about Jim and yourself, and ended up wasting a whole afternoon of test preparation.

CL: Right.

CO: So Sandra let's take a look at this together at your interpretations and your behaviors and see what alternative interpretations and behaviors might have resulted in getting the outcome you wanted. Would you like to do that with me?

CL: Okay. Sounds good.

CO: Great. Let's first look at your interpretations. Your first interpretation was that Jim knew you were studying but played his music anyway. Did that interpretation help you or hurt you in getting the outcome you wanted?

CL: I guess it hurt me because I made the assumption that he knew his music was too loud for me to concentrate, and yet he may not have realized it.

CO: Yes, I follow that. So what alternative interpretation or way of thinking might you have had that would have helped you get what you wanted?

CL: (pause) I'm not sure, but maybe that Jim wouldn't likely know how loud his music was and or that it was affecting me, unless he got some feedback to that effect.

CO: Feedback from you?

CL: Probably. I guess it would have to be from me since no one else was there to give it.

CO: Okay. Now, your second interpretation was that Jim didn't care what effect the music was having on you. Did that help or hurt you in getting the outcome you wanted?

CL: I guess it hurt me too because he seems to really care about me otherwise. I mean he is proud of my profession and really wants me to get the CPA designation.

CO: All right, then, what is an alternate interpretation that would have helped you get what you wanted, that is, finish the practice test and successfully study the rest of the afternoon.

CL: I guess it would be that Jim cares about me and if he knew his music was disturbing my studying he would turn it down.

CO: That follows. Now let's look at your behaviors in that situation. Your first behavior was to put in your ear plugs and try to ignore the music. Did that behavior hurt you or help you in getting you what you wanted?

CL: It clearly didn't help (laughs). I could still hear the music.

CO: What alternative behavior would have helped get you what you wanted?

CL: I just had to go over to his room and let him know the music was too loud.

CO: Then you became more upset and your asthma started flaring so, you took extra puffs of your inhaler. Did that behavior hurt you or help you in getting you what you wanted?

CL: It just made things worse. (pause) You know, I'm not what others would call an "assertive woman" so it's not all that easy for me to tell him what I need and want him to do.

CO: I hear that. It is difficult for you. But if you were to choose between having another bad flare-up of your asthma and all the stress associated with losing 4 hours of study time, and just going over and holding up a sign that says you can't concentrate because of the music, which would you choose?

CL: Obviously, the sign, which doesn't even require me to say what I want him to do. If he just knew the music was affecting my study, he'd have turned it down without being asked.

CO: That's wonderful. So, let's think about your next study time. How can it be different?

CL: Well, I need to do the practice exam again since I didn't complete it. I'm thinking I'll encourage Jim to go to his friend's place Saturday afternoon. There's bound to be some sporting event on the tube. If he decides to stay home, I'll mention I—and my asthma—need almost total quiet for that afternoon. (pause) Yes, I know what to do. (pause) So this is what this kind of counseling is all about? (pause) Not as bad as I thought. Thanks.

Case Commentary

Sandra came to the medical clinic with one objective: to get relief from anxiety that was aggravating her asthma. Based on her perception of the biological cause of her asthma she believed she needed a biological

44

treatment; that is, an antianxiety medication. Thus, Dr. Hamblin's talk of referral for psychological counseling was alien to her illness perception of causality, and it is not surprising that she objected to such a referral. Fortunately, Dr. Hamblin called in an onsite consultant. As Dr. Williams increased her awareness of an additional causative factor, the psychological cause, Sandra was much more receptive to a more psychologically based intervention. In short, as Dr. Williams helped Sandra expand her illness perception of causality, receptivity to counseling was significantly increased, and the outcome was positive and spared her the untoward side effects of the medication she was initially seeking.

Concluding Note

While illness perception research has expanded exponentially in the past 30 years, it has had minimal impact on the practice of individual and couples therapy inside and outside medical treatment settings. Unfortunately, this line of research has seemingly developed independently of an equally important line of research on the therapeutic alliance. The result is that few counselors and therapists are aware of the clinical value and utility of illness perceptions. Given the predictive value of illness perceptions on counseling outcomes, it seems that assessing clients' illness perceptions and then tailoring treatment accordingly is essential for effective counseling.

References

Bordin, E. (1994). Theory and research on the therapeutic alliance: New directions. In A. Horvath & L. Greenberg (Eds.), *The working alliance: Theory, research and practice* (pp. 13–37). New York, NY: Wiley.

Broadbent, E., Petrie, K. J., Main, J., & Weinman, J. (2006). The Brief Illness Perception Questionnaire (BIPQ). *Journal of Psychosomatic Research, 60,* 631–637.

Lambert, M., & Barley, D. (2002). Research summary on the therapeutic relations and psychotherapy outcome. In J. Norcross (Ed.), *Psychotherapy relationships at work: Therapists' contributions and responsiveness to patients* (pp. 17–32). Oxford, UK: Oxford University Press.

Leventhal, H., Diefenbach, M. & Leventhal, E. (1992). Illness cognition: Using common sense to understand treatment adherence and affect in cognitive interactions. *Cognitive Therapy and Research, 16,* 143–163

Leventhal, H., Leventhal, E., & Cameron, L. (2000). Representation, procedures and affect in illness self-regulation: A perceptual-cognitive model. In A. Baum, T. Revenson, & J. Singer (Eds.), *Handbook of health psychology* (pp. 19–47). Mahwah, NJ: Erlbaum.

Moss-Morris, R., Weinman, J., Petrie, K., Horne, R., Cameron, L., & Buick, D. (2002). The Revised Illness Perception Questionnaire (IPQ-R). *Psychology and Health, 17,* 1–16.

Sperry, L. (2006). *Psychological treatment of chronic illness.* Washington, DC: APA Books.

Sperry, L., Carlson, J., & Kjos, D. (2003). *Becoming an effective therapist.* Boston, MA: Allyn & Bacon.

Weinman, J. Petrie, K., Moss-Morris, R., & Horne, R. (1996). The Illness Perception Questionnaire: A new method for assessing illness perceptions. *Psychology and Health, 11*, 431–446.

5

STAGES OF CHRONIC ILLNESS[1]

Working with patients and families who are experiencing chronic medical conditions can be a challenge for many counselors who are otherwise proficient in treating clients and families with obvious psychological conditions. Without sufficient training and experience with chronic medical conditions, counselors tend to rely on what has worked for them in the past. Accordingly, they respond to patients and their families who are experiencing chronic medical conditions in the same or a similar way as they would to clients and families facing psychological conditions and issues. There is some similarity between therapeutic responses to those with psychological conditions and those with chronic medical conditions, but there are also many differences. This is because the therapeutic landscape of psychological conditions differs from the therapeutic landscape of chronic medical conditions.

Understanding the therapeutic landscape of chronic medical conditions begins with the distinction between a medical condition and a medical illness. Medical conditions are objective realities to which are applied medical diagnoses with identifiable signs. The experience of a medical condition, on the other hand, is referred to as a medical illness which often is difficult to describe except for symptoms, which can be vague. To be effective in working therapeutically with patients with chronic medical illness requires an understanding of the typical journey or phases that patients experience as they move from crisis to integration. Even though illness experience is subjective, research has nevertheless been able to identify the general boundaries of four phases of this experience (Fennell, 2003). This chapter sketches the phases of chronic medical illness and provides a framework for tailoring a therapeutic response to these phases. It begins with a discussion of the experience of chronic illness, including a

---

1. Adapted from Sperry, L. (2009). Therapeutic response to patients and families experiencing chronic medical conditions. *The Family Journal: Counseling and Therapy for Couples and Families, 17*, 180–184.

description of a phase model of chronic illness. Next, it describes a model of therapeutic responses to patients and their families based on each illness phase. Then, it illustrates this model with two case examples. Finally, it briefly discusses some practice implications of this model for individual and family counseling.

The Experience of Chronic Illness

The experience of having an acute disease, such as the common cold, is easy to describe because, for most people, it has the same sign and symptom presentation and follows a brief and predictable course. It begins with a nasal congestion and a sore throat, which within a day leads to a feeling of fullness with copious nasal discharge that irritates the nose. After 3 days the major signs diminish but the "stuffed up" feeling may continue for up to a week. During that time the individual may have a bit less energy. Essentially, symptom, course, and recovery are reasonably consistent and predictable for most people. On the other hand, a key characteristic of a chronic illness is its variability in terms of symptoms and course, and there may or may not be a recovery phase, depending on the medical condition and the individual. Needless to say, the experience of a chronic illness is much more variable than acute illness. This variability is confusing for medical personnel and counselors and can complicate both the therapeutic relationship and the treatment process (Sperry, 2006). Despite this variability, researchers have been able to articulate the experience of adjustment to a chronic medical condition from the patient's perspective in terms of a phase model.

A Phase Model of Chronic Illness

Fennell (2003) has described a phase model of chronic illness. She utilizes the term *phase* rather than *stage* because *stage* implies a forward moving progression whereas *phase* implies that both progression and regression are possible. These four phases are based on her clinical research with several hundred patients with a variety of chronic diseases and are briefly presented here.

> *Phase 1: Crisis.* The onset of illness triggers a crisis for which individuals seek relief through medical diagnosis and treatment, spiritual help, or substance abuse. Family, coworkers, and caregivers may respond with disbelief, revulsion, and rejection. In this phase the basic task is to deal with the immediate symptoms, pain, or traumas associated with this new experience of illness.
>
> *Phase 2: Stabilization.* A plateau of symptoms is reached, and individuals become more familiar with their illness. They attempt to

carry on their preillness activity level, which overtaxes them and contributes to relapses and the ensuing feelings of upset and failure. The basic task of this phase is to stabilize and restructure life patterns and perceptions.

Phase 3: Resolution. Amidst plateaus of symptoms and relapses individuals understand their illness pattern and others' response to it. There is initial acceptance that one's preillness sense of self will not return. In this phase the basic task is to develop a new self and to seek a personally meaningful philosophy of life and spirituality consistent with it.

Phase 4: Integration. Despite plateaus and relapses individuals are able to integrate parts of their old self before the illness to their new self. In this phase the basic task is to find appropriate employment if able to work, to reintegrate or form supportive networks of friends and family, and to integrate one's illness within a spiritual or philosophical framework. It also means achieving the highest level of wellness possible despite compromised or failing health status. Accordingly, integration means coming "to experience a complete life in which illness is only one aspect" (Fennell, 2003, p. 9).

Table 5.1 further articulates the medical, personal, and family implications as well as the basic therapeutic tasks of each stage.

Not every individual with a chronic illness manages to journey through all four stages. As Fennell (2003) points out, many chronically ill patients get caught in a recurring loop of cycling between phases 1 and 2 wherein each crisis produces new wounding and destabilization of the patient and the patient's family system. Such crises tend to be followed by a brief period of stabilization and, without intervention, a new crisis invariably destabilizes the system again. With appropriate therapeutic responding, chronically ill patients can be assisted to break this recurring cycle and move to phases 3 and 4.

Some patients, particularly those on the margins of society with limited resources and support systems, may never escape phase 1. They can be buffeted from crisis to crisis, and their only "relief" may be alcohol or drugs; relief that is temporary but only worsens their medical condition and further limits their access to effective treatment. "These individuals often lose everything they have … simply because they are sick and have not received the care and help they need" (Fennell, 2003, pp. 40–41).

Needless to say, an appropriate and effective therapeutic response is more necessary here than at any other illness phase. Such therapeutic response not only helps chronically ill patients in finding new meaning in life and the encouragement and coping skills to live that life with a

Table 5.1 Phases of Chronic Illness (adapted from Fennell, 2003)

Phase 1: Crisis

Medical	Onset of disease triggers a crisis –> seek relief through medical diagnosis and treatment
Patient	Shock, disbelief, disorientation, mood swings, isolation; external locus of control and external locus of treatment
Family	Family and caregivers experience disbelief, revulsion, and rejection
Basic Task	Deal with symptoms, pain, or associated traumas

Phase 2: Stabilization

Medical	Plateau of symptoms is reached, and individuals become more familiar with their illness
Patient	Attempts preillness activity level –> overtaxes and contributes to relapses and the ensuing feelings of upset and failure
Family	Family expects patient to return to past responsibilities –> disappointment and anger because patient does not resume prior responsibilities and successes –> divorce or stop support and assistance
Basic Task	Accept illness and comply with treatment regimen; stabilize and restructure life patterns

Phase 3: Resolution

Medical	Plateaus of symptoms and relapses but patient better understands illness pattern and others' reactions
Patient	Existential question: Why should patient live and how?; internal locus of control and internal locus of treatment; begin to accept that one's preillness self will not return
Family	Family begins to accept patient preillness self will not return and adjusts expectations of the patient; patient reconsiders or develops new friendships and significant others
Basic Task	Patient and family grieve loss of preillness self –> awareness and options to develop a new self and meaningful philosophy of life and spirituality

Phase 4: Integration

Medical	Some patients experience continued plateau or even improvement while others worsen
Patient	Integrates parts of preillness self into new self despite plateaus/relapses
Family	Family, friends, and significant others if possible; reduced or alternative work is sought; if on disability may seek to volunteer; but insist that what they do will be meaningful
Basic Task	Find appropriate employment; if on disability find volunteer activity, or live meaningfully; reintegrate or form supportive networks of friends and family; further integrate one's illness within a spiritual or philosophical framework

---

measure of dignity and a sense of wellness, but it can keep them alive while they escape this dangerous looping cycle.

Therapeutic Responses and Interventions

So what are these therapeutic responses and interventions? An essential intervention in working with those with chronic medical conditions is the elicitation of illness perceptions. Illness perceptions are one's instrumental beliefs about the causes, effects, time frame, cure, and control of the illness, and treatment outcomes (Leventhal, Diefenbach, & Leventhal, 1992). One's belief about the cause of illness is called an explanatory model. Expectations of how the illness should best be treated are based on this explanatory model. Noncompliance with treatment almost always reflects a discrepancy between the medical provider's plan for treatment and the patient's expectations (Sperry, 2006; Sperry, 2009b). The purpose of eliciting illness perceptions, explanatory models, and expectations is to identify the patients' view of their medical condition and understand their noncompliance. Noncompliance almost always indicates illness nonacceptance (Sperry, 2009b).

Movement beyond phase 2 requires that patients—and their families—accept their medical condition. Clinical experience shows that only when counselors and therapists understand the basis of patients' nonacceptance are they able to facilitate patients' acceptance of their illness. Various strategies, including cognitive restructuring, are useful in effecting illness acceptance (Sperry, 2009a). Space does not permit a discussion of other therapeutic responses and interventions. However, Table 5.2 summarizes some of the more common therapeutic responses and interventions useful with both patients and families for each of the four phases of chronic illness.

Case Illustrations

Case 1

Linda was a 38-year-old married white female with two children when she was diagnosed with multiple sclerosis (MS) 2 years ago. Over a period of several weeks Linda noticed that she had become increasingly fatigued, with blurry vision and, at times, had trouble walking. She had experienced fatigue and depression on and off since her mother died 6 years ago, but she had not experienced this degree of fatigue. She now had to push herself to meet her regular family and work responsibilities. She consulted with her family physician who could not find objective evidence of a disease process but suggested she cut back on work, relax more. Within 6 months her symptoms worsened and she had difficulty driving. Her family doctor

Table 5.2 Therapeutic Response to Patient and Family by Phase of Illness

Patient and Family Experience	Therapeutic Response
Phase 1: Crisis	
Patient	Address patient's symptomatic distress; elicit patient's illness perception, especially explanatory model and expectations
Family	Address family response to patient's health crisis
Phase 2: Stabilization	
Patient	Focus on (a) patient acceptance of his or her illness, and (b) treatment compliance
Family	Focus on family's acceptance of the patient's illness; and involve family in increasing treatment compliance; address marital discord and threats of separation or divorce
Phase 3: Resolution	
Patient	Focus on grieving patient's preillness self and relational issues; continue focus on treatment compliance, if indicated
Family	Help family to establish more realistic expectations of the patient; if needed address separation/divorce and custody issues
Phase 4: Integration	
Patient	Focus on assisting patient to forge a new sense of self as a whole person who happens to have a chronic medical condition
Family	Assist adjustment of family to patient's new friends and work or volunteer activity

referred her to a neurologist who, after a complete medical evaluation, made the diagnosis of MS.

Having a diagnosis provided Linda with a means to make sense of and explain her symptomatic experiences to others. Still she experienced feelings of shame, self-hatred, fear, and depression. She wondered if she was losing her mind. She also felt increasingly isolated from her husband, family, and coworkers. While her work supervisor was supportive, Linda feared that others would reject her so she was quite cautious in expressing both her pain and her fears at work and at home. Her physician suggested counseling or therapy might help her but she refused, thinking to herself that she just had some neurological symptoms (Phase 1).

Linda's physical symptoms began to stabilize and she recognized a pattern in her energy level, pain threshold, and mood swings. She experienced two physical relapses with sudden, increased intensity to her symptoms which were relieved with prescribed steroid medication.

She read widely to learn all she could about MS, she inquired into various investigational drug studies hoping to find anyone who would guarantee a cure, remove her symptoms, or more effectively cope with her situation. There was growing conflict with her family and a loss of patience with some of her care providers. Persistence of symptoms was increasingly frustrating for everyone. Her coworkers at the bank were annoyed that she couldn't "pull herself together" and her husband gave her the ultimatum to get well or get divorced. She experienced stigma for the first time in her life, but silently accepted others' labeling, misinformation, and nastiness. Still, Linda developed a support system consisting of three loyal friends, one of whom was a nurse. The nurse worked in a diabetes clinic and was familiar with the challenges patients and their families experienced in coping with a chronic medical illness. She urged Linda to get in touch with Gerald Weinstein, MS, LMHC, a licensed mental health counselor who had considerable experience working with chronic illness issues. Linda did take the advice and sought out this counselor for help with personal, family, and job concerns. During the second session she relinquished her illness denial and began to accept her MS (Phase 2)

This support and counseling worked: Linda began experiencing longer periods of stability and occasionally slight improvement, both of which were short-lived and were followed by relapses. She recognized that efforts to return to being her old, productive self inevitably led to relapse. As a result she became less focused on finding a cure and more on grieving the loss of her old self. With the help of her therapist, she struggled to find a new sense of meaning in life, and began keeping a journal of this new journey. When her husband Jared wanted a divorce claiming "You're not the woman I married," Linda was devastated. The counselor met conjointly with Linda and Jared for four sessions. In the first session Jared cried as he described the effect that Linda's health and behavior were having on him and their children. Recognizing that despite severe family stressors the couple retained a deep level of caring for each other, the counselor was able to educate Jared on how MS affects relations. He was able to help Jared better accept Linda's MS and to assist the couple in addressing childcare and housekeeping concerns. As family stressors abated and Jared renewed his commitment to the marriage, Linda was able to begin the process of assessing her friends, her job, and her hopes and dreams. This was a painful process but out of it a new self began to emerge. As time passed, Linda also felt increasingly more in control of her life and more assertive in confronting others' bias and stigmatizing comments (Phase 3).

Now confined to a wheelchair, Linda got better at recognizing and accepting the cyclic nature of her MS—plateau, improvement, and relapse. She came to view relapse as inevitable but no longer as a failure. She was also more able to incorporate salvageable parts of her preillness self with her newly emerging sense of self. She now identified herself to others as "a person who just happened to be experiencing MS" and no longer described herself as an "MS patient." The fact that she corrected her physician and others when they referred to her as an MS patient reflected this new view of self. In addition, she was able to integrate her suffering with a greater sense of compassion and respect. She was able to reestablish relationships with some of her formerly alienated extended family and friends. Finally, because of the increasing difficulty she experienced in working outside the home, she volunteered two mornings a week at an advocacy center for MS in the community (Phase 4).

Case Commentary. This is an accurate portrayal of a patient who experiences a chronic and progressively debilitating medical condition. It also portrays how a patient's family struggles with such a condition. Furthermore, this case portrays how a counselor's therapeutic response and interventions facilitated a patient's achievement of integration (Phase 4).

Although she initially refused counseling, Linda took the advice of a friend and sought out a counselor experienced in chronic illness. After eliciting her illness perceptions, Mr. Weinstein worked with her to help her accept her illness and relinquish her various denial beliefs and behaviors. This helped her progress to phase 2. Marital stressors were addressed in conjoint couples sessions in which Mr. Weinstein provided education about the impact of chronic illness on marriage and family life and helped the husband better accept Linda's MS. He helped Linda through the marital crisis, her reassessment of her life with MS, and the even more painful process of relinquishing her preillness sense of self. Furthermore, in assisting Jared and Linda to establish more realistic expectations for childcare and household responsibilities, the counselor facilitated Linda's movement into phase 3. Forging the beginnings of a new sense of self and assisting her in coming to terms with those who had become alienated from her was part of phase 4 work. It also included assisting her to accept life in a wheelchair and without a full-time job. Furthermore, Mr. Weinstein helped her husband and other family members to accept that Linda could no longer work, she would be permanently confined to a wheelchair, and she now had new friends. This was not easy for Jared and he overreacted toward Linda to such an extent that two more conjoint counseling sessions were needed. The fact that Linda now views herself as a whole person who happens to have MS reflects the integration that has occurred in her life. It is also a testament to the counselor's expert therapeutic responding.

Case 2

Jesse is a 28-year-old married Haitian American who is moderately obese. He has a history of untreated depression for about 3 years, and was diagnosed with diabetes mellitus Type 2 after being hospitalized for "blacking out" on the job 8 months ago. He was initially started on an American Diabetic Association (ADA) diet and exercise program, and when there was no change in his weight or glucose levels, oral antiglycemic drugs were begun.

He complained that the ADA diet excluded most of his "native foods" and he disliked doing blood sugar checks. Glycohemoglobin levels remained high despite the diet, exercise, and medication regimen. An endocrine consultation recommended an insulin pump. A week ago he was hospitalized again for "blacking out" on the job. Jesse's diabetes has worsened, his family is distraught, and medical professionals label him as noncompliant. Not surprisingly, his depression has worsened.

Case Commentary.   Like a large number of chronic illness patients, Jesse seems to be "stuck," and health care providers, particularly his family physician, have become "frustrated" by his noncompliance. Unlike Linda, Jesse is not experiencing high levels of wellness nor well-being. In terms of the illness phases, Jesse seems to be stuck "looping" between crisis (Phase 1) and stabilization (Phase 2), a common phenomenon among many patients.

Looping brings with it a sense of hopelessness with little or no prospect for the situation changing. If conventional counseling or therapy is available there is little guarantee that therapeutic responses will be appropriate and effective since relatively few counselors or other mental health professionals have the training and experience to understand and respond to the therapeutic landscape of chronic medical conditions.

However, if Jesse had access to a therapist who was able to elicit his illness perceptions and assist him toward illness acceptance and treatment compliance the situation could change dramatically. Probably, such therapy would require some collaboration with Jesse's family so that the family would also accept Jesse's illness and become a therapeutic ally in diet modification and other aspects of the treatment regimen. Furthermore, such collaboration with Jesse and his family would also entail considerable cultural sensitivity and competency of the counselor.

Practice Implications and Concluding Note

The case material just presented illustrates how patients progress or fail to progress through various phases of the chronic illness experience. Both cases demonstrate that the therapeutic landscape for psychological conditions differs from the therapeutic landscape for medical conditions. The case of Linda demonstrates how, with the help of a knowledgeable counselor, a patient can achieve a reasonably high level of wellness and well-being despite the ravages of an incurable medical condition.

The illness phase model and the therapeutic responding model have important practice implications for the practice of counseling. Both provide counselors with a framework in which to establish treatment goals and plan interventions, elicit essential information such as illness perceptions, collaborate with patients and their families to facilitate movement toward integration (Phase 4), and to anticipate patient and family resistance as well as counselor countertransference.

References

Fennell, P. (2003). *Managing chronic illness: Using the four phase treatment approach.* New York, NY: Wiley.

Leventhal, H., Diefenbach, M., & Leventhal, E. (1992). Illness cognition: Using common sense to understand treatment adherence and affect in cognitive interactions. *Cognitive Therapy and Research, 16,* 143–116.

Sperry, L. (2006). *Psychological treatment of chronic illness: The biopsychosocial therapy approach.* Washington, DC: American Psychological Association.

Sperry, L. (2009a). *Treatment of chronic medical conditions: Cognitive behavioral therapy strategies and integrative treatment protocols.* Washington, DC: American Psychological Association.

Sperry, L. (2009b). Lifestyle convictions and illness perceptions as predictors of treatment compliance and noncompliance. *Journal of Individual Psychology, 65,* 298–304.

6

ETHICAL CONSIDERATIONS[1]

A professional colleague shared a harrowing experience involving his young daughter who has been treated for juvenile-onset diabetes for most of her life. The colleague reported waiting with his wife and daughter in a hospital clinic waiting room for more than an hour for a scheduled consultation. The consultation with the clinic's health psychologist was requested by the daughter's endocrinologist in the hope of utilizing adjunctive psychological interventions to better stabilize the child's blood sugar levels. The appointment lasted only 10 minutes, and my colleague and his family left frustrated and upset. He was taken aback by the psychologist's aloofness and apparent lack of a bedside manner; that is, empathy and compassion. He shook his head and said, "That consultant was worse than most physicians. I was expecting that because he wasn't a physician, he would spend more time with us and be more helpful and receptive to my questions and concerns. After all, isn't that what mental health professionals are trained to do?"

He wondered if this consultant's behavior was normative for counselors and psychologists who practice in health care settings. Presumably, such behavior is not normative, but my colleague's query led me to reflect on the matter. There is no question that behavioral health and health-focused counseling with individuals, couples, and families is at the cutting edge of professional practice today (Sperry, 2005; Sperry, Lewis, Carlson, & Englar-Carlson, 2005). It is also a fact that providing such professional services requires knowledge and skill competencies above and beyond conventional training and licensure standards. What is also becoming clearer is that the perspective adopted by counselors and psychologists about professional and ethical practice can and does significantly affect their professional behavior with patients and clients.

---

1. Adapted from Sperry, L. (2005). Health counseling with individuals, couples, and families: Three perspectives on ethical and professional practice. *The Family Journal: Counseling and Therapy for Couples and Families, 13,* 328–331.

This chapter is about different perspectives on ethical and professional practice that influence the treatment process. In more than 40 years as a clinical supervisor and clinic director, I have observed that, irrespective of years of experience or professional discipline, counselors and therapists espouse different views or perspectives on the relationship of professional ethics and professional practice: They either view ethical practice and professional practice as integrally linked, they view the two as distinctly separate, or they espouse a view midway between these two extreme perspectives. The chapter provides detailed sketches of each of these three perspectives and implications for clinical practice.

Three Perspectives on Ethical and Professional Practice

I recall watching an episode of a sci-fi TV program about an engineer who was contracted by a large department store to program a humanoid to function as a customer service representative. The engineer's main responsibility was to design and test out three different computer chips that could be inserted into the humanoid that could estimate cost-efficiency and analyze customer reactions. The first chip activated a letter-of-the-law computer program in which the humanoid customer rep followed the store's return policy very strictly. A 4-week trial period was planned. At the end of the trial, data analysis indicated that cost-effectiveness was highest for this chip, but many customers felt put off by the seemingly mindless interpretation of store policy. For example, one customer who requested a return of an item purchased 15 days earlier and who had a store receipt was rejected because of the 14-day return policy. The second chip activated a spirit-of-the-law computer program in which the humanoid customer rep was very customer friendly and quite liberal in following the return policy. Customer response was uniformly positive with this approach and was only slightly less effective than the first. Finally, the third chip represented a mix where sometimes the rep followed the letter of the policy strictly and sometimes it did not.

Data analysis on this chip indicated that some customers were frustrated and disappointed and some were not. The day the trial period ended was the day before the stockholder's annual meeting. The store's president had decided that he would announce to the board the next day that a humanoid with the letter-of-the-law chip would now handle all customer returns because this chip had proved to be the most cost-effective. Ironically, that evening, a disgruntled customer who had been rejected for a refund called in a bomb threat at the store. The bomb squad team that responded to the threat unwittingly triggered a surge of electrical power that fried the humanoid, which was being recharged at the time. You have probably guessed that the letter-of-the-law chip was still inserted in the humanoid!

In many ways, this story line is akin to the three differing perspectives on ethics and professional practice. Although obviously not humanoids, the perspectives that counselors and therapists espouse about ethics and professional practice do program or influence their view of professional and ethical situations. Not surprisingly, these perspectives can result in differing clinical outcomes.

There are three such perspectives that characterize the current practice of counseling individuals, couples, and families. I refer to them as Perspectives I, II, and III (Sperry, 2007). Perspective I, analogous to Chip 1, and Perspective III, analogous to Chip 2, are polar opposites; Perspective II, analogous to Chip 3, is basically an intermediate position.

Perspective I

In this perspective, professional practice is viewed as disconnected from ethical practice. What really counts is professional practice; that is, assessment and intervention strategies and the like, whereas ethical codes and legal statutes are separate. At best, they are an inconvenience with which professionals must learn to live; at worst, they are redolent of malpractice suits or censure. Such individuals tend to view their professional work as a job and are often content to put in their time and be compensated to support their out-of-work life.

Providing services that are minimally to adequately competent is their goal. Typically, neither informal nor formal learning is a priority for them, and lifelong learning is simply a slogan that may apply to others. Thus, they will not ordinarily seek out supervision or consultation unless the situation demands it. It should not be surprising that they are likely to view formal continuing education requirements as impositions by their credentialing board or professional association rather than as an invitation and encouragement to grow in professional and personal terms. Their responsibility to monitor their level of competence seems to have little meaning for them, probably because they do not view ongoing education as necessary or important. Self-care is neither valued nor considered essential.

If attending in-house lectures or workshops is optional, they are unlikely to attend unless it relieves them of a work responsibility. If it is mandated, they may attend but may do so with some reluctance. To log the necessary hours for licensure renewal, they may search for the least expensive or most accessible workshops or training programs rather than base their choice on what knowledge or skill sets they need to enhance or develop. In short, they set their sights no higher than somewhere between a minimal to adequate level of competence. For individuals espousing Perspective I, it is not an issue of incompetence but, rather, a matter of limited motivation to progressively increase their level of competence in some but not all spheres of practice. Often, this means developing and maintaining a reasonable level of competence in the technical domain (i.e., techniques and interventions) but not the relational domains (i.e., establishing and maintaining effective relationships with patients or clients). The presumption is that therapeutic relationships are messy and fraught with danger.

It is not surprising, then, in this perspective that the focus of ethical thinking is limited to ethical codes, ethical standards, and legal statutes with an emphasis on compliance with enforceable rules and standards. Typically, one's personal and professional lives are separated, and invariably, one's personal ethics and professional ethics are also separated. Ethical sensitivity means awareness of professional misconduct, ethical problems, and ethical dilemmas. This perspective is grounded in the belief that there must be sanctions for misconduct. Accordingly, the goal is to avoid prohibited and slippery-slope behaviors, such as boundary crossings, and engage in risk management activities that reduce the likelihood of a malpractice lawsuit or professional censure. Ironically, this overemphasis on avoiding malpractice and censure invariably means that the counselor is really more focused on promoting his or her own welfare than on promoting the client's welfare.

Perspective III

In this perspective, professional practice is viewed as integrally linked to ethical practice. For those who view ethical practice and professional practice as integrally linked, sound professional practice is considered highly ethical practice, because ethical values inform professional practice. Accordingly, ethical values are consistent with best practices, research, clinical lore, and professional experience, but when there is potential conflict, ethical values trump clinical lore or clinical experience. Professional counselors and therapists operating from this perspective view competence as an ongoing, developmental process.

For the most part, professionals espousing this perspective view their professional work as a calling, as a commitment to making a difference in the lives of their clients. Accordingly, they are very invested in their work, and it provides them with considerable job and life satisfaction. Admittedly, they take the responsibility for monitoring their level of competence seriously and welcome opportunities to increase their expertise. Supervision, case consultation, and continuing education programs are important avenues for enhancing knowledge and skills. Although some of these individuals are voracious readers and consumers of the professional and research literature in their field, most others manage to find a way to stay current with new developments. These counselors and therapists are often sought out by others for supervision and consultation, roles that they take seriously and for which they are likely to have attained a high level of proficiency. Self-care is valued and considered essential in this perspective, because it is believed that as professionals take care of themselves, they are better able to care for others. Self-care and wellness are more likely to be a proactive rather than a reactive response.

This perspective provides a comprehensive focus wherein it is possible to integrate professional codes, as well as other ethical traditions, with one's personal ethics. Here, virtues and values are considered as important as ethical codes, standards, and rules. The focus is on positive behavior and virtues, ethical ideals, character development, and integrating one's personal philosophy of life with one's professional goals and career aspirations. In this perspective that values prevention, risk management is integrated with personal and professional development. Ethical decision making involves the professional, contextual, and ethical domains as well as personal, relational, and organizational considerations. Ethical sensitivity is essential in this perspective as is an integration of personal and professional ethical principles. Interestingly, individuals espousing Perspective III are more likely to be considered master therapists by their peers than those espousing the other two perspectives.

Master Therapists.   Master counselors and therapists are professionals who are viewed by others as practicing with the highest level of professional and ethical expertise. A landmark study of master therapists highlights the value they place on being exceptionally skilled practitioners (Skovholt & Jennings, 2004). A basic conclusion of the study is that these therapists were highly motivated to become experts in their field. Even after years of experience and training, these therapists placed a high value on building and maintaining their professional knowledge base and skill set. It was also noted that even though they had achieved what others would consider an expert level of practice, these master therapists were continually seeking formal and informal training to further broaden and enhance their clinical abilities. This constant desire and ongoing effort to find opportunities for learning and growth in their profession was a defining characteristic of these master therapists. Their drive for competency, combined with an awareness of their own limitations, inspired these therapists to become lifelong learners.

These therapists spoke of the importance of finding professional growth experiences beyond traditional didactic venues such as professional conferences and workshops. They particularly looked to consultation and supervision, as well as their own personal therapy, as important avenues for change, challenge, and inspiration. It was important for them to have others critically evaluate their work. They also "spoke eloquently of bolstering the accumulation of clinical experience with sustaining professional relationships [in order] to grow professionally" (Jennings, Sovereign, Bottoroff, & Mussell, 2004, p. 111).

For master therapists, their commitment to professional development meant more than just amassing years of clinical experience. For them, experience combined with clinical consultation, ongoing traditional academic training, and professional reflection yielded a deeper level of professional growth. Their commitment to professional growth appears to have bolstered their competence, which, in turn, they believe is an important ingredient in their ethically sensitive practice. It is interesting to note that the researchers in this study speculated that keeping current on new developments in the profession and exposing their work to others for feedback minimized the potential for unethical behavior among these master therapists.

Another study finding involved the relationship of competence and capacity for tolerance of ambiguity. These master therapists were less likely than other therapists to look for easy answers in their work with clients. Staying open to all experiences was another hallmark of competent practice for them. They seemed to be searching constantly for the uniqueness and intricacies of a situation. This appreciation of complexities has ethical implications that help to prevent premature closure, which involves the tendency to reduce anxiety by settling for the first solution that presents itself or using the same technique in virtually every situation.

Although premature closure is an effective anxiety reducer for the therapist, the premature solution or intervention chosen can be a poor fit for the client. Failure to be open to complexity and ambiguity leads to a narrowing of case conceptualizations and treatment interventions, which can result in less than competent work. Finally, there should be no doubt that these master therapists are unmistakably reflective of Perspective III.

Perspective II

This perspective represents a midway position between Perspectives I and III. Professional counselors and therapists operating from this perspective recognize that increasing competence is valuable either in terms of advancing their career or because the notion of being a lifelong learner has some appeal. Individuals here tend to view their professional work as either a career or a calling. To the extent to which their goal is to advance their career, they will become involved in informal and formal continuing education efforts. To the extent to which they recognize that their work involves making a difference in others' lives, they are also receptive to involvement in continuing education activities. Their involvement in continuing education efforts is largely more intense and active compared to those embodying Perspective I but not with the intensity or commitment of those in Perspective III. Self-care and wellness are more likely to be reactive responses to distress or burnout rather than proactive initiatives.

Individuals embodying this perspective are more likely to function in adequate or proficient stages of competence.

This perspective represents an effort to comply with ethical standards and rules while at the same time expressing some willingness to consider self-reflection, contextual considerations, and self-care. The extent to which professionals holding this perspective experience cognitive and emotional dissonance is a function of how much allegiance they have to Perspective I: The more allegiance, the less dissonance, and vice versa. Although these individuals may express some interest in integrating their personal and professional values, there is little commitment to undertaking such an effort.

The Transition from Perspective I to Perspective III

As professional ethics became part of the training of counselors and therapists in the late 1970s and early 1980s, it would be fair to say that Perspective I was the dominant mode in both teaching and professional practice. Although Perspective I remains common today, particularly among trainees and beginning counselors and therapists, Perspective II probably reflects the sentiments of an increasing number of practitioners today. Perspective III seems to reflect other trends in the field involving consolidation and integration; that is, integrative therapies that incorporate the multicultural and spiritual dimension in treatment, and so forth. Recent research suggests that master therapists and counselors live and model growth-based, positive ethics that are characteristic of Perspective III (Skovholt & Jennings, 2004). As such, they provide a useful and necessary example of professional practice to other aspiring counselors and therapists. A basic premise is that the natural progression from beginning to advanced therapist to master therapist and counselor involves movement from Perspective I or II to Perspective III.

Although these three perspectives appear to be discrete, it must be pointed out that ethical standards and legal statutes are not confined to Perspective I. All therapists and counselors, irrespective of the particular perspective they espouse, are expected to provide services reflecting a basic standard of care and mandatory ethical codes and standards.

Concluding Note

The article began with an unflattering anecdote about how not to practice health counseling with a family. Although it may be tempting to offer a specific analysis of the consulting health psychologist's behavior, there is insufficient information provided for such an explanation. However, generally speaking, we can say with some degree of confidence that effective professional practice is ostensibly good ethical practice because it fosters the client's or family's welfare above that of the professional. Furthermore, highly effective professional and ethical practice tends to be satisfying and gratifying for both client or family and professional. Finally, those practicing health-focused counseling and psychotherapy might well emulate the ethical and professional practice of master therapists. Among others things, it means espousing Perspective III.

References

Jennings, L., Sovereign, A., Bottoroff, N., & Mussell, M. (2004). Ethical values of master therapists. In T. Skovholt & L. Jennings (Eds.), *Master therapists: Exploring expertise in therapy and counseling* (pp. 107–124). Boston, MA: Allyn & Bacon.

Skovholt, T., & Jennings, L. (Eds.). (2004). *Master therapists: Exploring expertise in therapy and counseling.* Boston, MA: Allyn & Bacon.

Sperry, L. (2005). *Psychotherapy with chronic illness: A biopsychosocial therapy approach.* Washington, DC: American Psychological Association.

Sperry, L. (2007). *The ethical and professional practice of counseling and psychotherapy.* Boston, MA: Allyn & Bacon.

Sperry, L., Lewis, J., Carlson, J., & Englar-Carlson, M. (2005). *Health promotion and health counseling: Effective counseling and psychotherapeutic strategies.* Boston, MA: Allyn & Bacon.

7

SPIRITUAL CONSIDERATIONS[1]

Competence is an increasingly common term in professional parlance these days, whether the profession is law, medicine, management, psychology, or counseling. Professionals are increasingly expected to provide services that are clinically, culturally, ethically, as well as spiritually competent. A previous article (Sperry, 2011) addressed the first three of these areas of competence whereas this one addresses spiritual competence. Professional counselors who provide individual, couples, or family counseling, particularly when medical conditions are the focus, would do well to consider the implications of spiritual competence in their work (see also chapters 21, 22).

This chapter describes and illustrates spiritually competent practice. It begins with a description and definition of spiritual competence, as well as its requisite components: spiritual knowledge, spiritual awareness, spiritual sensitivity, and spiritual competency. Next, it describes the various spiritual competencies associated with counseling practice. Then, a case example illustrates spiritual competence in counseling with a family facing a serious medical condition.

Spiritual Competence: Components and Description

There is increasing discussion of spiritual competence today. Unfortunately, in much of this discussion there is definitional confusion over the meaning and conceptual boundaries of the term. Currently, it is not uncommon for spiritual awareness or spiritual sensitivity to be equated with or used synonymously with spiritual competence. Fueling this confusion is the fact that spiritual competence is rarely defined in the counseling literature, even in books devoted to the topic (e.g., Cashwell & Young, 2011). The exception is Robertson's operational definition which is the basis of the

---

1. Adapted from Sperry, L. (2011). Spiritually competent practice with individuals and families dealing with medical conditions. *The Family Journal: Counseling and Therapy for Couples and Families, 19,* 42–416.

Spiritual Competency Scale. She defines spiritual competency as a "level of competency (ability to carry out a task) that has been attained by gaining the knowledge, attitudes, and skills proposed by the ASERVIC *Spiritual Competencies*" (Robertson, 2008, p. 21). Otherwise, spiritual competence is discussed in global terms and assumed to be an aspect or manifestation of cultural competence (Lukoff & Lu, 1999). Over the past 30 years ACA has encouraged the development of the Multicultural Counseling Competencies which address several diversity variables including religion and spirituality. Nevertheless, spiritual competencies were greatly underrepresented. This prompted ASERVIC to develop stand-alone competencies that were specific to religion and spirituality (Robertson & Young, 2011).

In a previous article (Sperry, 2011), cultural competence was articulated as consisting of three interrelated components: cultural knowledge, cultural awareness, and cultural sensitivity, which are capacities and prerequisites that build on one another. Briefly, cultural knowledge involves acquaintance with facts about ethnicity, social class, acculturation, religion, gender, and age. Cultural awareness builds on cultural knowledge and adds the capacity to recognize a cultural problem or issue in a specific client situation. Cultural sensitivity is an extension of cultural awareness and involves the capacity to anticipate likely consequences of a particular cultural problem or issue and to respond empathically. Cultural competence builds on cultural sensitivity and adds the capacity to provide appropriate and effective action in a given situation resulting in positive treatment outcomes. In short, each component functions as a prerequisite for the subsequent component, such that a high level of cultural competence is dependent on high levels of its prerequisites.

Spiritual competence can similarly be described as consisting of three progressively interrelated components: spiritual knowledge, spiritual awareness, and spiritual sensitivity. Each component reflects specific capacities and builds on its prerequisite. Thus, spiritual knowledge is acquaintance with a wide range of spiritual beliefs, spiritual practices, and spiritual issues. Spiritual awareness is spiritual knowledge plus recognition of the spiritual dimension and specific spiritual considerations in one's self and in others. Spiritual sensitivity is spiritual awareness that involves empathic responding to the client's spiritual concerns. Furthermore, spiritual competence involves moving beyond spiritual sensitivity to initiating appropriate and effective actions. Table 7.1 summarizes these.

The value of distinguishing these prerequisite components of spiritual competence is the theoretically essential and necessary conceptual and definitional clarity that it offers. This definition is similar to but different from the definition of spiritual competence as it has been described in the social work literature as: "an active, ongoing process characterized by the following three, interrelated dimensions: (1) a growing awareness of one's own value-informed, spiritual worldview and its associated assumptions,

Table 7.1 Four Components of Spiritual Competence

Spiritual Knowledge	Acquaintance with various spiritual beliefs, practices, and issues
Spiritual Awareness	Spiritual knowledge (+) recognize spiritual considerations
Spiritual Sensitivity	Awareness (+) respond empathically
Spiritual Competence	Spiritual sensitivity (+) take appropriate and effective action

limitations, and biases, (2) a developing empathic understanding of the client's spiritual worldview that is devoid of negative judgment and, (3) an increasing ability to design and implement intervention strategies that are appropriate, relevant, and sensitive to the client's spiritual worldview" (Hodge & Bushfield, 2007, p. 106). In this three-dimensional definition, spiritual competence is understood to consist of the capacity for spiritual awareness (dimension 1), the capacity for empathic understanding (dimension 2) or what this article calls spiritual sensitivity (dimension 2), and the capacity for intervening (dimension 3) or what this article calls spiritual competence. Missing from this definition is the component of spiritual knowledge; that is, knowledge about spirituality and spiritual practices and an essential prerequisite for spiritual awareness.

Accounting for the component of spiritual knowledge is important, particularly if it is framed as a necessary prerequisite for other components of spiritual competence. For example, the first two of nine spiritual "competencies" previously promulgated by ASERVIC (Miller, 1999) are that a professional counselor should be able to explain the relationship between religion and spirituality, and that a professional counselor should be able to describe religious and spiritual beliefs and practices. Both of these reflect spiritual knowledge rather than spiritual awareness, spiritual sensitivity, or what this article is describing as spiritual competencies. The more recent version of the ASERVIC competencies continues to list the first of these two as a spiritual competency (Cashwell & Watts, 2010; Cashwell & Young, 2011).

Spiritual Competencies in the Practice of Counseling and Psychotherapy

As noted, there are two versions of the ASERVIC Spiritual Competencies, of which the first version consisted of nine competencies (Miller, 1999). When viewed from the components perspective described in this chapter, two would more accurately be considered spiritual knowledge, one spiritual awareness, three spiritual sensitivity, and three spiritual competence. The revision: "Competencies for Addressing Spiritual and Religious Issues in Counseling" (Cashwell & Watts, 2010) includes 14 competencies. Of these one would more accurately be considered spiritual knowledge, three spiritual awareness, five spiritual sensitivity, and five spiritual competence. These five competencies involve assessment, diagnosis, goals setting, and the utilization of spiritually sensitive treatment interventions. More specifically, these clinically focused spiritual competencies are:

- Assesses client's spiritual perspective by gathering information from the client or other sources;
- Makes a diagnosis and recognizes client's spiritual perspective can (a) enhance well-being; (b) contribute to client problems; or (c) exacerbate symptoms; sets goals with the client that are consistent with the client's spiritual perspective;
- Is able to (a) modify therapeutic techniques to include the client's spiritual perspectives, and (b) utilize spiritual practices when appropriate and acceptable to the client;
- Can therapeutically apply theory and current research supporting the inclusion of a client's spiritual perspective and practice.

Clearly, ASERVIC's revision is a significant accomplishment for the field of counseling, a feat that has not yet been matched in the fields of psychology, psychiatry, social work, or marital and family therapy. Nevertheless, some areas of competent practice are not addressed. These include case conceptualization, treatment monitoring of outcomes, collaboration with or referral to someone with additional spiritual expertise, and termination.

Following is a more complete list of competencies derived from Aten and Leach (2009), and specified by Sperry (2012):

- Develops an appropriate therapeutic alliance that is sensitive to the spiritual dimension;
- Maintains an appropriate therapeutic alliance and deals effectively with spiritual transference-countertransference, alliance ruptures, ambivalence, and resistance;
- Completes an integrative assessment and diagnosis which includes the spiritual dimension;
- Incorporates the spiritual dimension in an integrative case conceptualization;
- Incorporates the spiritual dimension in an integrative treatment planning and mutual goal setting;
- Implements appropriate spiritual and psychological interventions that reflect the integrative case conceptualizations;
- Refers to or consults with religious/spiritual resources, when indicated;
- Monitors and evaluates overall treatment progress and outcomes on all dimensions, including the spiritual dimension;
- Incorporates the spiritual dimension in the termination process.

Spiritually Competent Counseling of Individuals and Families with Medical Conditions

Spiritual competence has implications and applications in counseling practice, particularly for counseling with individuals and families experiencing a medical condition. Effective work with such clients presupposes the counselor can quickly and effectively assess a client's spiritual perspective, including their spiritual beliefs and their spiritual practices.

Spiritual Assessment

In my experience, the process of spiritual assessment of adults dealing with a wide variety of acute and chronic medical conditions is facilitated by use of the *Spiritual Perspective Scale* (SPS; Jesse & Reed, 2004; Reed, 1987). The SPS is a 10-item self-rating instrument designed to measure an individual's perceptions of the extent to which they hold certain spiritual views and engage in related spiritual practices (Reed, 1987). It can be administered either in a structured interview format or as a paper and pencil inventory. Each item uses a 6-point Likert-type scale that is anchored with descriptive words (i.e., 1 = Not at all or Strongly Disagree to 6 = All the time or Strongly Agree). One such item is: "I seek spiritual guidance in making decisions in my everyday life." Higher scores reflect a greater influence of the individual's spiritual perspective and more involvement with spiritual practices. The psychometric properties of the SPS are impressive with reliability (Cronbach's alpha) consistently rated above .90, and demonstrated criterion-related validity and discriminant validity (Reed, 1987).

Spiritual Crisis and Spiritual Coping Resources

Loss is common in those dealing with severe medical conditions. This is particularly evident in women who have lost a breast following mastectomy. Such losses are typically accompanied by doubts about personal identity and self-worth which can lead to a spiritual crisis in which the person's religious faith is shaken or abandoned. Research finds that 10% of women suffered a spiritual crisis associated with their breast cancer (Hegel et al., 2006). Fortunately, spiritual factors can provide life-affirming resources in women's response to the diagnosis of breast cancer as well as to their adjustment to its arduous treatment and life adjustment. In particular, religious and spiritual coping resources have proved essential to women who have experienced the loss of a breast following mastectomy (Gail, Kristjansson, Charbonneau, & Florack, 2009). These resources include prayer, the guidance of a spiritual leader such as a priest, chaplain, minister, or rabbi, the support of a spiritual companion or friend, and the support of a faith community.

Clinical Illustration

The following illustration is based on a case example appearing in *The Family Journal* (Sperry, 2010). A brief summary of the case is followed by a description of clinical and spiritual interventions and the spiritual competence demonstrated by the counselor.

Juanita H. is a 54-year-old married, first generation Mexican American female diagnosed with metastatic breast cancer. Following a mastectomy and removal of lymph nodes, she was to begin radiation and chemotherapy, but this was delayed for nearly 4 months because of poor wound healing. She had become increasingly depressed after the surgery, and her husband, who had faithfully accompanied Juanita to all her medical appointment before her surgery was no longer coming. Tearfully, Juanita recounted that they had fought almost constantly since the surgery and that "Jose won't even touch me anymore." Juanita's physician was stymied by his patient's worsening condition and could not explain her poor postoperative course of infections and slow wound healing. He also was not able to appreciate cultural factors or the marital difficulties. Frustrated, he decided to seek consultation from Serafina Garcia, PhD, who is licensed as both a mental health counselor and as a marital and family therapist. She had considerable experience working with clients wherein spiritual, cultural, and marital considerations have exacerbated their medical conditions.

In the initial consultation, Dr. Garcia identified Juanita's level of acculturation as low, and that her illness perceptions had "interfered" with effective treatment outcomes. Dr. Garcia also administered the *Spiritual Perspective Scale* as a structured interview during that first session. Because of Juanita's high scores on this scale, suggesting that spiritual beliefs and practices had been very important to her, Dr. Garcia conducted an extended spiritual assessment. She learned that Juanita had once been a devout, practicing Catholic who prayed the rosary daily, consistently attended Sunday mass, and had a special devotion to Our Lady of Guadeloupe. However, because a priest had berated her for using birth control after their fourth child was born, Juanita and her husband had left the Catholic Church. Juanita expressed remorse about leaving and missed "the church of my youth." Still she continued the rosary and her Our Lady of Guadeloupe novenas, at least until her mastectomy. Dr. Garcia learned that Juanita had experienced a spiritual crisis following the surgery in which she believed that God was punishing her "for using birth control." While Juanita's physician had known of her being estranged from her church, he had no idea that the surgery had triggered a spiritual crisis for her. Nor had it occurred to him that her spiritual resources might be utilized to positively influence health outcomes. In contrast, Dr. Garcia recognized these dynamics and would incorporate these religious coping resources in her counseling.

After the evaluation, Dr. Garcia discussed treatment recommendations with Juanita's physician. She indicated that Juanita was clinically depressed, but was probably not easily identified by other health professionals accustomed to prototypic DSM-IV-TR presentations. Instead, Juanita experienced primarily somatic symptoms not uncommon in immigrants from Mexico. This untreated depression together with untreated marital conflict most likely accounted for the rapid proliferation of the cancer and the retarded wound healing. Accordingly, immediate evaluation for possible antidepressant treatment was recommended. Also recommended was individual and couples counseling because marital discord can also retard wound healing. Spiritual practices and spiritual coping resources would also be incorporated. Dr. Garcia offered to provide this treatment to address depressive, spiritual, and relational issues, all of which appeared to be culturally influenced. Because of Juanita's estrangement from the Catholic Church, Dr. Garcia, with her client's consent, arranged for a colleague, a psychologically informed Spanish-speaking priest to visit with Juanita. He welcomed her back to the Church, reframed her belief that she was being punished by God, heard her confession, and administered the Eucharist and the sacrament of the sick. Along with Dr. Garcia's own counseling—individual and conjoint sessions with her husband—which included addressing Juanita's illness perceptions and her belief that God was punishing her, the consultation by the priest and the reinstatement of Juanita's spiritual practices, had a profound effect. Over the next 3 months Juanita's depression lifted, she began chemotherapy and radiation, she and her husband made progress on their marital issues, she returned to her church, and she increased her 5-year survival odds.

Concluding Note

Dr. Garcia's evaluation resulted in an integrative case formulation (Sperry 2012) that was considerably broader and more clinically useful than the physician's biomedical formulation, which had excluded essential cultural, family, and spiritual dynamics. Without such an integrative formulation and the integrative assessment upon which it was based, effective, tailored treatment interventions would likely not have been designed and implemented. In short, it is unlikely that conventional counseling or therapy would have achieved the same degree of clinical, cultural, and spiritual sensitivity and competence. Among other things, this case suggests that an integrative case formulation is a prerequisite for a high degree of clinical, cultural, and spiritual sensitivity and competence.

The case also suggests that Dr. Garcia's spiritual competence effectively complemented her clinical competence. She exhibited extensive spiritual knowledge upon which her spiritual awareness and spiritual sensitivity were based. Similarly, her high levels of spiritual awareness and spiritual sensitivity allowed her to recognize and empathically respond to Juanita's spiritual concerns which were missed by other health professionals involved in her case. What's more, her capacity to design and implement spiritual interventions that both extended her spiritual sensitivity and complemented her clinical competency reflects her high level of spiritual competence. Dr. Garcia's provision of counseling that was both clinically and spiritually competent as well as culturally sensitive is a testament to her commitment to diversity and her expertise as a counselor. As a result, Dr. Garcia was able to foster physical, emotional, and spiritual healing in a client and family experiencing a serious medical condition. Utilization of the competency of referral or consultation with a spiritual leader proved to be a key factor in the positive outcome.

Finally, this case illustrates some of the key points of this chapter. The first is that there are three prerequisite components of spiritual competence. The second is that there are several spiritual competencies including referral or consultation with a spiritual leader. The third is that counselors would do well to develop expertise in the components of spiritual competence and the various spiritual competencies.

References

Aten, J., & Leach, M. (Eds.). (2009). *Spirituality and the therapeutic process: A comprehensive resource from intake to termination.* Washington, DC: American Psychological Association.

Cashwell, C., & Watts, R. (2010). The new ASERVIC competencies for addressing spiritual and religious issues in counseling. *Counseling and Values, 55,* 2–5.

Cashwell, C., & Young, J. S. (2011). *Integrating spiritual and religion into counseling: A guide to competent practice* (2nd ed.). Alexandria, VA: American Counseling Association.

Gail, T., Kristjansson, E., Charbonneau. R., & Florack, P. (2009). A longitudinal study of the role of spirituality in response to the diagnosis and treatment of breast cancer. *Journal of Behavioral Medicine, 32,* 174–180.

Hegel, M., Moore, C., Collins, E., Kearing, S., Gillock, K., Riggs, R., … Ahles, T. (2006). Distress, psychiatric syndromes, and impairment of function in women with newly diagnosed breast cancer. *Cancer, 107,* 2924–2931.

Hodge, D., & Bushfield, S. (2007). Developing spiritual competence in practice. *Journal of Ethnic and Cultural Diversity in Social Work, 15,* 101–127.

Jesse, D. E., & Reed, P. G. (2004). Effects of spirituality and psychosocial well-being on health risk behaviors in Appalachian pregnant women. *Journal of Obstetric Gynecologic and Neonatal Nursing, 33,* 739–747.

Lukoff, D., & Lu, F. (1999). Cultural competence includes religious and spiritual issues in clinical practice. *Psychiatric Annals, 29,* 469–472.

Miller, G. (1999). The development of the spiritual focus in counseling and counselor education. *Journal of Counseling & Development, 77,* 498–501.

Reed, P. G. (1987). Spirituality and well-being in terminally ill hospitalized adults. *Research in Nursing and Health, 10,* 335–344.

Robertson, L. (2008). *The spiritual competency scale: A comparison to the ASERVIC spiritual competencies* (Unpublished doctoral dissertation). Submitted to the University of Central Florida.

Robertson, L., & Young, J. S. (2011). The revised ASERVIC spiritual competencies. In C. Cashwell & J. Young (Eds.), *Integrating spiritual and religion into counseling: A guide to competent practice* (2nd ed., pp. 25–42). Alexandria, VA: American Counseling Association.

Sperry, L. (2010). Breast cancer, depression, culture, and marital conflict. *The Family Journal, 18,* 62–65.

Sperry, L. (2011). Culturally, clinically, and ethically competent practice with individuals and families dealing with medical conditions. *The Family Journal, 19,* 212–216.

Sperry, L. (2012). *Spiritual dimension in counseling and psychotherapy* (2nd ed.). New York, NY: Routledge.

8

COMPLIANCE CONSIDERATIONS[1]

"Treatment compliance is arguably the greatest contemporary challenge to those engaged in the clinical practice of medicine.... Most people ... find it difficult to make major lifestyle changes or to use medications consistent over long periods of time, and thus few patients are fully compliant with physician's recommendations" (Becker, 1989, p. 416). Compliance or adherence is generally defined as the extent to which a person's behavior, such as keeping appointments, taking medications, or making lifestyle changes, coincides with medical or therapeutic advice. Statistics on noncompliance and its long term consequences stagger the imagination. It is estimated that only one-fourth of individuals with hypertension are under treatment and only about one-half of those actually control their blood pressure because only two-thirds use enough medication (Becker, 1989; Doherty & Baird, 1983). Counselors who deal with health-related and lifestyle change in their practice are no strangers to the phenomenon of compliance. This chapter describes an approach for effectively dealing with compliance issues in counseling within a family systems context. A straightforward and clinically useful therapeutic interviewing strategy for increasing compliance is described and illustrated.

Compliance

Early research on compliance emphasized the treatment regimen, health provider instructions, and later focused on clients' perception of their illness and expectations of treatment and then client–provider relationships. More recently, the focus has shifted to the influence of family dynamics. Families can be under- or overinvolved in the treatment process which can undermine compliance with treatment. If family members

---

1. Adapted from Sperry, L. (2006). Family-oriented compliance counseling: A therapeutic strategy for enhancing health status and lifestyle change. *The Family Journal: Counseling and Therapy with Couples and Families, 14,* 412–416.

are underinvolved they may not support the client sufficiently, whereas if they are overinvolved they may limit the client's exercise of personal responsibility. Furthermore, disturbances in the family or in the client's relationship with the family can significantly impact a client's compliance. Even in the absence of family dysfunction, client–family interaction patterns can undermine compliance such as when a resentful client refuses to comply in order to spite partners. Or, family members may undermine a client's compliance with a weight management regimen by giving gifts of candy, teasing the weight-reducing client, or continuing to use off-limit ingredients such as salt and sugar in preparing meals (Doherty & Baird, 1983).

The terms *family compliance counseling* and *family-oriented compliance counseling* are used by Doherty and Baird (1983) to describe the process of involving the family in order to foster compliance so as to enhance health status and lifestyle change. They insist that an adequate understanding of compliance involves the "therapeutic triangle" consisting of the health care provider, the client, and the client's family, and that compliance emerges in a cooperative therapeutic alliance or system from which the client derives information, support, and resources needed to adhere to an agreed upon treatment regimen. They state that the main purposes of family compliance counseling are: (a) to educate client and family about the disease and treatment regimen; (b) to provide a forum for client and family members to share their emotional reactions and concerns about the disease and regimen; and (c) to facilitate an agreement among family as to how the client will be supported in adhering to the treatment program. In addition, they offer a six step process for conducting family-oriented compliance counseling (Doherty & Baird, 1983). The approach they describe is primarily psychoeducational. In the following sections, a psychotherapeutic strategy is offered which can be utilized alone or in conjunction with their approach.

Enhancing Compliance

The therapeutic interviewing strategy advocated for use in health counseling involving individual, couple, and family issues derives from the cognitive behavior analysis system of psychotherapy (CBASP). CBASP was developed by McCullough (2000) for chronic depression, extended to other psychiatric conditions by Driscoll, Cukrowicz, Reardon, and Joiner (2004), and applied to medical and health counseling issues by Sperry (2005). Whereas other therapeutic approaches tend to assist clients to cope with or work through past and present conflicts, CBASP encourages clients to work toward achieving what they want or desire to happen in their lives. This approach fosters collaboration as counselor and client work together to achieve the therapeutic goal (Driscoll et al., 2004). Counselors can utilize this basic therapeutic strategy to process situations and issues as they arise in any counseling context whether it is a single, unscheduled 10- to 15-minute encounter or in scheduled sessions that are part of ongoing counseling.

This therapeutic strategy is clinically useful in quickly and easily reviewing a problematic situation and coming up with alternative ways of achieving the medical and health outcomes that those with medical and health-related issues desire. Unlike clients who present themselves for conventional individual, couples, or family therapy, medical clients are not as receptive to more traditional psychotherapeutic treatment strategies that are longer in duration and less focused than the treatment strategy described and illustrated here. Whether the issue involves treatment compliance, denial of illness, difficulty with a medical provider, or remission of symptoms, counselors who have some knowledge of illness dynamics and are sensitive to both the treatment concerns of medical clients and can utilize appropriate intervention strategies can find work with individuals, couples, and families facing health issues and crises to be very rewarding. Utilization of this interview strategy was described and illustrated with a couple in which denial of the illness exacerbated relational conflicts and the chronic disease (i.e., systemic lupus erythematosus, in one partner; Sperry, 2005). In the case illustration that follows, treatment noncompliance is the issue.

Case Illustration

June T. has been referred to Jackson Tierney, a family counselor, who practices in an outpatient medical clinic of a local hospital. He specializes in counseling medical clients who are not responding adequately to their treatment regimen for any number of reasons, including compliance issues. Jackson has been quite effective in utilizing a straightforward interview strategy with such clients and their families. He typically works with clients between one and three sessions. June is an elementary school teacher who has been married for 8 years and she and her husband Jeff have no children. She was diagnosed with diabetes mellitus, Type 2 about 3 months ago and was begun on a diabetes diet plan to control her blood sugar and at the same time started the clinic's weight management program with the hope of losing 25 pounds. The hope was that with regular monthly medical monitoring and attendance at a weekly weight group she could get down to and maintain her target weight. Achieving and maintaining both diet and weight could significantly reduce the likelihood that she would need insulin injections and would slow the progression of her chronic illness. After 6 weeks she had lost a total of nearly 14 pounds, but then started gaining weight. Although June could provide no explanation for the gain, her physician suspected compliance

COMPLIANCE CONSIDERATIONS

was the issue and arranged for Jackson to meet with her. They met for a brief session and arranged for a follow-up meeting to include her husband. The following transcription picks up about 10 minutes into that session. Prior to this, June described how disappointed she was with her weight gain even though she attended the weight management group meetings religiously and was following the diet pretty closely. Jackson asked her to describe what it was like when she relapsed. She teared up and said it was awful and she was so frustrated.

Counselor:	I hear your frustration June. Can you describe a recent situation that illustrates it.
June:	Sure. I was really excited because I was getting really close to achieving my target goal for the weight management program after losing another 6 pounds in the past 2 weeks. I told Jeffrey that this time I really felt like celebrating. He said lets go out for the evening. I said great and was hoping it would for dancing, but he took me to his favorite Italian restaurant. Then, he wanted to order for both of us. And he orders pasta. After the waiter took our order, Jeffrey berated me for flirting with the waiter. I said I was only being friendly. Then we got into a fight and I was so mad, I didn't say another word and when the food came I just stuffed myself. It was two days before we started talking again and by then I had gained back about 5 pounds in those 2 days.
Counselor:	What did this mean to you? What were you thoughts or interpretations?
June:	I was thinking: I just wanted to go out dancing not out to eat. Doesn't he know I'm on a low carb diet and shouldn't be eating pasta.
Counselor:	OK, and what other thoughts might you have had?
June:	What's he trying to do, sabotage my success or something? He's always just so jealous when I talk to other men.
Counselor:	So what did you do, what were your behaviors?
June:	Well, I was hurt that he ordered food I shouldn't be eating. And, I was so angry when he said I was flirting and I wouldn't say anything more to him. Also, and I'm embarrassed to say it, I stuffed myself.
Counselor:	June, what were you hoping would happen that evening?
June:	I just wanted to enjoy my success at losing weight and spend a romantic evening with my husband.
Counselor:	What actually happened?
June:	I didn't get to go dancing and I stuffed myself and probably gained back most of the weight I lost.
Counselor:	Did you get what you expected?

June: No. I absolutely did not get what I wanted.

Counselor: Jeff, please tell us your take of that evening.

Jeff: All right. Well, I wanted to take her out and celebrate because she was so happy. We got to the restaurant and I thought I'd be really smooth and debonair so I offered to order dinner for us both. Then I ordered the stuff I know that she really used to enjoy. She didn't say much to me but was overly friendly with the waiter. Anyway, after he left I told her that it was disgusting that she was flirting again. She got mad and wouldn't talk to me the rest of the evening. What a bummer.

Counselor: So what was your interpretation of that situation?

Jeff: Well, she doesn't tell me directly what she wants me to do. She should know after all these years that I'm not good at mind reading. And, she shouldn't flirt, especially in front of me. It drives me crazy.

Counselor: Were there any other thoughts you might have had?

Jeff: Probably that this weight management thing is for the birds. That it causes more trouble than it's worth.

Counselor: I hear that, Jeff. So what did you do, what were your behaviors?

Jeff: Well, I ordered the kind of food that she—actually both of us—really used to enjoy. And, I got really angry and told her not to flirt anymore. Then, I spent the rest of the evening fuming. I was a victim of her silent treatment, again.

Counselor: Now, what did you want to happen that night?

Jeff: I just wanted us to enjoy dinner and spend a quiet evening together with her.

Counselor: What actually happened?

Jeff: Nothing worked out. My evening was ruined.

Counselor: Did you get what you expected and wanted?

Jeff: Not by a long shot.

Counselor: It seems that both of you wanted to celebrate June meeting her target goal. What I also heard is that June wanted Jeff to recognize that when celebrating she didn't want to eat a big feast, but rather go dancing. And, Jeff expected June to tell him directly how she wanted to celebrate since he's not a good mind reader.

Jeff: Yeah, sometimes she just clams up and then gets upset. I guess I wouldn't have objected to going dancing, at least after I had eaten something. But I didn't know what she wanted.

June: Well, you make up your mind so fast, and you seemed to have forgotten that I'm on a weight management program to control my diabetes. You know I don't want to have to take pills and insulin shots.

Counselor: It's clear that you are both still feeling frustrated with the way this turned out. I'd like to analyze this situation with you, with the hope of coming up with some alternate interpretations for it. Would that be all right with you? (both nod affirmatively) Jeff, you wanted to celebrate June's success by taking her to eat and spend a quiet night alone with her. Is that right?

Jeff: Yes, but I also wanted her to remind me that doing the Italian food wasn't a good way to celebrate. I didn't make the connection that she wanted to go dancing to help her keep fit and maybe even lose some more weight. I admit, sometimes I'm a little dense.

Counselor: Let's take a closer look at your interpretations. First, she doesn't tell you directly what she wants you to do. Did that interpretation help you or hurt you in terms of getting what you wanted?

Jeff: Well, I guess it hurt me. It's true that she doesn't tell me stuff and I'm terrible at mind reading.

Counselor: Can you think of another interpretation that might have helped you get what you wanted?

Jeff: Maybe I could have thought, why not ask her how she'd like to celebrate. Particularly, since she brought the idea of celebrating in the first place.

Counselor: How might asking that have helped you get what you wanted?

Jeff: Well, I guess it would have led to a conversation in which we could have talked about the pluses and minuses of different ways to celebrate. You know going out for a big feast versus going dancing or doing something else.

Counselor: Okay. Let's look at your second interpretation. You said she shouldn't flirt, especially in front of you. Did this interpretation help you or hurt you?

Jeff: That one did really hurt me because every time it comes up it never gets resolved. I guess I'm overly sensitive—and maybe jealous. I really don't want to lose her.

Counselor: Lose her? What do you mean?

Jeff: You know, she's lost a lot of weight now and I see guys looking at her figure. And, I don't like it at all.

Counselor: Your other interpretation was that June's weight management program was for the birds and that it causes trouble. Did that help you or hurt you get what you wanted?

Jeff: It just made things worse. I guess I'm worried that the more she loses weight she'll be more attractive to others and who knows what will happen. (Pause) I don't want her to lose interest in me and turn to someone else.

Counselor: I hear that and will come back to it. Turning to your behaviors; did ordering the pasta for her help or hurt in getting you what you wanted?

Jeff: It's obvious now that it hurt me. I just didn't make the connection and she didn't say anything. It seemed like the right thing to do at the time.

Counselor: How about getting angry and telling her not to flirt anymore. Did that help you or hurt you?

Jeff: It hurt. I'm starting to see that things get worse when I'm so sensitive—she would say I was being jealous. And, facing her silent treatment is just like being rejected.

Counselor: Like being rejected. (Pause)

Jeff: Nothing good comes out of it. (Pause) It just dawned on me that what I most fear happening is something that I'm actually promoting

Counselor: How is that?

Jeff: I mean when I don't really attend to her needs, when she doesn't tell me and I don't ask her what she wants, she seems to give other people, particularly guys, more attention. And, when I tell her to stop flirting, she reacts by giving me the cold shoulder. Then I really feel rejected. Maybe that's why I'm so sensitive to her losing weight. When she was heavier she was probably less attractive to others. So I'm not keen on her doing this weight management program. Oh, man.

Counselor: Yes, it seems like there is a pattern here: as you're less attentive to her needs, that is, you don't ask her what she wants or expects, she may be more responsive to those who give her attention. And, so far, to the extent that she loses weight in this diabetes-weight management program, you experience it as a loss to you, and so you view the program as a source of trouble rather than helping her regain and maintain her health. (Pause) So what alternative might there be to getting angry and telling her not to flirt?

Jeff: I guess it all goes back to being more proactive and finding out what she's thinking and what she wants rather than assuming that if she doesn't say anything that everything is all right and I can just make decisions for us both. If I'm more attentive and ask her, it will probably make it much easier for her to tell me what she needs and wants.

Counselor:	That follows. I could anticipate that the alternatives you came up with might help you achieve this.
Jeff:	Yeah, seems like they might.
Counselor:	(Turning to June). Okay, June, in this situation, your first interpretation was that you didn't want to go out to eat but to go dancing. Is this right?
June:	Yes, it is.
Counselor:	Did these thoughts help you or hurt in terms of getting what you want?
June:	(Pause) Well, it did hurt me because it made me feel like I had to go along with his dinner plans instead of just telling him that I really wanted to go dancing. I guess a better interpretation would have been to be more assertive and say what was on my mind.
Counselor:	That sounds reasonable. Your second interpretation was that he was trying to sabotage your success by ordering you a high carb pasta dinner. Did this help or hurt you in terms of getting what you wanted?
June:	Well, it definitely hurt because I know he really liked that pasta dish, and I also used to like it a lot before going on this program. I guess I thought I would hurt his feelings if I said what I really needed was just a small high protein meal and then some exercise, like dancing.
Counselor:	Sure. Your third interpretation was that Jeff is always jealous when you talk to other men. Is that accurate?
June:	Pretty much. And it hurt because I've no intention to leave Jeff or have an affair or anything, but I get angry when he says that I'm flirting when I'm just being friendly and he starts attacking me as being unfaithful. I really love him but I can't take that attacking so I just back off and don't give him any attention until things cool down which is usually the next day or so. I didn't know until just now that he feels rejected by me. That's never been my intention. And, it hurts me that he doesn't have more faith in me. (Pause) Maybe, when he starts to say I'm flirting with others that I could think that I don't have to say anything or defend myself, but rather I can use it as a cue to smile and start paying more attention to him.
Counselor:	How might this alternative interpretation help you?
June:	Well, it would show that I really care for him and it would probably short circuit his defensiveness and feeling rejected. It'd also help me feel less lonely and misunderstood.

Counselor: That makes sense. Let's look at one of your behaviors. You said you were angry and hurt and then you stuffed yourself. Did that help or hurt you?

June: It really hurt because I went back into my emotional eating pattern. That night I did pig out but fortunately didn't gain back all the weight I lost. But it was a setback.

Counselor: What alternative behavior might you have employed?

June: Well, what I learned in my weight management group is to use those two negative feelings anger and hurt as cues to move away from food, take a walk, take some deep breaths, and clear my head. Those things have worked for me already in other situations that haven't involved Jeff. Now, I need to do them when I'm with him.

Counselor: That sounds very appropriate. (Pause) June, is there anything that Jeff said that you'd like to speak to or comment on?

June: Yes. I guess I mentioned it already. (Looking directly at Jeff) I didn't know that you felt so rejected when I gave you the silent treatment. And, I never got the sense that you really wanted me to succeed in this diabetes-weight management program. When you said that as I succeeded in losing weight you felt even more jealous and rejected. Well, it makes more sense to me. (Pause) Isn't there some way for me to lose weight and reduce the progression of my diabetes without you feeling so bad?

Counselor: Jeff, is there anything that June said that you'd like to speak to or comment on?

Jeff: Yeah. It's really reassuring to hear that you really love me and want to stay with me. This has been tough talking about this stuff but it has been helpful. (Pause) And, I guess I really am in favor of you staying in your diabetes program and getting healthier.

Case Commentary

The case demonstrates the reality of the treatment compliance triangle, and that one or more family members can make the difference between compliance and improved health outcomes or noncompliance and reduced health outcomes. In this example, Jeff's role—particularly his interpretations and behaviors—in the triangle was critical in understanding June's noncompliance. By utilizing the CBASP interview strategy, the counselor was able to engage both Jeff and June in the collaborative process of reviewing a critical situation in a nondefensive and helpful manner.

Concluding Note

Compliance is unquestionably a formidable challenge for all health care providers, including counselors and therapists. Because family dynamics clearly impact a client's compliance with a treatment regimen for both medical conditions and lifestyle change, a case was made for use of family-oriented compliance counseling. After noting a psychoeducational approach to family-oriented compliance counseling, a psychotherapeutic strategy to accomplish similar outcomes was described and extensively illustrated with a session transcription.

References

Becker, L. (1989). Family systems and compliance with medical regimen. In C. Ramsey (Ed.), *Family systems in medicine* (pp. 416–431). New York, NY: Guilford.

Doherty, W., & Baird, M. (1983). *Family therapy and family medicine.* New York, NY: Guilford.

Driscoll, K., Cukrowicz, K., Reardon, M., & Joiner, T. (2004). *Simple treatments for complex problems.* Mahwah, NJ: Erlbaum.

McCullough, J. (2000). *Treatment for chronic depression: Cognitive behavioral analysis system of psychotherapy.* New York, NY: Guilford.

Sperry, L. (2005). A therapeutic interviewing strategy for effective counseling practice: Application to health and medical issues in individual and couples therapy. *The Family Journal: Counseling and Therapy for Couples and Families, 13,* 477–481.

9

MOTIVATIONAL INTERVIEWING[1]

Rates of nonadherence with medical treatment are as high as 80%. Consequently, nonadherence, also called noncompliance, is a problem with significant consequences for patients and their families. Because it has significant psychosocial impact, counselors and psychotherapists are referred or asked to consult on such cases. Recently, motivational interviewing (MI) has been found to be an effective adjunctive treatment in dealing with nonadherence issues, particularly when delivered in a family context. Accordingly, those engaged in individual and family counseling would do well to develop competence in motivational interviewing and utilize it in their work.

This chapter begins with a definition and description of MI and its principles and skill sets. Then, it describes nonadherence with medical regimens, the failure of conventional approaches, and the value of MI as an intervention delivered in a family context in increasing treatment adherence. A clinical example and session transcription illustrate this intervention.

Motivational Interviewing: The Basics

MI was originally developed in the 1980s by William Miller, PhD to help clinicians address clients' problematic alcohol and substance use issues (Miller & Rollnick, 2002). Essentially, MI is a strategy for helping clinicians change what they say so that clients can change what they do. Evidence continues to mount that MI is a clinically effective and economically efficient intervention that guides clients toward change across a wide spectrum of health-related behaviors ranging from diet, medication

---

1. Adapted from Sperry, L. (2012). Motivational interviewing, non-adherence with medical treatment, and families. *The Family Journal: Counseling and Therapy for Couples and Families, 20,* 306–308.

compliance, risky sexual practices, to self-management of chronic medical conditions (Rollnick, Miller, & Butler, 2008).

MI is defined as "a client-centered, directive method for enhancing intrinsic motivation to change by exploring and resolving ambivalence" (Miller & Rollnick, 2002, p. 25) and as a collaborative conversation that strengthens a client's motivation and commitment to change (Miller & Rollnick, 2009). These definitions reflect MI's humanistic and client-centered roots and the three core ingredients that, together, represent the "spirit" of motivational interviewing. These ingredients are: (a) a collaborative partnership, a relationship built on shared understanding, caring, respect, and trust; (b) support of the client's autonomy, recognizing that the true power for change rests within the client; and (c) an evocative approach to counseling that draws out the client's own motivations and capacities for change, in contrast to telling him or her what to do or why. MI is similar to other client-centered approaches, like health coaching and health counseling, in engaging and activating clients to take a more active role in their own self-care, self-management of chronic conditions, preventive care, and treatment of acute and chronic conditions.

There are four principles of MI which are easily remembered with the acronym RULE: (a) **R**esisting the urge to direct the client with lecture, persuasion, or demands; (b) **U**nderstanding the client's motivation by exploring the values, needs, aspirations, abilities, and ideas; (c) **L**istening with empathy; and (d) **E**mpowering by exploring the client's past experience, setting achievable goals, and problem-solving to overcome barriers to change. These principles clearly reflect the collaborative, respectful, evocative spirit of MI (Miller & Rollnick, 2009).

Specific MI skills are related to these principles. The most basic and important MI skills are the OARS skills: **O**pen-ended inquiry (e.g., "Tell me about your reasons for change"); **A**ffirmations (e.g., "I'm impressed with your efforts to try despite all the obstacles you are facing"); **R**eflections as in reflective listening; and **S**ummaries. Reflection is considered the most useful MI skill. When using reflections (e.g., "It sounds like you're really frustrated") a clinician can deepen rapport, particularly when patients express strong emotions or values. Clinicians can also strategically employ reflections to reinforce or affirm the patient's expressed desire, reasons, ability, or need for change. Selective reflection of a patient's "change talk" has been shown to be a key ingredient of MI's positive effects. Summaries are a special type of reflection that recaps the client's story and can help transition an interaction toward a specific action or plan. Other skills include developing discrepancies, rolling with resistance, and promoting "change talk" (Miller & Rollnick, 2002).

Research and clinical experience indicates that intensive training and follow-up supervision or coaching is essential in achieving proficiency in MI skills (Martino, Ball, Nich, Frankforter, & Carroll, 2008). For this reason, initial MI training should occur over at least two sessions with direct coaching, and with the provision that participants practice skills between sessions and utilize a learning process that includes reflection, feedback, and additional skill practice. Thereafter, additional coaching can promote skill refinement (Rosengren, 2009).

Utilizing MI in Families with Treatment Noncompliance

Failure to follow advice from health care professionals, called treatment noncompliance or nonadherence, is a significant problem. Research indicates that 50% of patients in the United States do not comply with the health care plan for treatment such as medication, while nearly double that number fail to comply with dietary restrictions, exercise, or other restrictions of health-compromising behaviors (DiMatteo, Giordani, Lepper, & Croghan, 2002). Typically, health education was the approach or strategy most commonly used to increase treatment adherence.

Unfortunately, this approach is insufficient in changing patients' behavior probably because it is persuasive, prescriptive, and focused on providing general advice. In contrast, a more collaborative, family-centered approach which focuses on the family's beliefs, values, and health behaviors; and enhances the family's self-efficacy and skills, is more likely to increase treatment adherence. Research comparing these two approaches showed a 64% success rate with knowledge or general advice alone and an 85% success rate for the more collaborative, family approach (Burke & Fair, 2003).

Because it is a collaborative approach that empowers patients, MI has become the intervention of choice in increasing treatment adherence to medical regimens (Rollnick et al., 2008). Furthermore, using MI with the patient's family is noted to be superior to using MI with individual patients (Gance-Cleveland, 2005). In short, MI is a useful adjunctive intervention that augments both health education as well as other counseling interventions.

Illustration of Utilizing MI in Families with Treatment Noncompliance

Key: hypertension patient (PT), wife (WF), counselor (CO)

CO: Please, tell me what you have noticed since we met last time.	focusing discussion
PT: I have to be honest. I have not done the salt reduction thing at all. There is no good excuse. I just haven't done it. I've done okay with the other goals, just not salt.	Brief mention of success embedded in sustain talk

CO: You're feeling pretty good about *two* of the three goals you set.

Selectively reflecting change talk

PT: Yeah, I've been good about my exercise. That's been easier than I thought it would be. I'm also doing pretty good at not overeating at home. Sometimes I overdo it, but not as much as before.

PT expanding on several areas of success

CO: You are persistent and you've found quite a bit of success so far.

Affirmation

PT: I guess so, except with the whole salt thing.

Sustain talk regarding salt-reduction goal

CO: I appreciate your honesty. Tell me more about reducing salt intake. What kind of things have gotten in the way?

Open-ended question

PT: I guess I'm just lazy. Not using the salt shaker is not easy. Food doesn't taste right without it. And, it kills me when I'm eating lunch with my coworkers and they use salt like it's going out of style.

Sustain talk: PT finds it hard to adjust: struggles when around salt users

CO: It's hard seeing others who apparently aren't on a low salt diet use it. Being around them makes you not want to use salt too.

Reflection: Expressing empathy and rolling with resistance

PT: Yes, exactly. I mean, later on I kick myself for salting everything because 1 know that raises my blood pressure. My hypertension is not silent like most people. I get a strange sensation in my temples when my pressure is really high, like after salty meals. I guess I should really cut down and choose less salty foods. But that's mostly what the cafeteria serves. Maybe I should take a lunch to work. It could cut down on high salt foods. But I'd need help with that (looking over to his wife, Ginny).

Increasing change talk. Listing cons of not adhering to his treatment plan
Identifying barriers for success with possible solution involving wife

CO: So on a scale from 1 to 10, how important is it for you to reduce salt use?

Assessing importance of salt reduction goal

PT: Probably a 4 or so. Maybe a 7 or so

Sustain talk and

when I feel that sensation. That's when I wish I had the salt substitute with me.

change talk

CO: What is it about that sensation that makes it more important for you?

Open-ended question focusing on change talk

PT: It means that my pressure is way up and increases my immediate risk of stroke. Stroke runs in my family. Or, until I can reduce salt use maybe ·I could take the salt substitute with me and use it in the cafeteria.

Reason to be serious about salt reduction
Acknowledges possibility of better choices

CO: So, you could choose to take a low salt lunch to work with you. Or, you could use the salt substitute at the cafeteria. Both are steps in the right direction, you are thinking about making different choices.

Summarize the two options. Affirming the effort

WF: Well, you were really good at dinner last night. You'd didn't roll your eyes when you used the salt substitute like you have in the past. That was great!

Wife expresses support

PT: Actually, I guess I'm getting more used to it. It doesn't taste like the real thing. But that's all right. (pause) I really should take a lunch with me to work. But, I'm not really into packing one myself. Maybe, if Ginny could help. But I know in the past she wasn't keen on doing that.

More change talk, eliciting help from wife

WF: Now, I would be happy to pack your lunch for you. In the past it was different because I was trying to get three kids off to school so I just didn't have time to make a lunch for you too. But, I could do it now that the kids are on their own.

Supporting change talk

CO: It sounds like you are interested in taking your own lunch because you know it will be healthier for you. Ginny has agreed to pack you a low salt lunch.

Summarize

PT: Yeah. I think that can make a big difference. But, I'm gonna need some seasoning too, at least until my taste buds adjust to less seasoning. And, I

PT developing change plan, identifies another barrier

feel funny about taking a salt-
substitute shaker to work with me.
I know I'll get those looks from
the guys.

CO: So you feel good about taking a healthy lunch but not so good about the looks you might get from others if you take a salt substitute shaker with you to work. Still, you're open to to this option over eating high salted foods in the cafeteria.

Double-sided reflection ending with change talk

PT: Yes, I am.

Change talk

WF: I just saw that our grocery now carries the salt substitute in small packets. I could put a packet or two in with your lunch.

Family generating change plan

PT: Yes, that could help make this whole thing a lot easier.

Strengthening plan

CO: So, on a scale of 1 to 10, how confident are you about your new lunch plan?

Assessing confidence of change plan

PT: 10/10. I know this is going to work.

Change plan

CO: When do you think you can start?

Seeking commitment with start date

PT: Ginny, can we start this tomorrow?

Seeking help from wife

WF: Absolutely.

Support

CO: Looks like you two have a plan that you are excited about.

Reflection and summary

Concluding Note

This session transcription illustrates the application of MI as a powerful intervention for increasing treatment adherence in a family counseling context. Had the patient's response to the counselor's scaling question been 4 of 10 or so, rather than the reported 10 of 10, the counselor would have proceeded to process this with a response like "And what would need to happen for it to be 8 of 10?" and so on until a reasonable change plan was in place. In this case and many others, MI has proven to be an invaluable and necessary competency that all counselors and clinicians would do well to add to their therapeutic armamentarium.

References

Burke, L., & Fair, J. (2003). Promoting prevention: Skill sets and attributes of health care providers who deliver behavioral interventions. *Journal of Cardiovascular Nursing, 18*(4), 256–266.

DiMatteo, M., Giordani, P., Lepper, H., & Croghan, T. (2002). Patient adherence and medical treatment outcomes: A meta-analysis. *Medical Care, 40*(9), 794–811.

Gance-Cleveland, B. (2005). Motivational interviewing as a strategy to increase families' adherence to treatment regimens. *Journal for Specialists in Pediatric Nursing, 10*(3), 151–155.

Martino, S., Ball, S., Nich, C., Frankforter, T., & Carroll, K. (2008). Community program therapist adherence and competence in motivational interviewing. *Drug and Alcohol Dependence, 96*, 37–48.

Miller, W. R., & Rollnick, S. (2002). *Motivational interviewing: Preparing people for change* (2nd ed.). New York, NY: Guilford.

Miller, W. R., & Rollnick, S. (2009). Ten things that motivational interviewing is not. *Behavioural and Cognitive Psychotherapy, 37*(2), 129–140.

Rollnick, S., Miller, W. R., & Butler, C. (2008). *Motivational interviewing in health care: Helping patients change behavior.* New York, NY: Guilford.

Rosengren, D. (2009). *Utilizing motivational interviewing skills: A practitioner workbook.* New York, NY: Guilford.

10

CASE CONCEPTUALIZATION[1]

In her initial session with a Hispanic couple, a counseling intern learned that they had recently lost their 3-year-old son to acute myeloid leukemia, an aggressive childhood cancer. The counselor began the session by eliciting the parent's thoughts and feelings about their son's death. In describing the days before and after his death they expressed feelings of guilt and insisted that they could have done something to save him. Upon hearing their guilt producing thought, the counselor vigorously began disputing it. Near the end of the session, the father showed agitation, and the mother had become withdrawn and despondent. They left the session feeling worse than when they came. Unfortunately, the intern had not addressed the shift that occurred in the parents' affect as the session progressed, and so it was not surprising that the parents did not keep their follow-up appointment.

This case illustrates that providing effective counseling can be a complex and challenging process. When delivered effectively, it can facilitate symptom reduction and improve personal and relational functioning, but when delivered poorly, it can be harmful, especially to vulnerable clients like these parents. Anxious to apply interventions she learned in a weekend CBT workshop, the intern had not developed an accurate and appropriate family case conceptualization. Had she done this she would have elicited and explored their goals for family counseling and recognized and addressed their reactions. Moreover, instead of quickly focusing on disputing the parent's maladaptive belief, she might have listened empathically to them and involved them in a collaborative decision about their readiness to process their maladaptive belief. Presumably, this intern had not conceptualized the case because she had decided that the "right" focus should be on the parent's guilt. Failure to develop an adequate and appropriate case conceptualization is not just a shortcoming of trainees, it is

---

1. Adapted from Sperry, L. (2013). Family case conceptualization and medical conditions. *Family Journal: Counseling and Therapy for Couples and Families, 21,* 74–77.

common enough among experienced practitioners that it has been dubbed "therapist drift" (Waller, 2009).

This chapter begins by the describing case conceptualization and its increasing role in counseling practice today. Then, it introduces family case conceptualization and the importance of a comprehensive family assessment as a precursor to an accurate family case conceptualization. After that, it illustrates, with a case example, the use of the family case conceptualization when the presenting issue is a medical condition.

Case Conceptualization

Interest in case conceptualization has increased exponentially since the early 1990s. Then, counselors and other practitioners might include a case conceptualization in a written report or case presentation, but it was not required. Today, however, case conceptualizations are an expected part of counseling practice. What accounts for this rapid shift in practice patterns? Tracy Eells, the eminent case conceptualization researcher, offers three reasons for this shift (Eells, 2012). First, is the increasing accountability demanded of practitioners in which payers base treatment reimbursement on a case conceptualization with a realistic treatment plan. Second, there is the increasing scientific basis of psychotherapy and the ready availability of empirically supported treatments. The expectation is that practitioners will base their practice on scientific knowledge and demonstrate it in evidence-based practice, and case conceptualizations provide a framework for such practice. The third reason is the expectation of formal diagnoses that are based on diagnostic manuals, such as DSM-IV-TR or ICD-9. These manuals primarily describe symptoms, but not causes, precipitants, maintaining factors, or treatment strategies. Case conceptualizations provide a structure for explaining the client's symptoms and concern in a way that integrates theory and research and fills the gap between diagnosis and treatment (Eells, 2012).

There have been an increasing number of articles and books on case conceptualization since the early 1990s. Eells describes the very first of these books, *Psychiatric Case Formulation* (Sperry, Blackwell, Gudeman, & Faulkner, 1992), as having "influenced a generation of mental health practitioners" (Eels, 2012, p. xii). He also notes that the commonly used designation "case formulation" from the past is gradually being replaced with the designation "case conceptualization." In this discussion, however, *case conceptualization* is also used as an umbrella designation for three components: a diagnostic formulation, a clinical formulation, and a treatment formulation (Sperry, 1989, 2010; Sperry et al., 1992; Sperry & Sperry, 2012).

A *diagnostic formulation* is a descriptive statement that answers the "What happened?" question. This formulation identifies the presenting problem, its triggers, and the client's maladaptive pattern (e.g., a predictable style of thinking feeling, acting, and coping in stressful circumstances). It can also include a formal diagnosis or a five axes DSM diagnosis.

A *clinical formulation,* is an explanatory statement that answers the "Why did it happen?" question. The clinical formulation articulates and integrates the intrapsychic, interpersonal, and systemic dynamics to provide a clinically meaningful explanation of the client's maladaptive *pattern,* and a statement of the causality of their behavior. An effective clinical formulation effectively links the diagnostic and treatment formulations.

A *cultural formulation* also provides an explanation for the client's presentation, but from a different perspective than the *clinical formulation.* It describes the impact of cultural factors on the client and answers the question, "What role does culture play?" It provides a cultural explanation of the client's presentation as well as the impact of cultural factors on the client's personality and level of functioning and vice versa (Sperry, 2010; Sperry & Sperry, 2012).

A *treatment formulation* is an explicit blueprint for treatment interventions. Informed by both the answers to the questions, "What happened?" and "Why did it happen?" the answer to the question "What can be done about it, and how?" is the treatment formulation. A well-articulated treatment formulation provides treatment goals and focus, a treatment plan, treatment interventions, as well as predictions about the course of treatment and its outcomes.

The most clinically useful case conceptualizations are those that emphasize the unique context and the needs and resources that the individual brings to treatment. Such case conceptualizations can be informed by a theoretical framework (e.g., CBT, dynamic, or solution-focused), or one that is sufficiently broad and can integrate and incorporate and biological, psychological, and social factors, the biopsychosocial model (Sperry, 2004). In addition, the best case conceptualizations are characterized by having high *explanatory power* (i.e., the degree to which the formulations sufficiently explain a pattern ranging from "poor" to "highly compelling") and high *predictive power* (i.e., anticipate likely treatment issues such as difficulty with engagement, termination, transference enactment, etc.) (Sperry & Sperry, 2012).

Family Case Conceptualization

Family case conceptualizations incorporate family or systemic dynamics. It has only been in the past few years that family case conceptualizations have been described and illustrated in the family therapy literature (Carlson, Sperry, Lewis, 2006; Sperry, 2004, 2005). Family case conceptualizations are also referred to as "systemic case conceptualizations" (Gehart, 2010, p. 18).

Only recently have core family therapy textbooks begun to discuss the family case conceptualization (Bitter, 2009; Gehart, 2010). Gehart indicates that a family case conceptualization is the first step in providing competent family therapy, in which practitioners "conceptualize the situation with the help of theory" (2010, p. 1). Like individual case conceptualizations, the most useful family case conceptualizations "focus on the unique contexts, needs, and resources of the individual family members and the system as a whole" (Bitter, 2009, p. 374). Not surprisingly, such systemic case conceptualizations are based on a detailed, systemic assessment. The following elements are common in such a comprehensive systemic assessment:

1. Client Factors
   a. Personality dynamics and level of functioning
   b. Personal strengths and resources
2. Family Structure and Interaction Patterns
   a. Couple subsystem dynamics and functioning
   b. Parental subsystem dynamics and functioning
   c. Family resources and strengths
3. Cultural Factors and Intergenerational Patterns
   a. Ethnicity, identity, and acculturation levels of family members
   b. Social, familial, and acculturative stress
   c. Discrimination, trauma, and abuse history
   d. Parent–child relations
   e. Health status, treatment, and substance use history
4. Narrative and Social Discourses
   a. Dominant discourses
   b. Identity narratives
   c. Other discourses

See Gehart (2010) for a similar but different systemic assessment framework.

Case Example: Family Case Conceptualization of a Medical Condition

Jeff was a 14-year-old Caucasian male with whom I had just begun working in individual psychotherapy at a child and adolescent outpatient clinic. Jeff was diabetic. Following clinic policy, I met Jeff and his mother for the first session and learned from Jeff's mother that he "did not seem to be adjusting to the divorce very well." She was referring to her recent divorce from her husband of 15 years. Jeff and his identical twin brother, Jon, were living with their mother in the family home, after their father had moved out and into a nearby apartment. While it was arranged that the twins could see their father on weekends, Jeff seemed increasingly quiet and "less connected" with his family and his friends. Jeff had very little to say at this first meeting but was considerably more verbal the next time we met, which was the first of 12 planned individual sessions. My impression was that a good therapeutic alliance was forming. Four days later, I got an urgent call from Jeff's mother saying he had been hospitalized, and she entreated me to join her at the hospital because she "wasn't sure Jeff was going to make it." Reportedly, the pediatric endocrinologist who consulted on the case told the parents that Jeff had nearly died from a diabetic coma and that his body was unlikely to sustain another incident such as this.

I met both parents later that afternoon at bedside. Jeff was just coming out of the coma and was groggy, although there was a slight smile on his face when his mother thanked me for coming to be with Jeff. Apparently, three days after our last session, Jeff had gone into a diabetic coma. Earlier that day he had been with his father, who announced that he was getting married in 6 weeks. Jeff said nothing and left and, unknown to anyone, stopped taking his insulin. Two days later he was found unconscious in his room by his mother, who rushed him to the emergency room where he was diagnosed with life-threatening diabetic ketoacidosis and slipped into a coma.

Jeff's coma had mobilized his parents immediately, who stayed by his bedside and, putting their differences aside, planned how they could support Jeff as best they could. His father volunteered that he would move back into the family home to be available to Jeff as he recovered. The family would be back together again, at least for a while, as Jeff undoubtedly wanted. Although his father did not verbalize it, it was not unreasonable to anticipate that after the situation stabilized he would move back to his apartment and go forward with his wedding plans.

This was my first experience in which an adolescent family member's illness served the purpose of reuniting parents who had separated or even divorced. In my subsequent family therapy training I would learn that this is not an uncommon family dynamic. However, I was trained neither to conceptualize this family dynamic nor to anticipate likely outcomes. If I had received such training in family case conceptualization, here is how the conceptualization and treatment plan might have looked.

Family Case Conceptualization Statement

Family Clinical Formulation.   Pattern analysis reveals that when his parents divorced and his father subsequently spoke of remarriage, Jeff had responded by going off his diet and stopping his insulin. The result was diabetic ketoacidosis, which can result in coma and death if not aggressively treated. An evaluation of individual dynamics reflects his self-view of being weak and physically defective in a world that is dangerous, where the unexpected happens, and where people try to be caring but let him down and hurt him. His strategy is then to seek comfort and safety using whatever means and at whatever cost to him. His self-harming behavior is his way of drawing his family back together where he can feel secure, connected, and cared for. In terms of systemic dynamics, it appears that the family's narrative is one of independence and self-reliance wherein everyone it is expected to take care of themselves and their own needs. This narrative "permits" the parents to find other partners and go on with their individual lives if the marriage doesn't work out. Similarly, it is acceptable that Jeff's sister is living independently in another state. Unfortunately, Jeff's schemas are a poor fit with the family narrative. Even his hobbies reflect his need for security (coin collecting) and connectedness and caring (scouting) rather than independence and self-reliance.

Family Treatment Formulation. Based on the clinical formulation above, the following short-term and longer term treatment goals can be specified. Given that Jeff's health behavior of blood sugar drops and diabetic ketoacidosis and coma is relationally specific to his father's talk of his prospective remarriage and have not generalized, a conservative treatment strategy would be to focus on the short-term goal of reducing or modifying this trigger. This could involve a few sessions with parents in which they are coached to reduce "triggering" future health crises. It had been elicited that the parents no longer spoke with each other but would channel information about themselves through Jeff and so the therapist would help them understand the overall pattern and find ways of communicating directly with each other.

Next, treatment would include individual sessions with Jeff that would focus on his defectiveness and rejection schemas, and sessions that would include his parents in which the family schema or narrative of independence and self-reliance would be addressed. Coming from the narrative therapy tradition, restorying involves focusing on previously unexamined or unemphasized aspects of those experiences (White & Epston, 1990). The resulting story includes pieces of meaning and understanding that are new or different and that allow for a positive shift in the original family narrative. In this case, restorying would involve a bit less emphasis on the independence and more emphasis on achievement, obedience, and loyalty. It would also emphasize more relaxation and recognition of each other's uniqueness.

In addition, the parents would be coached about the value of regularly scheduling time together with Jeff, at least once a week, to show their support and caring for him. Even when remarriage occurred, this planned family time together was preferable to emergency meetings in the hospital, and certainly less life threatening. Efforts to achieve such family time would likely fail if this intervention preceded work on the family narrative.

Finally, health-focused counseling (Sperry, 2009) is directed at maintaining stable blood sugar levels and adherence to the diet and insulin regimen. Attempts to provide this kind of counseling prior to parent coaching and focus Jeff's schemas would most likely have been futile.

Case Commentary

In this example, the family case conceptualization did guide treatment planning and implementation. The parents were quite responsive to parent coaching sessions and work on the family narrative, as was Jeff. The result was that Jeff's health stabilized and has remained stable for 2 years. Although his father did remarry about a year ago, the family regularly continues to meet weekly. It is noteworthy that the pattern analysis provided a framework not only for planning interventions based on the clinical formulation, but just as importantly, it also offered a strategy and rationale for sequencing the interventions. As was previously noted, it is counterintuitive to offer health counseling interventions last rather than first, as this case illustrated.

Concluding Note

That case conceptualization has and will continue to impact professional counseling is an established fact. Although it is an essential aspect of counseling practice, some trainees and experienced counselors fail to develop accurate case conceptualization, and "therapist drift" occurs often to the detriment of clients. The description of family case conceptualization should be of particular interest to counselors and other practitioners working with couples and families. Such case conceptualizations are critically important when couples and families are dealing with medical conditions. Conceptualizing cases in a way that incorporates family dynamics, client dynamics, and the impact of the medical condition on the client and family was illustrated in the case of Jeff and his family.

References

Bitter, J. (2009). *Theory and practice of family therapy and counseling.* Belmont, CA: Brooks/Cole.

Carlson, J., Sperry, L., & Lewis, J. (2006). *Family therapy techniques: Integrating and tailoring treatment.* New York, NY: Routledge.

Eels, T. (2012). Foreword. In L. Sperry & J. Sperry, *Case conceptualization: Mastering this competency with ease and confidence* (pp. xi–xii). New York, NY: Routledge.

Gehart, D. (2010). *Mastering competencies in family therapy: A practical approach to theories and clinical case documentation.* Belmont, CA: Brooks/Cole.

Sperry, L. (1989). Integrative case formulations: What they are and how to write them. *Journal of Individual Psychology, 45,* 500–507.

Sperry, L. (2004). Case conceptualizations: The missing link between theory and practice. *The Family Journal: Counseling and Therapy for Couples and Families, 20*(10), 1–6.

Sperry, L. (2005). Case conceptualization: A strategy for incorporating individual, couple, and family dynamics in the treatment process. *American Journal of Family Therapy, 33,* 353–364.

Sperry, L. (2009). *Treatment of chronic medication conditions: Cognitive-behavioral therapy strategies and integrative treatment protocols.* Washington, DC: American Psychological Association.

Sperry, L. (2010). *Core competencies in counseling and psychotherapy: Becoming a highly competent and effective therapist.* New York, NY: Routledge.

Sperry, L., Blackwell, B., Gudeman, J., & Faulkner, L. (1992). *Psychiatric case formulations.* Washington, DC: American Psychiatric Press.

Sperry, L., & Sperry, J. (2012). *Case conceptualization: Mastering this competency with ease and confidence.* New York, NY: Routledge.

Waller, G. (2009). Evidence-based treatment and therapist drift. *Behaviour Research and Therapy, 47*(2), 119–127.

White, M. & Epston, D. (1990). *Narrative means to therapeutic ends.* New York, NY: Norton.

11

CULTURALLY SENSITIVE TREATMENT[1]

While most clinicians report that cultural sensitivity and culturally sensitive treatments are important in providing culturally competent care to clients, couples, and families, very few clinicians report that they actually provide culturally sensitive treatment (Hansen et al., 2006). Arguably, there are various reasons for this, but a likely explanation is that few clinicians have had adequate training and experience with culturally sensitive treatment. Such training would include assessment of such factors as cultural identity, level of acculturation, family dynamics, and "explanatory models," indications for the use of various types of culturally sensitive treatment, and a method of selecting if, when, and how to utilize such treatments. The value of such training and experience is particularly evident when clients present with health issues or medical conditions (Sperry, 2006). This chapter addresses these factors and provides a clinically useful strategy for selecting such treatments. It begins by briefly distinguishing cultural intervention, culturally sensitive therapy, and culturally sensitive intervention. Then it provides a strategy, in the form of guidelines for making such decisions. A case example illustrates the use of this strategy.

From Cultural Sensitivity to Cultural Competence

Training programs today seem to be effective in promoting cultural sensitivity; that is, awareness of how cultural variables may affect the treatment process, but they do not seem to be as effective in promoting cultural competency; that is, the capacity to translate cultural sensitivity into action that results in effective treatment. This is the consensus among most of the clinicians and supervisors I have spoken with recently as well as the

---

1. Adapted from Sperry, L. (2010). Culture, personality, health, and family dynamics: Cultural competence in the selection of culturally-sensitive treatments. *The Family Journal: Counseling and Therapy with Couples and Families, 18,* 316–320.

conclusion of a recent large-scale survey of practicing clinicians (Hansen et al., 2006).

Becoming culturally competent involves such essential skills as the accurate assessment of cultural identity, level of acculturation, family dynamics, explanatory model, and personality dynamics as they influence a client's presenting problem and the identification and selection of the best "fit" for culturally sensitive treatment. Selecting appropriate cultur-ally sensitive treatment presupposes the clinician has accurately assessed cultural identity and level of acculturation. The term *cultural identity* refers to an individual's self-identification and sense of belonging to a particular culture or place of origin, while acculturation is the process and degree to which a client integrates new cultural patterns into his or her original cultural patterns (Paniagua, 2005). Level of acculturation can be deter-mined based on the client's language, generation, and social activities, as these factors are assessed by instruments such as the Brief Acculturation Scale (Burnam, Hough, Karno, & Telles, 1987). It also presupposes the clinician can accurately assess personality and relevant family dynamics. Since family conflicts and marital discord can arise from different levels of acculturation among family members and spouses leading to anxiety, depression, and noncompliance with medical regimens, it is essential that the clinician identify "discrepancies in levels of acculturation among fam-ily members and clients' perceptions of 'elevated levels of acculturative stress'" (Paniagua, 2005, pp. 170–171). Eliciting a client's explanatory model, the personal explanation of the cause of his or her problems, symp-toms, and impaired functioning is essential in working with any client who presents with a health issue or medical condition, and particularly those with lower levels of acculturation (Sperry, 2006). Related to the explanatory model is the concept of "illness perceptions," which are a cli-ent's belief about his or her illness in terms of its identity or diagnostic label, its cause, its effects, its time line, and the control of symptoms and recovery from it (Sperry, 2008). Often, such client explanations and ill-ness perceptions reflect key cultural values, beliefs, sanctions, and taboos that, if they are not heeded, can interfere with the treatment process and outcomes.

Types of Culturally Sensitive Treatments

Based on a comprehensive assessment of the factors and dynamics that impact the client's presenting problem, the clinician may select a conventional or a culturally sensitive treatment. This section briefly describes three types of culturally sensitive treatment (Sperry, 2010).

Cultural Intervention

A cultural intervention is a healing method or activity that is consistent with the client's belief system regarding healing and has the potential to effect a specified change. Some examples are: healing circles, prayer or exorcism, and involvement of traditional healers from that client's culture. Sometimes, the use of cultural interventions requires collaboration with or referral to such a healer or other experts (Paniagua, 2005). Still, a clinician can begin the treatment process by focusing on a core cultural value, such as *respito* (respect) and *personalismo* (friendliness), in an effort to increase *clinician's achieved credibility*; that is, the cultural client's perception that the clinician is trustworthy and effective.

Culturally Sensitive Therapy

Culturally sensitive therapy is a psychotherapeutic intervention that directly addresses the cultural characteristics of diverse clients, such as beliefs, customs, attitudes, and their socioeconomic and historical context. Because they utilize traditional healing methods and pathways such approaches are appealing to certain clients. For example, *cuento therapy* addresses culturally relevant variables such as *familismo* and *personalismo* through the use of folk tales (*cuentos*) and is used with Puerto Rican children. Likewise, *Morita therapy*, which originated in Japan, is now used throughout the world for a wide range of disorders ranging from shyness to schizophrenia. These kinds of therapy appear to be particularly effective in clients with lower levels of acculturation.

Culturally Sensitive Intervention

A culturally sensitive intervention is a Western psychotherapeutic intervention that has been adapted or modified to be responsive to the cultural characteristics of a particular client. Largely because of the structured and educational focus, diverse clients seem to find cognitive behavior therapy (CBT) interventions acceptable, and these are most often modified to be culturally sensitive (Hays & Iwamasa, 2006). For example, particularly in culturally diverse clients with lower levels of acculturation, disputation and cognitive restructuring of a maladaptive belief are seldom the CBT intervention of choice, whereas problem solving, skills training, or cognitive replacement interventions (Sperry, 2010) may be more appropriate.

Strategy for Selecting a Culturally Sensitive Treatment

Here is a strategy for selecting culturally sensitive treatment when indicated. This strategy includes seven specific guidelines and is particularly valuable when health issues or medical conditions are present.

1. Elicit or identify the client's cultural identity, level of acculturation, explanatory model (i.e., belief about the cause of their illness, such as bad luck, spirits, virus or germ, heredity, early traumatic experiences, chemical imbalance in brain, etc.), and treatment expectations. Also, elicit the client's personality dynamics, particularly as they influence the treatment process.

2. Identify family dynamics and the level of acculturation of family members who have direct influence on the client. Also, elicit their explanatory models of the client's health or medical problem and their own expectations for treatment. Then, estimate the difference, if any, between the client and family members on these parameters, and its actual or potential effect on the client's response to treatment.

3. Develop a cultural formulation framing the client's presenting problems within the context of the overall family's cultural identity, acculturation levels, explanatory models, treatment expectations, and the interplay of culture and the client's personality dynamics.

4. If a client identifies (cultural identity) primarily with the mainstream culture, has a high level of acculturation, and there is no obvious indication of prejudice, racism, or related bias, consider conventional interventions as the primary treatment method. However, the clinician should be aware that a culturally sensitive treatment may (also) be indicated as the treatment process develops.

5. If a client identifies largely with the mainstream culture, has a high level of acculturation, and there is an indication of prejudice, racism, or related bias, consider culturally sensitive interventions or cultural interventions for the cultural aspect of the client's concern. In addition, it may be useful to utilize conventional interventions for related noncultural concerns (i.e., personality dynamics).

6. If a client identifies largely with her or his ethnic background and the level of acculturation is low, consider cultural interventions or culturally sensitive therapy. This may necessitate collaboration with or referral to an expert or an initial discussion of core cultural values.

7. If a client's cultural identity is mainstream and the acculturation level is high, but that of his or her family is low, such that the presenting concern is largely a matter of cultural discrepancy, consider a cultural intervention with the client and the family. However, if there is an imminent crisis situation, consider conventional interventions to reduce the crisis. After it is reduced or eliminated, consider intro-

ducing cultural interventions or culturally sensitive therapy (Sperry, 2010).

Case Illustration: Strategy for Selecting
Culturally Sensitive Treatment

Marques is a 23-year-old single, first generation Haitian American male. He presented at a mental health clinic with complaints of sadness and was evaluated by a licensed mental health counselor who was a middle aged Caucasian male. His mood was depressed and he admitted experiencing increased social isolation, low energy, and hypersomnia, sleeping 10 to 12 hours per night. Marques also noted that he was also having difficulty dealing with a "tough situation." He presented as shy and passive while his mood was sad with constricted affect. He is the oldest of three siblings and since migrating from Haiti has lived with his mother and younger sister in a predominantly Haitian community.

The counselor elicited his explanatory model and health beliefs. Marques believed that his depression was primarily due to distress and disappointment about law school, having withdrawn at the semester break of his first year despite having a full scholarship. He was tearful in describing his exclusion from a study group and the complaints of white students that minorities were admitted only because of affirmative action. This was particularly troubling to Marques since he had high LSATs and a 3.9 GPA in his undergraduate studies. He believed he could not return to school because of fear of reexperiencing racism. Marques disclosed that when he was in sixth grade in a U.S. school he was hit in the head with a rock during a confrontation between a white and Haitian student; and afterwards avoided all confrontations. Accordingly, the counselor was not surprised that he had refused to confront the law school situation, and instead quietly withdrew. His treatment expectations were to "get rid of the sadness," to be less troubled by others' criticism, and to better face "tough situations." Marques identified himself as a "middle class American of Haitian heritage" and demonstrated a high level of acculturation. After securing his written consent, the clinician interviewed Marques's mother and his younger sister. They likewise exhibited high levels of acculturation and also believed that Marques's depression stemmed from his withdrawal from law school. His mother shook her head and said that, while Haitian men tend to be less dominant than Haitian women, she "couldn't understand why he's so shy and passive, especially when wronged by others. He's been this way since he was a kid." This description seems consistent with the dynamics of the avoidant personality.

To complete this initial evaluation, the counselor arranged for a routine medical consultation for Marques because it had been nearly 2 years since he had completed an annual medical checkup. The results of that evaluation were positive for a diagnosis of hypothyroidism. The physician conjectured that Marques's thyroid had been underfunctioning for a year or more and was hopeful this chronic medical condition could be controlled by Synthroid, which Marques agreed to take as prescribed. Because low energy and depression are common symptoms of hypothyroidism, the counselor evaluated Marques's symptoms over the next 4 weeks. By then, lab tests indicated that his thyroid levels were in the normal range. However, while he had returned to his previous energy level, he continued to experience sad feelings and was still socially isolated.

In terms of a clinical and cultural formulation, his depressive symptoms and social isolation appeared to be triggered and exacerbated by his experience with racism leading to his withdrawal from school. Prominent was his avoidant behavior, which seemed to be exacerbated by both his avoidant personality as well as cultural beliefs, which appeared to be operative in his response to Caucasian law students.

Figure 11.1 visually depicts the relative impact of cultural dynamics, personality dynamics, and medical condition on Marques as he presented for counseling. Note that personality dynamics were rated as high while cultural dynamics were rated as midrange, and as such were considered contributory to his initial presentation. In contrast, family dynamics was rated as low and considered noncontributory. His medical condition was contributory but to a lesser extent than culture or personality.

Based on this evaluation, a treatment plan was developed in which both conventional and culturally sensitive treatments were included. This

Influence of Cultural Dynamics

low   high
<--- X ----------------------------------->

Influence of Personality Dynamics

low   high
<-- X ------------>

Influence of Family Dynamics

low   high
<----- X --->

Influence of Health Factors

low   high
<------------------------- X --->

Figure 11.1   Influence of cultural dynamics, personality dynamics, family dynamics, and health factors on the presenting problem in the case of Marques.

mutually agreed upon treatment plan involved four treatment targets. The first was the depressive symptoms which would be addressed with CBT and continuation of thyroid medication. The medical consultant doubted that an antidepressant was indicated, but left that option open to reconsideration at the judgment of the counselor. The second target was his avoidant personality style and behaviors that were culturally influenced for which a culturally sensitive intervention would be directed at dealing more effectively with tough situations such as experiences of prejudice and racism. The clinic's Haitian male therapist would be involved with this treatment target as well as the third target in which he would serve as a cotherapist with Marques's Caucasian counselor in group therapy. This third target involved the personality component of Marques's avoidant personality style for which conflict resolution and assertive communication skills training would be a central part of the group work. The fourth target involved career exploration including the possibility of reinstatement in law school. His therapist would consult with and involve the school's minority affairs director, who was an African American male.

Case Commentary

As a result of the assessment and cultural formulation, it was determined that Marques would be best treated with conventional interventions aimed at personality dynamics *and* a culturally sensitive intervention aimed at cultural dynamics. However, had Marques's explanatory model of depression and his treatment expectations been more culture-based, and his personality dynamics less dominant, consideration would have been given to a cultural intervention. Similarly, if there was a discrepancy of acculturation levels between Marques and his mother and younger sister or interfering family dynamics were operative, cultural interventions and family interventions might have played a more prominent role in the treatment plan.

Concluding Note

A case was made for the importance of counselors and other mental health providers to become more culturally sensitive and culturally competent with regard to determining the need for and selection of culturally sensitive treatment when indicated. Utilizing the selection strategy described and illustrated in this article is quite demanding, particularly when the client presentation involves a chronic medical condition and family dynamics. Among other things, it requires the acquisition of a number of skill sets and competencies including the assessment of cultural identity, level of acculturation, explanatory model and illness perceptions, cultural formulation, as well as assessment of family dynamics, and medical and psychological symptoms. Nevertheless, this strategy has the potential to increase cultural sensitivity and foster cultural competence in mental health providers.

References

Burnam, M., Hough, R., Karno, M., Escobar, J., & Telles, C. (1987). Acculturation and lifetime prevalence of psychiatric disorders among Mexican Americans in Los Angeles. *Journal of Health and Social Behavior, 278*, 89–102.

Hansen, D., Randazzo, K., Schwartz, A., Marshall, M., Dalis, D., Frazier, R., … Norvig, G. (2006). Do we practice what we preach? An exploratory survey of multicultural psychotherapy competencies. *Professional Psychology: Research and Practice, 37*, 66–74.

Hays, P., & Iwamasa, G. (2006). *Culturally responsive cognitive-behavioral therapy: Assessment, practice, and supervision.* Washington, DC: American Psychological Association.

Paniagua, F. (2005). *Assessing and treating cultural diverse clients: A practical guide.* Thousand Oaks, CA: Sage.

Sperry, L. (2006). *Psychological treatment of chronic illness: The biopsychosocial therapy approach.* Washington, DC: American Psychological Association.

Sperry, L. (2008). *Treating chronic medical conditions: Cognitive behavioral strategies and integrative protocols.* Washington, DC: American Psychological Association.

Sperry, L. (2010). *Highly effective therapy: Developing essential clinical competencies in counseling and psychotherapy.* New York, NY: Routledge.

12

THERAPEUTIC STRATEGY[1]

Learning to do effective individual psychotherapy as well as couples and family counseling/therapy is a complex undertaking for most trainees. When health and medical issues are part of the clients' presentation, another level of complexity is added to the treatment process. Needless to say, guiding trainees to deal with health issues along with psychological considerations in the counseling process can be a daunting challenge not only for trainees but also for their instructors and clinical supervisors. Fortunately, focused therapeutic methods and techniques continue to be developed and some of these appear to offer considerable promise to the practice of health-focused counseling and psychotherapy (Sperry, 2006; Sperry, Lewis, Carlson, & Englar-Carlson, 2005). One of these methods is a straightforward and easily learned interviewing strategy derived from the cognitive behavior analysis system of psychotherapy (CBASP). CBASP was developed by McCullough (2000) and initially targeted to the treatment of chronic depression. Recently, this approach has been extended to several other mental disorders as well as to psychological issues involving parents, children, and couples (Driscoll, Cukrowicz, Reardon, & Joiner, 2004).

To date, this approach has not been extended to health issues. Accordingly, this chapter endeavors to describe the application of the approach to medical and health issues which I have found useful with individuals and couples. The article begins by briefly describing a nine steps interview strategy that adapts and extends the method described by McCullough (2000). Then it applies this strategy to medical and health issues that arise in the context of counseling. Specifically, it illustrates the use of the interview strategy with a couple experiencing relational discord that is

---

1. Adapted from Sperry, L. (2007). Utilizing a family-sensitive cognitive behavioral intervention with chronic illness: The impact of family dynamics and therapy on medical symptoms. *The Family Journal: Counseling and Therapy with Couples and Families, 15*, 56–61.

exacerbated by the wife's chronic illness, systemic lupus erythematosus (SLE), commonly referred to as lupus. A transcription of a conjoint session demonstrates the use of this interview strategy.

A Nine Step Interview Strategy

The nine step strategy functions as a "cognitive map" in the counseling process. The map guides the counseling process by providing a focus or sense of direction for therapeutic discussion. This interview strategy can also be likened to training wheels on a bicycle. Counselors and trainees can utilize this basic therapeutic strategy to process situations and issues as they arise in any counseling context whether it is a single, unscheduled 10- to 15-minute encounter or in scheduled sessions that are part of ongoing counseling. In a longer counseling session or ongoing series of sessions, the nine step interview strategy is utilized in a cyclic fashion, by repeating the nine steps, for each situation, conflict, or concern of the client. In short, this therapeutic interview method becomes the core strategy for the entire counseling processing.

The cognitive map consists of nine steps in the form of questions initiated by the counselor or therapist. These nine steps are:

Step 1: Can you describe what happened?

Step 2: What was your interpretation of [your thoughts about] the situation?

Step 3: What were your behaviors? [what did you say, what did you do?] Your feelings?

Step 4: What were your expectations [what did you want or hope would happen]?

Step 5: What actually happened?

Step 6: Did your behaviors and thoughts help or prevent [hurt] you from getting what you wanted?

Step 7: It didn't sound like it did. Can we analyze this together to see what happened and what might be different?

Step 8: How did your behaviors [thoughts/ interpretations] help get you what you wanted? OR How did your behaviors [thoughts/ interpretations] prevent [hurt] you from getting you what you wanted? OR Were your expectations realistic?

Step 9: What thoughts might have better helped you get what you wanted? OR What behaviors might have better help you get what you want the next time a situation like this comes up? OR How can your expectations be modified to be more realistic?

Illustration: A Couple with Relational Discord
and Systemic Lupus Erythematosus

Carol and Tom had been married for 6 years and had been experiencing relational difficulties for nearly 2 years. The latter period coincided with Carol's diagnosis and the beginning of her treatment for lupus (SLE). It is noteworthy that her diagnosis was made during the course of fertility treatments she had been undergoing for some 3 years. The couple's hopes and plans for a family seemed to all but disappear as her illness was diagnosed and appeared to take center stage in their lives. Even though her doctors told her she had a milder form of the disease, Carol intermittently experienced severe joint pain and headaches, along with chronic fatigue. Most of the time she had little energy to do even routine chores, and it soon became clear that continuing with her professional work was becoming all but impossible. On the advice of her physician she had resigned from her elementary school teaching position a year and a half ago. She could still do basic things such as fixing meals and light cleanup but not much more. Nevertheless, there were days when she felt energetic enough to think she was actually getting better and would set out to take on tasks she had easily accomplished in the past. Inevitably, she would overdo it and exacerbate her condition. Although relational discord occurred occasionally before the diagnosis, it predictably had increased as Carol's symptoms worsened and were exacerbated by various demands in the home and in the relationship. While Carol had largely accepted her illness, Tom had not. On the one hand he accepted the doctor's assessment that SLE would limit Carol's functioning, but on the other hand he expected that she would continue to do many things for him that he had become accustomed to in the past. Her submissive style and lack of assertive communication only seemed to compound matters.

Carol's physician referred the couple for couples therapy, recommending that they meet with a counselor whose training and experience were in health-focused counseling and psychotherapy. The counselor quickly recognized that Carol's illness not only impaired her functioning but magnified the influence of her personal style of submissiveness on relational dynamics which predictably had a negative impact on their functioning as a couple. He had two therapeutic goals. The first was to increase the couple's understanding of their personal and interpersonal dynamics and the interplay and impact of SLE on them as individuals and as a couple. The second was to modify their relational pattern vis-à-vis the challenge of the chronic illness they both faced. Because of its effectiveness with similar health-related cases, he chose to begin the therapeutic process with the nine step interview strategy.

The following transcription describes the application of this approach during their fourth conjoint session.

Counselor: It's nice to see the two of you again. How have things been lately?

Tom: (Silence) … Carol, as usual, seems to be waiting for me to take the lead. But I would really like it if she would respond to your question.

Counselor: I hear you, Tom. You don't feel that the responsibility for responding should be yours alone, and you wish that Carol would take the initiative sometimes.

Carol: Sure, I'll start off. Well, what happened is that Tom came home from work, and he was in a bad mood. Maybe, he had a bad day at the office. Whatever it was, he was grousing about dinner. Earlier I had decided not to cook and hoped that we might go out for a change. After all, I had a little more energy than usual that day, which doesn't happen too often. I had spent a few hours cleaning the house that afternoon, and I was starting to drag and my joints had really become inflamed. My medication doesn't help at times like that and I was too fatigued to cook dinner. He told me he was hungry and tired and wondered why dinner wasn't ready.

Counselor: What did this mean to you? What were you thinking?

Carol: Well, I thought that I, when I'm not feeling well that I shouldn't have to cook a meal, but I also knew better than to presume we'd go out to eat without asking Tom first. I also thought that he seldom appreciates the housework I do when I'm feeling well or really badly. I also assumed he was angry with me for being inconsiderate of the hard day he probably had at work and that he was tired. This made me feel guilty. So. I immediately apologized for not being considerate and started to put together a quick meal. But, I let him know by the tone of my voice that I was upset and I started tearing up, just on the verge of crying.

Counselor: What actually happened?

Carol: Tom became frustrated that I was upset, and we got in an argument. He had no idea what was happening inside me. We ended up ordering takeout and ignored each other the rest of the evening.

Counselor: What did you expect to happen?

Carol: I wanted him to hug and kiss me when he got home, and then I wanted to relax and go to our favorite restaurant. I really wanted some acknowledgment of the work I did around the house and the pain I endured in the process. I hoped that we could enjoy dinner out and relax after a long day.

Counselor: Did you get what you expected?

Carol: I clearly didn't get what I wanted.

Counselor: Tom, please tell us your version of the story.

Tom: All right. Well, I walked through the door, and Carol was lying on the couch watching TV. There was nothing in the kitchen for dinner like there usually is, so I asked her when we were going to eat. She got all upset and started apologizing and crying. For the life of me I couldn't understand why she was so upset. After I picked up our food order, she told me that she had wanted to go out. Then we started arguing.

Counselor: So what was your interpretation of that situation?

Tom: I thought that she got upset again for no reason. When I finally figured out she wanted to go to dinner, I couldn't understand why she didn't just tell me that she was tired and in pain. After all, even though we've been married 6 years I still can't read her mind. Very well, anyway. I thought that I did not need her picking a fight after I had such a long day. So I went and picked up some takeout and sat on the couch to watch the evening news. My tone of voice may have been a little gruff, but I wasn't upset with her at first. I guess I didn't say much to her the rest of the evening because I was in a bad mood after having an awful day at work.

Counselor: What did you want to happen when you got home that night?

Tom: I just wanted to come home after a hard day at the office, have a good meal, and take it easy for the rest of the evening. It didn't really matter to me if we ate out or ate at home. Instead, I arrived home, got into an argument with my wife, and went to sleep frustrated and angry.

Counselor: Did you get what you expected and wanted?

Tom: Absolutely not.

Counselor: It seems that both of you wanted to spend a relaxing evening together. What I also heard is that Carol wanted you to appreciate the work she did around the house especially when it triggered so much pain and fatigue. And, Tom expected Carol to tell him directly her idea about the situation, whether it was to eat at home or go out.

Tom: Yeah, she never tells me what she wants. Instead, she gets upset, and leaves me clueless. I wouldn't have objected to going out to eat, but I didn't know what she wanted.

Carol: Well, you were so irritable and gruff that I assumed you were mad at me for not having dinner ready the minute you got home. You don't even notice that I was in pain from spending half the day cleaning. You know that doing that usually exacerbates my SLE.

Counselor: It's clear that you are both still feeling frustrated with the way this turned out. I'd like to process this situation with you, with

111

the hope of coming up with some alternate interpretations for it. (Pause) Tom, you wanted to come home, have dinner with Carol, and settle in for the night, is that right?

Tom: Yes, but I also wanted her to tell me she was in pain and her plans for dinner, rather than getting her feelings hurt for no reason.

Counselor: Let's take a closer look at these interpretations. First, you thought or concluded that she was upset again for no reason. Did that interpretation help you or hurt you in terms of getting what you wanted?

Tom: (Pause) Well, I guess it hurt me. I assumed she was being unreasonable and noncommunicative and that just made me angry.

Counselor: Can you think of another interpretation that might have helped you get what you wanted?

Tom: Maybe I could have concluded that she was upset and probably had a reason for it which means I should try to find out what's wrong. That would have helped me because I wouldn't have become so angry and maybe we could have talked calmly about things rather than argue.

Counselor: Okay. Let's look at your second interpretation. You said that you didn't appreciate her picking a fight with you for no reason. Did this interpretation help you or hurt you?

Tom: That one really hurt me because, I assumed again that she was the one who was being unreasonable and that I had nothing to do with it. I guess I was being selfish because I was irritable and angry about my bad day at the office. Maybe if I had been more sensitive and observant of her fatigue and pain—and the clean house—I wouldn't have hurt her feelings. That would have avoided the argument.

Counselor: Next, you said that your tone of voice was unpleasant when you got home. Is that correct?

Tom: It is. (Pause) I think I follow what you're getting at. I guess it hurt me because it probably made her think that I was angry with her. Maybe I should have made it clear that I wasn't upset with her right as soon as I got home, instead of the way I treated her.

Counselor: Good. You also said that you picked up some takeout and then ignored her for the rest of the evening.

Tom: Yeah, and that hurt me because it hurt her feelings even more which made everything worse. If I hadn't been so stubborn and talked to her about it, we might have resolved it within a few minutes instead of ruining the whole evening.

Counselor: Would changing this behavior have also helped you achieve your other expectation which was for her to tell you what she wanted?

Tom: That's interesting. Maybe it would have helped. But ultimately that would really depend on her. I guess that may not be a realistic expectation

Counselor: I can understand that you want her to feel comfortable telling you what she wanted, but it may be a realistic goal for you because it relies on her behavior, which, as you know, is beyond your control. Can you think of a related but more realistic expectation?

Tom: Sure. I guess it would be that I wouldn't dump my own bad mood on her. That would probably make it much easier for her to tell me what she needs and wants.

Counselor: That follows. I could anticipate that the alternatives you came up with might help you achieve this.

Tom: Yeah, I can too.

Counselor: Okay, Carol, in this situation, you wanted to go out to dinner with Tom and then spend a nice evening together. You also said that you wanted him to acknowledge your pain when you exert yourself cleaning the house. Is this right?

Carol: Yes, it is.

Counselor: The first interpretation you gave was that you really should have known better than to plan to go out without first asking Tom. Did this thought help you or hurt in terms of getting what you want?

Carol: (Pause) Well, it did hurt me because it made me feel like I had to ask permission from him instead of just telling him that I would like to go out to dinner. I guess a better interpretation would have been to think that he would be tired from a hard day at the office and would probably enjoy eating out somewhere.

Counselor: That sounds reasonable. Your second interpretation was to assume that he must be angry with you. Did this help or hurt you in terms of getting what you wanted?

Carol: Well, it definitely hurt because my own feelings were hurt when I thought he was angry. If I had just thought that he might have had a bad day and his irritability and moodiness had nothing to do with me, I probably wouldn't have gotten so upset.

Counselor: Sure. Your third interpretation was that Tom didn't even care about all the time and resulting pain you'd experienced from cleaning the house. Is that accurate?

Carol: Uh hmm. Again, this one hurt me. I didn't get what I wanted because I ended up feeling so bad and upset. Instead, I should have thought that he just walked in the door and probably didn't have a chance to even notice the cleaning that I had done or my pain and fatigue. Then, I would not have been upset, and maybe he wouldn't have gotten so frustrated and we could have had a nicer evening together.

Counselor: Will this new interpretation help you with your expectation, which was for him to acknowledge your work around the house?

Carol: Well, it might, but I can't really make him say anything no matter what I do. So maybe it's not a realistic expectation

Counselor: I agree, you can't control anyone else's behavior. Can you think of an alternate expectation?

Carol: I guess that one of my expectations might be to shut down verbally when I'm not feeling well and tired because it too often leads to unnecessary arguments.

Counselor: Sounds good. Hopefully, these new interpretations might help you.

Carol: Yes, it probably will, assuming I can actually do it.

Counselor: You also said that you immediately apologized to him for not being a good wife and then began trying to quickly put together a meal. Is that accurate?

Carol: Yes. I know what I did wasn't helpful because it only made him more upset with me because he had absolutely no idea why I was upset. It would have been much better if I had just told him that I understood that he had a tough day at work and that I wanted to go out for dinner.

Counselor: You also noted that you let him know you were upset by his tone of voice and that you were on the verge of crying. Did this help or hurt, did it get what you hoped for?

Carol: It hurt because he usually ignores me when I act like this. I should have just told him about my pain and fatigue. Then we probably could have resolved things much sooner.

Counselor: You've both done some really good work today. What are each of you thinking right now?

Carol: Well, it's clear that we both make assumptions about the other instead of just talking. And, it seems to lead to discord rather than harmony.

Tom: I agree. It seems we are so accustomed to fighting with each other that we expect negative reactions and emotions from each other when what we really want to do is have a relaxing time together.

Counselor: Was working through this situation helpful?

114

Tom:	Definitely. I now see how I contributed to the argument. And, that blaming her was off the mark and made things worse.
Carol:	It was helpful to realize that my being submissive and nonassertive can actually hurt our relationship. I've been this way in the past assuming that being submissive would reduce the chance of us fighting. But, it actually promotes discord.
Counselor:	A real irony. (Pause) Is what you've learned today applicable to other situations?
Tom:	It sure makes me more aware of how I come across to her. I've got to find other ways to let her know about things that get to me at work without taking it out on her and hurting her feelings. She might even feel more comfortable asserting herself with me then.
Carol:	It's becoming clearer to me that if I could be a bit more assertive and tell Tom when and how my SLE is acting up, we would probably get along much better.
Counselor:	Well, we've done a lot this session. And, it seems like things are going in the direction you hoped they would.

Case Commentary

The case demonstrates that an illness or health concern can impact individual and couple functioning while also magnifying the influence of the personality style of one or both spouses. In this instance, Carol's submissive and nonassertiveness style amplified the effects of her chronic illness which together served to increase relational discord. Utilizing the interview strategy facilitated an exploration of the thoughts, behaviors, feelings, and expectations of each spouse in a nonthreatening manner. Furthermore, the strategy surfaced the unrealistic expectations that each spouse had for the other in a way that engendered little or no resistance. This was an important consideration given that other interventions and approaches to eliciting and processing such dynamics can and often do trigger resistance. It is also worthwhile to note that Tom's recognition of his unrealistic expectations of Carol should facilitate his resistance to accepting of her illness, something that has heretofore fueled their relational discord.

Concluding Note

The interview strategy described and illustrated in this article appears to have considerable promise for individual therapy and couples therapy/counseling which involves medical and health related issues. The fact that it is a straightforward and easy to use map for guiding the counseling process in the midst of complex issues and concerns makes it a promising option for use in educational programs that train counselors and therapists in addition to its clinical utility for experienced counselors and therapists.

References

Driscoll, K., Cukrowicz, K., Reardon, M., & Joiner, T. (2004). *Simple treatment for complex problems: A flexible cognitive behavioral analysis approach to psychotherapy.* Mahwah, NJ: Erlbaum.

McCullough, J. (2000). *Treatment for chronic depression: Cognitive behavioral analysis system of psychotherapy.* New York, NY: Guilford.

Sperry, L. (2006). *Psychological treatment of chronic illness.* Washington, DC: American Psychological Association.

Sperry, L., Lewis, J., Carlson, J., & Englar-Carlson, M. (2005). *Health promotion and health counseling* (2nd ed.). Boston, MA: Allyn & Bacon.

13

COMBINED TREATMENT
Medication and Psychotherapy[1]

Because medication is viewed as being as effective as psychotherapy and
less costly, it is increasingly utilized in the treatment of common psychiatric presentations in primary care settings, particularly chronic depression.
However, chronic depression remains one of the most difficult-to-treat
psychiatric conditions, and in the past there has been little therapeutic
success in reversing chronic depression in a medical patient even with
medication (Sperry, 1995). More recently, both clinical experience and
research suggest that the combination of medication with psychotherapy
or couples or family therapy is the more effective strategy. This chapter
describes combined treatment with an emphasis on chronic depression.
It begins by profiling three levels of depression. Then, it describes some
specialized couples and family therapeutic interventions that appear to
be quite effective when mild to moderate depression is present in a partner or family member. Next, it discusses combined treatment modalities
and suggests why medication plus specialized therapeutic interventions is
effective when depression is severe and chronic. Finally, it suggests some
reasons why some combined treatment approaches may be more effective
than other approaches.

Mild, Moderate, and Severe Depression

There are three levels of severity and impairment in depression among
couple partners or family members. The first is referred to as "mild"
depression. Individuals with this form of depression have rather acute,
time-limited problems or symptoms; that is, they are relatively high-
functioning individuals with no previous psychiatric histories, and their
depression follows clear precipitants. Such individuals tend to be good

---

1. Adapted from Sperry, L. (2004). Using medication and psychotherapy to optimize treatment
   outcomes for difficult, depressed couples and families. *The Family Journal: Counseling and Therapy with Couples and Families, 12,* 189–203.

candidates for various individual, couples, or family interventions. They also have good prognoses and are likely to respond favorably to treatment and return to baseline in a reasonably short period of time. Needless to say, these are ideal candidates for couples therapy.

The second level is "moderate" depression. Individuals with this form have longer term depression and typically have responded initially but later relapsed or have had partial response to treatment; that is, they were depressed and came out of it fully or partially and then became depressed again, sometimes without clear precipitants. When depressed, their functioning is in the moderate range of impairment, but otherwise, they can usually hold jobs and maintain interpersonal relationships, particularly during good periods. They may receive both psychotherapy and medication, but they need longer term or intermittent treatment.

The third level is called "difficult" or "chronic" depression. Unlike moderately depressed individuals, these persons tend to be more impaired and appear "resistant" to generic treatments and have long, usually unremitting patterns of chronic depression and severe impairment, with little or no response to medication alone. They are among the highest utilizers of medical services and carry diagnoses such as major recurrent depression, dysthymic disorder, chronic depression, and "double" depression. Unlike mildly or moderately depressed clients, these individuals typically have histories of early trauma or neglect, comorbid personality disorders, insecure attachment styles, and significant social skills deficits. They are very difficult to engage in treatment and exhibit little or no motivation and readiness for change.

Couple and Family Approaches for the Mildly and Moderately Depressed

A number of research studies have been undertaken involving the treatment of depression in couples and family members. Most of the studies reported on interventions targeting couples in which one of the partners met criteria for depression. One such study was the London Depression Intervention Trial. In this trial, couples were randomly assigned to individual cognitive behavioral therapy (CBT), medication, or systemic couples therapy. A partner was considered "depressed" if he or she scored 11 or higher on the Beck Depression Inventory (BDI). Manualized systemic couples therapy was found to be significantly better than either manualized CBT or medication (Jones & Asen, 2000). The explanation for this finding was that a specialized treatment focus (i.e., couples dynamics in systemic couples therapy) is superior to a generic psychotherapeutic treatment (i.e., CBT). Because it appears that the majority of couple partners would be classified as mildly to moderately depressed on the basis of their BDI scores, this research has little clinical relevance for chronically depressed couples and families.

Other researchers have also addressed the treatment of depression in couples and families. Beach (2001) and colleagues developed what they called a "scientific foundation" for the treatment of depression in couples and families. Banawan, O'Mahen, Beach, and Jackson (2002) reported on empirical support for the efficacy of behavioral marital therapy and reviewed several other specialized approaches targeting single-modality approaches to depression in couples and families. They offered a strictly psychosocial formulation of depression and described stress generation theory to explain the link between depression and marital discord. Unfortunately, Banawan et al. gave no description of the criteria they used for determining the type and severity of depression studied, nor did they mention the use of medication or combined treatment modes. Presumably, their theory and research are not applicable to chronic depression.

Combined Treatment: Medication and Psychotherapy

Combined treatment refers to treatment whereby both psychotherapy and medication, or a related biological treatment, are provided to a moderately depressed or difficult client. Combined treatment is the treatment of choice for difficult clients (Thase, 2003). There are two ways of providing combined treatment: in a split treatment mode or in an integrated treatment mode. Split treatment mode refers to a psychotherapist providing psychosocial interventions while a psychiatrist or primary care physician manages medication. Integrated treatment mode refers to both psychotherapy and medication management being provided by a psychiatrist. Note that integrated treatment does not necessarily mean "integrative treatment." When I use the term *integrative treatment* in this chapter, I mean treatment that is specialized and tailored to the unique needs and expectations of a client.

Currently, it is unclear which mode is better and which is more cost effective. Some research addresses the question, but only a few retrospective studies, and with equivocal results, have been published. Unfortunately, the answer won't be available until randomized trials are undertaken. However, on the assumption that it lowers costs, the split treatment mode is favored by most managed care organizations. Perhaps a more basic consideration is the question of whether combined treatment is indicated for a particular case. On the basis of research, it appears that combined treatment is clearly indicated for severe, recurrent, or chronic depression; obsessive-compulsive disorder, bipolar disorder, and schizophrenia; and quite likely for bulimia and panic disorder. However, there is little evidence that combined treatment is indicated for milder depressive and anxiety disorders (Thase, 2003).

A Specialized Treatment Approach for Difficult, Chronically Depressed Clients

This section briefly describes a recent treatment approach that includes focused strategies that can optimize treatment outcomes for difficult clients. The cognitive behavioral analysis system of psychotherapy (CBASP; McCullough, 2001) was developed specifically for individuals with long-term, chronic depression. As will be noted, when combined with medication, it is the most potent form of treatment for chronic depression currently available. Recent research offers an explanation as to why cognitive restructuring and disputational strategies, empathic understanding, and analytic interpretations have little or no impact in the treatment of chronically depressed adults.

Because chronically depressed individuals are perceptually disconnected from their social environments and tend to function at the preoperational level of cognitive and emotional development, they do not respond to therapeutic interventions that assume a connection to their environments and higher levels of development. CBASP was developed specifically to address the idiosyncratic pathology of these clients. The major goal of treatment is to systematically demonstrate to them that everything they do has environmental consequences, including the effects they have on their therapists.

CBASP uses situational analysis to modify the structural preoperational level of functioning of patients. Other methods are utilized to teach such patients to discriminate between the behavior of negative significant others and that of therapists. Another client outcome goal is learning to generate empathy. In sessions, therapists using CBASP endeavor to exacerbate clients' pathological patterns and in so doing intensify their experiences of the behavioral consequences they unwittingly produce.

Although sharing some commonalities with CBT and interpersonal psychotherapy, CBASP is significantly different from both in that it was developed specifically to target the unique pathology of chronic depression. It appears that some of the therapeutic strategies of CBASP may have applicability to other conditions, such as severe anxiety disorders and personality disorders. Controlled research studies have demonstrated the effectiveness of this approach with the chronically depressed. In a national study of 681 chronically depressed patients at 12 sites, CBASP, combined with the antidepressant nefazodone (Serzone), improved mood in 85% of patients after only 3 months of treatment. This combined treatment was significantly more effective than either medication or psychotherapy alone for treating chronic depression. Patients were treated with the medication twice a day, had 16 to 20 sessions of CBASP, or had the combined treatment. Those in the study had been depressed continuously for at least 2 years, and most had experienced chronic depression for an average of 20 years. Over the 12-week study period, 55% of the medication-only group reported positive responses, and 52% of the CBASP-only group experienced treatment responses, whereas 85% of those who took medication and underwent CBASP had positive responses to treatment (Keller et al., 2000).

Prior to this research, several other studies on combined treatment had been completed. Usually, they combined a generic form of CBT and medication and tested the combination against therapy alone and medication alone. Although it was expected that combined treatment would be superior to either therapy or medication alone, the expectation was not borne out (Thase, 2003). The key finding of the CBASP nefazodone study was that when working with difficult clients, effective treatment outcomes require tailored treatment; that is, interventions that are custom fitted to particular clients. This explains why generic treatments, such as CBT, have only limited effectiveness in the treatment of difficult clients. There are some data to suggest that CBASP and other specialized couple and family therapy approaches can be effectively utilized alone with mild to moderately depressed clients. However, to achieve optimal outcome effectiveness with difficult clients who are chronically depressed, these approaches probably need to be combined with medication, as is the case with CBASP. Currently, only one randomized, controlled trial of combined treatment has been completed, which involved CBASP and nefazodone. It is highly unlikely that such studies will be undertaken on the other three approaches. The reason is cost. The price tag for completing the 3-month trials of CBASP and nefazodone was reportedly $23 million (Thase, 2003).

Brain–Mind Connections in the Treatment Process

This section briefly describes why specialized treatments such as CBASP and medication work so well with difficult clients who are chronically depressed. The long-standing mind–brain dichotomy in mental health seems to be giving way to the beginnings of integration. "The increased use of pharmacologic and psychotherapeutic treatments is reflective of the recognition that the brain is the organ of the mind.... The disorders treated by psychiatrists and other mental health clinicians are disorders of brain function and often require combined or integrated interventions" (Beitman, 2003, p. xv). The implication is that therapy can change the brain. Is it true, and if so, how does it occur? Yes, it is true, and speculation has been offered as to the mechanisms of change. I'll look briefly at two explanations of the mechanisms of change.

The first mind–brain explanation is based on the extensive research of Eric Kandel (1998), the Nobel laureate, physician, and psychiatric researcher. He concluded that psychotherapy is a powerful biological

121

intervention, a conclusion based on research indicating that learning produces alterations in gene expression that change the strength of neuronal connections and structural changes that alter the anatomical pattern of interconnections between the nerve cells of the brain. This means that psychotherapy produces long-term behavior changes by altering gene expression, which results in structural changes in the brain.

In family systems language, changes in family dynamics and subsystems influence these brain changes. In order for family patterns to change, new memories of relating differently must occur. Because these relational changes are also biological changes, sufficient time is required in order to consolidate these changes into long-term memories. Because they are biological processes, they take time to occur, and they occur slowly sometimes, and after enough of them accumulate, they achieve a jump in growth. The holding environment provides the safety to expose the brain to different path possibilities and the time necessary for them to grow into long-term brain structure (Schaefer, 2003, p. 149). Because changing family patterns require building new memories of relating, changes must occur in many brain subsystems, or else the therapeutic effect will recede after therapy ends. In other words, psychotherapeutic processes that produce gradual changes in affect, motivation, and relational behavior are reflected in modifications in neural structure. Thus, like medication and other biological interventions, specific therapeutic interventions produce functional and structural changes in the brain. Furthermore, it appears that "pharmacotherapy and psychotherapy may be synergistic for change by promoting consolidation of the biological substrate of their individual and combined efforts" (Blinder, 2003, p. 179).

A second mind–brain explanation offers additional insight into how specific therapeutic interventions influence the brain. In their efforts to normalize neuronal functioning and brain circuits with medication and therapeutic interventions, neuroscience researchers have come to conceptualize treatment processes in terms of either "top-down" or "bottom-up" strategies. Top-down refers to treatment efforts that are primarily focused on cortical structures and neural tracts (top), which also can influence subcortical circuits, particularly in the limbic system (down). Similarly, bottom-up refers to treatment efforts that are largely focused on limbic circuits, which also can produce changes in cortical circuits (Fawcett, 2002). Of particular promise are recent efforts to normalize the expression of under- and overmodulated maladaptive personality traits with medication and behavioral interventions. For example, top-down treatment strategies typically utilize standard psychotherapies (i.e., cognitive therapies and dynamic therapies) to enhance cortical influences on limbic circuits. The goal is to undo negative learning, particularly maladaptive beliefs, and to increase the modulating or normalizing effects of emotional responses. Bottom-up treatment strategies typically involve the use of psychotropic medication in order to modulate harmful and other overmodulated behavior patterns and emotional states by normalizing the activity of limbic structures. However, focused CBTs appear to be as effective as medication as bottom-up strategies and secondarily as top-down strategies. Combining specialized treatment approaches with medication has been shown to have a significant synergistic effect, as noted in the CBASP and nefazodone study (Keller et al., 2000).

Concluding Note

A specialized psychotherapeutic treatment approach such as CBASP appears to be much more effective than generic psychotherapeutic or systemic approaches because it is tailored to specific mind–brain targets—both top-down and bottom-up targets—and when combined with medication produces a potent, synergistic treatment outcome for difficult, chronically depressed clients. Even though there have been no published reports of specialized couple or family treatment interventions combined with medication, it is quite likely that when combined with medication, these specialized systemic interventions will be similarly effective in the treatment of difficult, chronically depressed couples and families.

References

Banawan, S., O'Mahen, H., Beach, S., & Jackson, M. (2002). The empirical underpinnings of marital therapy for depression. In J. Harvey & A. Wenzel (Eds.), *A clinician's guide to maintaining and enhancing close relationships* (pp. 133–155). Mahwah, NJ: Erlbaum.

Beach, S. (Ed.). (2001). *Marital and family processes in depression: A scientific foundation for clinical practice.* Washington, DC: American Psychological Association.

Beitman, B. (2003). Introduction. In B. Beitman, B. Blinder, M. Thase, M. Riba, & D. Safer (Eds.), *Integrating psychotherapy and pharmacotherapy: Dissolving the mind-brain barrier* (pp. xv–xix). New York, NY: Norton.

Blinder, B. (2003). Psychodynamic neurobiology. In B. Beitman, B. Blinder, M. Thase, M. Riba, & D. Safer (Eds.), *Integrating psychotherapy and pharmacotherapy: Dissolving the mind-brain barrier* (pp. 141–160). New York, NY: Norton.

Fawcett, J. (2002). Schemas or traits and states: Top down or bottom up? *Psychiatric Annals, 32*(10), 567.

Jones, E., & Asen, E. (2000). *Systemic couples therapy and depression.* London: Karnac.

Keller, M. B., McCullough, J. P., Klein, D. N., Arnow, B., Dunner, D. L., Gelenberg, A. J., … Zajecka, J. (2000). A comparison of nefazodone, the cognitive behavioral-analysis system of psychotherapy, and their combination for the treatment of chronic depression. *New England Journal of Medicine, 342,* 1462–1470.

McCullough, J. P., Jr. (2001). *Skills training manual for diagnosing and treating chronic depression: Cognitive behavioral analysis system of psychotherapy.* New York, NY: Guilford.

Schaefer, P. (2003). Medicating the ghost in the machine. In P. Prosky & D. Keith (Eds.), *Family therapy as an alternative to medication: An appraisal of pharmland* (pp. 139–158). New York, NY: Brunner-Routledge.

Sperry, L. (1995). *Psychopharmacology and psychotherapy: Strategies for maximizing treatment outcomes*. New York, NY: Brunner/Mazel.

Thase, M. (2003). Conceptual and empirical basis for integrating psychotherapy and pharmacotherapy. In B. Beitman, B. Blinder, M. Thase, M. Riba, & D. Safer (Eds.), *Integrating psychotherapy and pharmacotherapy: Dissolving the mind–brain barrier* (pp. 111–139). New York, NY: Norton.

Part II

INTEGRATED BEHAVIORAL
HEALTH

Treatment of Common Medical Conditions

14

ARTHRITIS[1]

Arthritis is a common chronic medical condition characterized by damaged joints and persistent pain. It affects nearly 43 million Americans or approximately one of every six individuals. As the nation's population ages, arthritis is expected to affect 60 million people by 2020. Arthritis is a complex disorder that comprises more than 100 distinct conditions and can affect individuals at any stage of life, and it is estimated to cost almost $65 billion annually in medical care and lost productivity (National Center for Chronic Disease Prevention and Health Promotion. 2000). As a chronic disease, arthritis is characterized by an uncertain prognosis, an uncertain course, and a significant impact on individual and family dynamics. Accordingly, a biopsychosocial perspective provides a unique insight into this disease as well as integrative treatments that can reduce its physical, psychological, family, and interpersonal effects (Sperry, 2006). This chapter briefly describes osteoarthritis, rheumatoid arthritis, and juvenile arthritis in terms of their biopsychosocial features, with an emphasis on individual, couple, and family dynamics. Since psychological interventions are central to effective integrative treatment, these dynamics can be addressed in individual and family counseling. A case example illustrates these points.

Medical Aspects and Treatment of Arthritis

Osteoarthritis and Rheumatoid Arthritis

Two of the most common forms are osteoarthritis and rheumatoid arthritis. Osteoarthritis affects approximately 65% of older adults, while rheumatoid arthritis affects only about 5% of the total population.

---

1. Adapted from Sperry, L. (2009). Treating patients with arthritis: The impact of individual, couple, and family dynamics. *The Family Journal: Counseling and Therapy with Couples and Families, 18,* 263–266.

Osteoarthritis alters the hyaline cartilage and causes loss of the articular cartilage of the joint as well as irregular growth to the connecting bone structures. This disease begins asymptomatically before age 40 and afterwards nearly everyone experiences some pathological changes in their weight bearing joints. While men and women are equally affected by it, the onset is sooner in men. Pain is the earliest reported symptom, which is increased by exercise and relieved by rest. Morning stiffness lasts 10 to 30 minutes and lessens with movement. As the disease progresses, joint motion decreases, and tenderness and grating sounds—called crepitus—appear. As articular cartilage is lost in the joint ligaments become lax. Ligaments which effectively supported the joint before the disease progressed now become lax or loosened resulting in the joint becoming less stable and increasing the risk of complications, such as fractures if the individual falls. Pain and tenderness are experienced that arise from the changes in the ligaments and tendons (National Center for Chronic Disease Prevention and Health Promotion, 2000).

Medical treatment includes medications to reduce inflammation, pain, and swelling as well as physical therapy and exercise. Rehabilitation techniques are also employed for the purpose of preventing dysfunction and decreasing the severity or duration of disability. Interestingly, psychological factors are more strongly associated with disability than the disease process itself. Self-management appears to be an important part of the treatment regimen. Usually this involves a patient education component in which information about the disease and its manifestation and progressive course is provided. This can be accomplished in face-to-face contact, phone contact, or by computer programs or written materials.

Juvenile Arthritis

When arthritis occurs in children younger than age 16, it is called juvenile arthritis. Approximately 285,000 children in the United States have some form of the disease. The most common form is juvenile rheumatoid arthritis which is an autoimmune disease in which the lining of the joint—called the synovial membrane—becomes inflamed and enlarged, limits movement, and causes pain and tenderness. Enzymes released by the inflamed membranes cause further damage by eroding the bone and cartilage. Such joint and bone damage can cause problems in a growing child. If the growth areas of the bones are affected, the bones may grow at different rates so that one bone may develop abnormally in shape or size. The unfortunate result is that one leg may be permanently shorter than the other. Common symptoms include persistently swollen and tender, pain when moving joints, stiffness or decreased ability to move joints, and limping. Medical treatment is based on the severity of the condition and may include multiple medications. Physical therapy may be recommended to keep the joints moving as freely as possible (National Center for Chronic Disease Prevention and Health Promotion, 2000).

Individual Dynamics in Arthritis

Psychological factors influencing pain and disability have been noted in patients with arthritis. These include depression, stress, coping strategies, and illness perceptions (Keefe et al., 2002; Schiaffino, Shawaryn, & Blum, 1998; Sperry, 2009). This section briefly describes these dynamics as they influence the patient's experience of arthritis.

Depression

Depression is common among arthritis patients and influences overall adjustment to arthritis (Keefe et al., 2002). Some 15 to 17% of patients with rheumatoid arthritis report depressive symptoms, and those who are depressed had significantly poorer functioning and more arthritis-related physician visits and hospitalizations (Katz & Yelin, 1993). Disease activity and arthritis-related physical limitations have been found to predict depression in patients with rheumatoid arthritis. Depression is found to predict a moderate to large amount of variance in physical and psychological disability, even controlling for disease status. Furthermore, arthritis patients with a prior history of major depression are more likely to report higher levels of current pain (Keefe et al., 2002).

Stress

Stress is often blamed for disease flare-ups in rheumatoid arthritis patients. While no consistent link has been found between the two, there is agreement that stress is important in understanding how patients adjust to arthritis. The relationship between stress and depression was much stronger in rheumatoid arthritis patients than in osteoarthritis patients, and rheumatoid arthritis patients demonstrate more psychological and physiological reactivity to interpersonal stress than osteoarthritis patients as measured by cortisol and interleukin-6 levels (Keefe et al., 2002).

Coping Styles

Individuals have different ways of coping with their illness. Coping style can be classified as active vs. maladaptive coping. Different styles of coping show different relations to positive and negative affect; while active coping was only related to positive affect, maladaptive coping was related to both increased negative affect and decreased positive affect (Keefe et al., 2002). It has been found that active coping is predictive of positive affect while affective regulation is correlated to negative affect (Hamilton, Zautra, & Reich, 2005).

Illness Perceptions

Illness perceptions are subjective beliefs that form the basis for an individual's coping efforts, treatment compliance, and emotional responses (Schiaffino, Shawaryn, & Blum, 1998). A dynamic relationship exists between illness representations and illness experience. For example, patients with rheumatoid arthritis who believed their arthritis to be curable and, to some extent, "their own fault" reported higher levels of depression (Schiaffino et al., 1998). This finding is consistent with research on learned helplessness and perceived control in which self-blame occurs when best efforts fail. Because such representations and related beliefs are depressogenic and interfere with treatment, they must be therapeutically examined, challenged, and modified with psychotherapeutic interventions (Sperry, 2009).

Couple and Family Dynamics in Arthritis

Osteoarthritis and Rheumatoid Arthritis

Besides the aforementioned psychosocial factors, arthritis impacts and is impacted by family dynamics. The impact of adult-onset rheumatoid arthritis and osteoarthritis on family role functioning and the performance of household responsibilities is well documented (Reisine, 1995). Family members may not understand how arthritis can reduce the patient's functioning and capacity to handle his or her predisease roles and responsibilities. The arthritis patient has a distressing reaction, feeling that she is bringing less to the marital relationship than her healthy partner. The patient may believe that she is "holding back" the healthy spouse from being fulfilled. Feelings of insecurity arise along with shame and guilt or the patient may believe that the partner is resentful of what their life as a couple has become due to illness. A vicious cycle develops with the feeling of inadequacy and the continual need to apologize. Negative or critical remarks from husbands correlated with higher ratings of pain and disability for women with rheumatoid arthritis (Griffin, Friend, Kaell, & Bennett, 2001). Furthermore, negative spousal interaction was more predictive of patient adjustment than supportive spousal interactions, and a patient's inability to meet spousal expectations seems to contribute to depressive symptoms (Bediako & Friend, 2004). Needless to say, such role changes, doubts, and distress in the marital relationship and subsequent marital discord increase the probability of divorce. On the other hand, among patients with rheumatoid arthritis, higher daily emotional and social support from family members is related to higher levels of psychological well-being and less depression (Keefe et al., 2002).

Recently reported research on arthritis and illness perception studied the impact of a couple's illness perception on the wife/patient's psychological adjustment. It was found that the better the match or congruence of the couple's illness perception concerning the patient's personal control over rheumatoid arthritis the better was the psychological adjustment in women. Psychological adjustment was higher in wives from couples with similar optimistic beliefs about personal control, illness coherence, and rheumatoid arthritis consequences, when compared to those in couples where both partners held similar pessimistic beliefs (Sterba et al., 2008). An obvious implication of this study is that couples or family counseling that increases partners' understanding of illness perceptions may be beneficial in reducing marital distress and in increasing the patient's overall psychological health and well-being.

Research on family interventions strongly suggests the importance of including the patient's spouse in treatment approaches and focusing on relationship issues. Inclusion of a close family member, such as the patient's spouse, in family-oriented interventions for chronic medical conditions can be more efficacious than focusing solely on patient-oriented interventions. A review of 12 randomized, controlled studies with various illness populations, including arthritis, showed evidence that family-oriented interventions were more beneficial (Martire, 2005). Research also shows that a couple-oriented intervention for osteoarthritis was more efficacious than a similar patient-oriented intervention in enhancing spouses' support of patients and their positive and negative responses to patient pain. Following the intervention, patients in the couple-oriented intervention reported a greater decrease in their spouses' punishing response, such as anger and irritation, than did patients in the patient-oriented intervention (Martire, Schulz, Keefe, Rudy, & Starz, 2008). Again, the implication is that family and couples interventions can and do positively impact the patient's as well as the couple's well-being.

Juvenile Arthritis

Besides swollen and painful joints in the child or adolescent, the entire family is impacted by the disease in a variety of ways. These include the financial burden associated with this disease. It also includes the need for more medical care, mental health services, or education services than other children in the family require. It involves additional time demands in providing special care to the child. Juvenile arthritis inevitably impacts the parent's employment in terms of absences and sick days the parent must take because of medical appointments or treatments for the young patient. In terms of the young patient, there are missed school days because of the child's flare-ups and medical appointments. These absences may require extra child care expenses. Because of missed school time due to illness, tutoring may be needed which can be another financial drain. Many children or adolescents with juvenile arthritis will also experience significant emotional, developmental, or behavioral problems related to their illness. These and other related considerations are experienced as quite distressing by most young patients and their families. Needless to say, individual and family counseling may be indicated for some children and adolescents with juvenile arthritis and their families (Szer, 2002).

Integrative Treatment of Arthritis

Effective treatment of arthritis involves an integration of medical interventions with psychoeducational, and psychosocial interventions, including family counseling. Psychoeducational strategies such as relaxation training and skill training in cognitive pain management, problem solving, and social skills can be incorporated (Sperry, 2009). Because of the significant psychological component, counseling or referral for individual therapy and family counseling are commonly intervention choices today.

Case Illustration

Jolanda R. is a 52-year-old married African American female who has been self-treating her osteoarthritis for some 3 years without much relief. In fact, her disease has progressed to the point that she can barely get out of bed in the morning without assistance. Her husband, exasperated by her complaints about pain, has regularly urged her to see a specialist. As her condition worsened, she reluctantly made an appointment at a downtown arthritis clinic. James Shilling, MD, the clinic's rheumatologist, diagnosed her with osteoarthritis with mild spinal stenosis.

Dr. Shilling immediately began her on a combination antiarthritic drug regimen. Recognizing that she was also moderately depressed, he prescribed an antidepressant, but Mrs. R. refused it. The rheumatologist expressed his concern about the impact of depression on her pain symptoms, and Mrs. R. agreed to a consultation with the clinic's psychotherapist, Jessie Samuels, PhD. Dr. Samuels met with Mrs. R. that same day and assessed her mental status, her illness perceptions, and her support system. She confirmed a diagnosis of depression related to medical condition, marital conflict, and problematic illness perceptions. She indicated that successful treatment of severe arthritis included family involvement and asked that Mrs. R. bring her husband to their next appointment.

Dr. Samuels noted that Mrs. R., like many other arthritis patients, had conflicting "cure/control" and "cause" illness perceptions; that is, that their condition is curable but it is their fault they are arthritic because of overuse, poor diet, or lack of exercise. The results of such conflicting beliefs include an increasing sense of helplessness and depression. Just prior to meeting with Jolanda and her husband, she gave Mr. R. a short illness perception questionnaire about his beliefs about Jolanda R.'s arthritis and treatment. When they met with Dr. Samuels she explained to the couple how Jolanda R.'s illness perceptions were influencing her health and well-being. She also indicated that there were differences between the couple in their illness perceptions regarding both "cure/control" and "cause." She furthered noted that the clinic utilized an integrated treatment approach because it had found that medications alone were seldom sufficient for effective treatment of arthritis unless psychoeducational and psychosocial treatments were combined with the medication. More specifically, she indicated that the couple's conflicting illness beliefs needed to be therapeutically addressed to enhance their marital relationship and Jolanda's health and well-being. She noted that if the illness perceptions were not addressed, neither the depression nor arthritis pain could be effectively treated, as these beliefs will continue to interfere with the overall treatment. Accordingly, Dr. Samuels proposed a plan of working with the couple, and also meeting with Mrs. R. separately. The couple agreed to this plan, and Dr. Samuels utilized CBT strategies to process the conflicting illness perceptions and related marital discord. Within 2 months, Mrs. R.'s pain and depression had diminished and the dosage of her medications was reduced. A follow-up plan was set in which she would continue to be monitored by Dr. Shilling every 2 months and would check in with Dr. Samuels in 4 months.

Concluding Note

Arthritis in its various forms is a chronic medical condition which can significantly impact individual patients and their families. Arthritis and other chronic medical conditions not only have significant psychosocial features and sequelae, but are far more prevalent than behavioral and psychiatric disorders combined. Therefore, it will be incumbent on family counselors and other mental health professionals to become more knowledgeable and better equipped to effectively deal with these chronic medical conditions because it is the rare counseling and psychotherapy client who does not have at least one comorbid medical condition.

References

Bediako, S. M., & Friend, R. (2004). Illness-specific and general perception of social relationships in adjustment to rheumatoid arthritis: The role of interpersonal expectations. *Annals of Behavioral Medicine, 28*(3), 203–210.

Griffin, K, Friend, R., Kaell, A. T., & Bennett, R. S. (2001). Distress and disease status among patients with rheumatoid arthritis: Roles of coping styles and perceived responses from support providers. *Annals of Behavioral Medicine, 23*, 133–138.

Hamilton, N., Zautra, A. J., & Reich, J. (2005). Affect and pain in rheumatoid arthritis: Do individual differences in affective regulation and affective intensity predict emotional recovery from pain. *Annals of Behavioral Medicine, 29*, 216–224.

Katz, P. P., & Yelin, E. H. (1993). Prevalence and correlates of depressive symptoms among persons with rheumatoid arthritis. *Journal of Rheumatology, 20*, 790–796.

Keefe, F., Smith, S. J., Buffington, A. L. H., Gibson, J., Studts, J. L., & Caldwell, D. S. (2002). Recent advances and future directions in the biopsychosocial assessment and treatment of arthritis. *Journal of Consulting and Clinical Psychology, 70*(3), 640–655.

Martire, L. (2005). The "relative" efficacy of involving family in psychosocial interventions for chronic illness: Are there added benefits to patients and family members? *Families, Systems, & Health, 23*(3), 312–328.

Martire, L., Schulz, R., Keefe, F., Rudy, T., & Starz, T. (2008). Couple-oriented education and support intervention for osteoarthritis: Effects on spouses' support and responses to patient pain. *Families, Systems, and Health, 26*(2), 185–195.

National Center for Chronic Disease Prevention and Health Promotion. (2000). *Chronic diseases and their risk factors: The nation's leading causes of death, 1999.* Bethesda, MD: Author.

Reisine, S. (1995). Arthritis and the family: The impact of arthritis. *Arthritis Care and Research, 8*(4), 265–271.

Schiaffino, K. M., Shawaryn, M. A., & Blum, D. (1998). Examining the impact of illness representation on psychological adjustment to chronic illnesses. *Health Psychology, 17*(3), 262–268.

Sperry, L. (2006). *Psychological treatment of chronic illness.* Washington, DC: American Psychological Association.

Sperry, L. (2009). *Treatment of chronic medical conditions. Cognitive behavioral therapy strategies and integrative protocols.* Washington, DC: American Psychological Association.

Sterba, K., DeVellis, R., Lewis, M., DeVellis, B., Jordan, J., & Baucom, D. (2008). Effect of couple illness perception congruence on psychological adjustment in women with rheumatoid arthritis. *Health Psychology, 27*(2), 221–229.

Szer, I. (2002). Psychogenic rheumatism in adolescents. *Drug Benefit Trends, 14*(12), 32–36.

15

ASTHMA[1]

Asthma is a common chronic respiratory condition characterized by a reversible airway obstruction and airway responsiveness to a variety of irritants. An asthma attack involves such common symptoms as wheezing and tightness or pressure in the chest, and the condition can be life threatening if not properly treated. The course of this disease is highly variable depending on the individual's unique symptoms, triggers or precipitants of symptoms, health status, and the individual's capacity for self-management. As a result, asthma sufferers and their family can experience acute exacerbations of their condition as distressing and helpless and will seek out emergency room treatment when symptoms worsen: Nearly 75% of those emergency room visits for asthma are avoidable (Pleis & Lethbridge-Cejku, 2006). Statistics like this reflect a failure to adopt a biopsychosocial perspective of asthma. Besides providing a unique insight into factors that predispose, trigger, and maintain this chronic medical condition, the biopsychosocial perspective favors integrative treatments that can reduce its physical, psychological, and family and interpersonal effects (Sperry, 2006).

This chapter briefly describes asthma in terms of its biopsychosocial features, with an emphasis on individual, couple, and family dynamics. Since psychological interventions are central to effective integrative treatment, these dynamics can be addressed in individual and family counseling. A case example illustrates these points.

Medical Aspects of Asthma

An asthma attack is usually accompanied by tissue inflammation, mucous congestion, and constriction of the smooth muscles in the airways.

---

1. Adapted from Sperry, L. (2009). Treating patients with asthma: The impact of individual and family dynamics. *The Family Journal: Counseling and Therapy with Couples and Families, 17,* 350–354.

Whether caused by airway edema, acute bronchoconstriction, chronic mucous plugs, or changes in the lung itself, airflow obstruction and airflow hyperresponsiveness are signature features of this disease. Airway obstruction is due to a combination of factors including spasm of airway smooth muscles, edema of airway mucosa, increased mucous secretion, or infiltration of the airway walls. It results in an "asthma attack." Although there is great variability in symptomatology, an asthma attack begins with spasms of wheezing, coughing, and shortness of breath. Tightness or pressure in the chest, dyspnea or subjective difficulty or distress in breathing, and wheezing are commonly present during an asthma attack (Sperry, 2009).

The prevalence of asthma in the United States is about 5% among adults and 7% among children, although the incidence appears to be increasing. Morbidity and mortality increase disproportionately among the indigent in inner city areas. Approximately 25% of asthmatics experience severe symptoms, the greater majority of whom are women, ethnic minorities, those with the least education, smokers, and those receiving care from nonspecialists. In comparison to those with mild to moderate asthma, those with severe symptoms also tend to have less of an understanding of the asthma, its clinical manifestations, and the means to control asthma attacks. Asthma is the leading cause of hospitalization among children and is responsible for more absenteeism from school than any other chronic illness (National Center for Chronic Disease Prevention and Health Promotion, 2000).

Just as symptoms are varied, the experience of this disease state varies widely. Most commonly, in at least 50% of cases, asthma sufferers experience a reaction within seconds after exposure to a trigger, and this reaction continues for approximately an hour. There is also a delayed reaction that begins 4 to 8 hours after exposure that lasts for hours or even days. Chronic inflammation causes the airways of these individuals to become hyperresponsive to allergens, physical exertion, cigarette smoke, molds, and even breathing cold air. Psychological factors including crying, screaming, failed expectations, or relational stress may trigger symptoms (Sperry, 2006).

The course of this disease is highly variable depending on the individual's unique symptoms, triggers, or precipitants of symptoms, health status, and their capacity for self-management of this condition. Thus, it should not be too surprising that nearly 75% of emergency room admissions for asthma are avoidable. Furthermore, approximately 40% of asthmatics do not utilize appropriate symptom management strategies when their symptoms worsen. Upwards of 60% of asthmatics are poor at judging the extent of dyspnea (National Center for Chronic Disease Prevention and Health Promotion, 2000).

Effective medical treatment usually involves a management protocol. It consists of assessing the severity of the illness, controlling environmental factors to avoid or minimize triggering symptoms or exacerbations, using medication to manage exacerbations and reverse and prevent airway inflammation, utilizing patient education and self-management methods, and monitoring the course of therapy. The goal of such treatment is to prevent chronic symptoms, maintain lung or pulmonary function as near to normal as possible, prevent exacerbations, minimize the need for emergency room visits and hospitalization, and avoid the adverse effects of treatment. Recovery from this condition is typically defined as movement into the normal range of pulmonary function (National Center for Chronic Disease Prevention and Health Promotion, 2000). Needless to say, even small improvements can be clinically significant. The focus of traditional medical treatment is entirely on management rather than on cure.

Self-management is a key component in effective asthma management. It involves at least two goals. The first goal is to assist these individuals to self-manage their asthma at home and to work through treatment adjustment in response to changes in their symptoms. Patient education is a necessary prerequisite for effective self-management (Sperry, 2009). It includes basic facts about asthma, the role of quick-response and long-term control medications, correct use of metered-dose inhalers, and strategies for decreasing environmental exposure, a reduce plan for acute episodes, and involvement of family and significant others in the treatment process. Equally important is the second goal which is the development of the asthmatic's skills, judgment, and the confidence necessary for engaging in self-management activities and for collaborating with health care providers.

Individual Dynamics in Asthma

Comorbid Psychopathology

Comorbid psychopathology is known to exacerbate asthma and decrease quality of life (Lehrer, Feldman, Giardino, Song, & Schmaling, 2002). These same researchers have noted that family disorganization is another exacerbant. More specifically, anxiety, panic attacks, and depression are the most common comorbid conditions experienced by asthma patients.

Anxiety. Individuals with asthma seem particularly prone to experiencing anxiety (Lehrer et al., 2002). Anxiety symptoms appear to result in respiratory effects consistent with acute asthma exacerbation. The relationship appears to be reciprocal in that an emotional state can trigger asthma or can be triggered by asthmatic responses (York, Fleming, & Shuldham, 2006).

Panic Attacks. One of the most commonly studied negative emotions in asthma is panic (Carr, Lehrer, & Hochron, 1995). The incidence of panic disorder among patients with asthma is approximately 10% (Lehrer et al., 2002). Panic disorder patients report seven times more physician visits and twice as many lost work days as the general population. An excessively high panic response, such as rapid breathing, can lead to hyperventilation-induced asthma exacerbation that can then result in overuse of asthma medication and decreased effectiveness. It was found that among asthmatics, dyspnea may predict panic better than catastrophic thinking (Carr et al., 1995). A surprising observation is that panic symptoms may be adaptive in patients who have asthma as patients with low asthma-related panic have increased asthma mortality. It was further suggested that reduction of panic symptoms may be contraindicated in asthma patients with acute distress, and that asthma symptoms in patients with comorbid panic disorder should be closely monitored during treatment for panic symptoms (Carr, Lehrer, Hochron, & Jackson, 1996).

Depression. There is growing consensus that there is increased prevalence of depression among patients with asthma despite variable reports ranging from 1 to 45% (Opolski & Wilson, 2005). Depression appears to contribute to respiratory consequences consistent with asthma while contentment is related to effects that relieve airway constriction. Depression may also play a role in asthma self-management. It has been established that depressed patients with chronic illness are three times more likely to be noncompliant with regard to medical treatment (Opolski & Wilson, 2005). The bidirectional association between depression and asthma can result in a deteriorating cycle.

Illness Perceptions

Illness perception or representation is one of the most promising factors in understanding asthma and is a key consideration in both the medical and psychological treatment of this chronic medical condition (Sperry, 2006). Illness perceptions are the patients' internal representations about their medical condition; that is, their understanding of it and its symptoms, cause, illness duration, impact or consequences, curability, and their ability to control it. Illness perceptions and treatment beliefs of asthmatics tend to be sensitive predictors of their treatment compliance, particularly medication noncompliance, and beliefs about the necessity of medication and concerns about its potentially adverse effects and by negative perceived consequences of illness. While social, demographic, and personality factors explain very little of the variance in compliance, illness perceptions and treatment beliefs have been shown to be substantial independent predictors of compliance with asthma treatment (Horne & Weinman, 2002). Another study found that compliance with inhaler use was predicted by age, gender, and illness perceptions about the controllability of their condition, and about the duration of their medical condition (Jessop & Rutter, 2003). Finally, the number of inhaler prescriptions was significantly associated with patients' beliefs about the necessity of their asthma medication, acceptance of their illness, as well as belief in a long illness duration and high morbidity (Byer & Myers, 2000).

Family Dynamics in Asthma

Besides the aforementioned individual dynamics, asthma impacts and is impacted by systemic factors, particularly family and couple dynamics. Increasingly, systemic factors involved in asthma have been of interest to both researchers and family counselors and therapists. A special issue of *Family Process* (Fiese, 2008) was devoted to asthma with articles focusing on such systemic considerations as integration of individual needs into the family, developmental trajectories of risk and resilience, cultural adaptation in family therapy, and supportive and destructive patterns of interaction. A major theme of the special issue was that asthma is an exemplar in the study of family health because of its potential to affect multiple members of the family, its comorbidity with psychological problems, and its disproportionate influence on minority and low-income families (Fiese, 2008).

Family dynamics involving asthma patients, especially parent–child relationships, are commonly studied by health researchers. Unfortunately, space does not allow more than the brief mention of a few of these studies. A particularly intriguing study involved children brought to a pediatric emergency room with and without asthma symptoms. The findings suggested that children with asthma were at risk for depression and that depression may worsen asthma severity. It was recommended that children with asthma in distressed families or high stress situations should be screened for depression, and that children with persistent asthma should be screened for depression and family relational distress. The study also found that family relational intervention was likely to be efficacious in the treatment of both childhood depression and asthma (Wood et al., 2006).

Researchers have noted that family disorganization is a major exacerbant of asthma (Lehrer et al., 2002). For example, dyspnea is commonly observed in asthma patients prior to the onset of an asthma attack. While clinicians have noted that asthma attacks can be triggered by high levels of affective or emotional expression in family members, research has not borne out that clinical observation until recently. A study found that the severity of dyspnea was directly related to levels of affective expression in family members of asthmatic patients, particularly their spouses (Furgał et al., 2009). Severity of dyspnea was assessed with the Borg scale while family functioning, including affective expression, was assessed with the Family Assessment Questionnaire. As predicted, the higher the level of affective expression, the greater severity of the patient's dyspnea. The researchers conclude that dyspnea constitutes a specific form of emotional communication between spouses. The obvious implication is that counselors and other clinicians would do well to consider that family affective expression can not only exacerbate but also trigger dyspnea in asthmatic patients (Furgał et al., 2009).

So what role, if any, should family counseling and therapy play in asthma treatment? A fascinating research study was recently reported. Asthma psychoeducation is a promising intervention in asthma treatment. These programs, which are largely disease-focused with little or no concern for family dynamics, are relatively effective in symptom reduction. In an attempt to boost the effectiveness of such programs, a study evaluated a novel asthma psychoeducation program which incorporates family therapy (Ng et al., 2008). A randomized wait list-controlled crossover clinical trial design was used to study children with stable asthma and their parents. Outcome measures included exhaled nitric oxide, spirometry, and adjustment to asthma for children, and perceived efficacy in asthma management, anxiety and depression scales, and a quality of life scale for parents. Repeated measures found a significant decrease in airway inflammation, and an increase in patient's adjustment to asthma as well as perceived efficacy in asthma management for parents. Significant improvements in both symptom-related measures and mental health and relationship measures were observed, and serial trend analysis revealed that most psychosocial measures continued to progress steadily after intervention. In other words, family therapy significantly augmented gains from psychoeducation. Not surprisingly, the researchers concluded that family therapy should be incorporated into asthma psychoeducation programs (Ng et al., 2008).

Research on family interventions strongly suggest the importance of including the patient's spouse in treatment approaches and focusing on relationship issues. Inclusion of a close family member, such as the patient's spouse, in family-oriented interventions for chronic medical conditions can be more efficacious than focusing solely on patient-oriented interventions. A review of 12 randomized, controlled studies with various illness populations, including asthma, showed evidence that family-oriented interventions were more beneficial (Martire, 2005). Again, the implication is that family and couples interventions can and do positively impact the patient's as well as the couple's well-being. Of particular importance is that couples or family counseling that increases partners' understanding of illness perceptions may be beneficial in reducing marital distress and in increasing the patient's overall psychological health and well-being (Sperry, 2006).

Case Illustration

Paula J. is a 29-year-old married female with a 14-year history of asthma. Her asthma has worsened recently. About 3 months ago, she had started working in a pet store owned by a family friend. While she enjoys working with the animals and her fellow employees she has become noticeably aware of her exposure to animal dander in the store. Needless to say, she quickly found her allergic response to the dander further complicated her asthma. Seven weeks ago and again last week she experienced full-blown asthma attacks which were so severe she ended up in the emergency room. Prior to this time, her asthma was reasonably well controlled on medication and an inhaler, but now it was poorly controlled. Her internist, Dr. Samuels, proceeded to prescribe medications to control her new allergy but Paula didn't tolerate the side effects and stopped taking it. She was referred to an allergist who suggested a desensitization treatment but Paula balked at the prospect of undergoing weekly treatment for three or more years. Paula had now missed several days of work and she agreed that both physical and emotional stressors, her dander allergy and her marital discord, were complicating her asthma. Since additional medication did not seem to help much, Dr. Samuels referred Paula to his colleague, Joanna Ibrahim, PhD, a mental health counselor specializing in chronic respiratory illnesses, to deal with Paula's much more challenging chronic health condition.

Dr. Ibrahim undertook a biopsychosocial assessment which included the Illness Perception Questionnaire-Revised (Horne & Weinman, 2002). Based on the assessment, she engaged Paula in developing a workable treatment plan. She noted that Paula was only partially accepting of her medical conditions and that she rated the consequences or impact of her asthma and allergies as only minimal and believed that she had only minimal control over her symptoms. Her view of the causality of her asthma was that it "was just hereditary" and she did not make any connection to stress. In short, while her internist assessed her asthma–allergy condition as severe, Paula downplayed her asthma, which is not uncommon among those in illness denial. She reported that she had begun smoking at age 15 and it appears that it somehow triggered her first asthma attacks. Asthma was diagnosed by her female pediatrician who advised Paula to stop smoking, which she did on her own. Dr. Ibrahim noted her high need for attention and other histrionic features. From the history, the therapist surmised that Paula would act out against an authority figure who made demands on her, particularly about health matters. For example, both Paula's father and husband reportedly berated her for not using her inhaler. Her husband Joey was especially convinced that Paula's asthma had worsened over the years he had known her because of her refusal to follow her treatment regimen. In apparent defiance she refused to use her inhaler, or use it properly, which inevitably led to full-blown asthma attacks. In short, marital conflict seemed to be the trigger or exacerbant. In Dr. Ibrahim's experience, it was not unusual for a partner to "accept" his or her partner's illness, while the other person continued to deny it. Such an "acceptance-denial" pattern would often become an ongoing source of conflict for the couple, as it appeared to be in this case. Finally, the counselor concluded that ethnic and other cultural factors did not seem to be operative in her medical condition.

While Paula's asthma was typically triggered by stress and allergens, it remained potentially life threatening because she would "forget" to carry an inhaler with her or failed to use it in an effective manner when she had access to one. Accordingly, illness denial, problematic illness representations, and noncompliance with her inhaler became main treatment targets. An equally important target was marital discord. The fact that Paula had a previous success at a lifestyle change effort (smoking cessation) and was able to easily engage with both individual and group sessions suggested the prognosis would be moderate to high, at least for the first two treatment targets.

Interventions consisted of individual CBT sessions focused on increasing illness acceptance and modifying her illness representations. They also processed relational issues with her husband and her father. Aware of how her histrionic dynamics could interfere with treatment, Dr. Ibrahim was careful to frame her feedback to Paula in ways that fostered collaboration. Paula also participated in one of Dr. Ibrahim's psychoeducation groups that focused on symptom perception training, psychoeducation, and relaxation and mindfulness. That Paula was able to keep a diary of symptoms and triggers and learn in a group session to use an inhaler effectively, suggested that she was sufficiently engaged in the treatment process.

As treatment proceeded, Paula made progress on all treatment targets except for relational issues. Dr. Ibrahim discussed the value of conjoint sessions with her husband. She agreed to meet for a "few" such sessions if they were related to her asthma control. Her husband, Joey, also agreed to participate. Accordingly, the couple met with Dr. Ibrahim about couples issues that impacted Paula's asthma. They identified a "relation defeating" pattern in which Paula would be experiencing some stress and begin to wheeze after which Joey would demand that she use her inhaler. Both agreed that "demanding" treatment compliance with the inhaler only made things worse. The therapist asked Paula what Joey might say or do that she would consider helpful. Paula said that Joey could show his concern and care for her by gently suggesting that she engage in a preventive health behavior, such as controlled breathing. Joey was agreeable to this "relation building" pattern plan. The conjoint work also focused on how the couple could engage in other "relation building" actions such as "dating" each other (Sperry, Carlson, & Peluso, 2006). Focusing on "relation building" behaviors paid off as Joey refrained from making demands, and Paula began to use an inhaler properly and effectively. Within 3 months, Paula had accepted her illness, modified her illness perceptions, and was engaging in positive health behaviors. Her condition was stabilized and a plan for monthly and then quarterly follow-up with Dr. Samuels and Dr. Ibrahim was made.

Concluding Note

Asthma in its various forms is a chronic medical condition which can significantly impact individual patients and their families. Asthma and other chronic medical conditions not only have significant psychosocial features and sequellae, but are far more prevalent than behavioral and psychiatric disorders combined. Therefore, it will be incumbent on family counselors and other mental health professionals to become more knowledgeable and better equipped to effectively deal with these chronic medical conditions because it is the rare counseling and psychotherapy client who does not have at least one comorbid chronic medical condition. The case example illustrates how a counselor can utilize individual and couples therapeutic interventions to increase illness acceptance, modify illness perceptions, and reduce relational discord, while increasing health and well-being.

References

Byer, B., & Myers, L. (2000). Psychological correlates of adherence to medication in asthma. *Psychology, Health and Medicine, 5,* 389–393.

Carr, R. E., Lehrer, P. M., & Hochron, S. M. (1995). Predictors of panic-fear in asthma. *Health Psychology, 14*(5), 421–426.

Carr, R. E., Lehrer, P. M., Hochron, S. M., & Jackson, A. (1996). Effect of psychological stress on airway impedance in individuals with asthma and panic disorder. *Journal of Abnormal Psychology, 105,* 137–141.

Fiese, B. (2008). Breathing life into family processes: Introduction to the special issue on families and asthma [Special issue]. *Family Process, 47*(1), 1–5.

Furgał, M., Nowobilski, R., Pulka, G., Polczyk, R., de Barbaro, B., Nizankowska-Mogilnicka, E., & Szczeklik, A. (2009). Dyspnea is related to family functioning in adult asthmatics. *The Journal of Asthma, 46*(3), 280–283.

Horne, R., & Weinman, J. (2002). Self-regulation and self-management in asthma: Exploring the role of illness perceptions and treatment beliefs in explaining nonadherence to preventer medication. *Psychology and Health, 17,* 17–32

Jessop, D., & Rutter, D. (2003). Adherence to asthma medication: The role of illness representations. *Psychology and Health, 18,* 595–612.

Lehrer, P., Feldman, J., Giardino, N., Song, H-S., & Schmaling, K. (2002). Psychological aspects of asthma. *Journal of Counseling and Clinical Psychology, 70,* 691–711.

Martire, L. (2005). The "relative" efficacy of involving family in psychosocial interventions for chronic illness: Are there added benefits to patients and family members? *Families, Systems, & Health, 23*(3), 312–328.

National Center for Chronic Disease Prevention and Health Promotion. (2000). *Chronic diseases and their risk factors: The nation's leading causes of death, 1999.* Bethesda, MD: Author.

Ng, S., Li, A., Lou, V., Tso, I., Wan, P., & Chan, D. (2008). Incorporating family therapy into asthma group intervention: A randomized waitlist-controlled trial. *Family Process, 47*(1), 115–130.

Opolski, M., & Wilson, I. (2005). Asthma and depression: A pragmatic review of the literature and recommendations for future research. *Clinical Practice and Epidemiology in Mental Health, 1,* 1–18.

Pleis, J., & Lethbridge-Cejku, M. (2006). Summary health statistics for U.S. adults: National Health Fitness Survey, 2005. National Center for Health Statistics. *Vital Health Statistics, 10,* 232.

Sperry, L. (2006). *Psychological treatment of chronic illness.* Washington, DC: American Psychological Association.

Sperry, L. (2009). *Treatment of chronic medical conditions: Cognitive behavioral therapy strategies and integrative protocols.* Washington, DC: American Psychological Association.

Sperry, L., Carlson, J., & Peluso, P. (2006). *Couples therapy.* Denver, CO: Love.

Wood, B., Miller, B., Lim, J., Lillis, K., Ballow, M., Stern, T., & Simmens, S. (2006). Family relational factors in pediatric depression and asthma: Pathways of effect. *Journal of the American Academy of Child & Adolescent Psychiatry, 45*(12), 1494–1502.

York, J., Fleming, S., & Shuldham, C. (2006). Psychological interventions for children with asthma. *Cochrane Review, 23,* 67–81.

16

BREAST CANCER[1]

Breast cancer is the most common form of cancer and the second leading cause of death in middle aged women. Several nonmedical or psychosocial factors can exacerbate the course of this disease and complicate its treatment and recovery. These factors include clinical depression, cultural factors, and marital factors, particularly marital conflict. Accordingly, this segment highlights these individual, cultural, and systemic dynamics. A case example illustrates key points. Individual and couples therapy has become an essential adjunctive for effective medical treatment and clinical outcomes of cancer. Given that an increasing number of clients referred to or presenting for individual and family therapy have some form of cancer, clinicians would do well to recognize these individual, cultural, and family dynamics and have the capacity to effectively address them. This chapter begins with a brief description of medical factors and treatment considerations in breast cancer.

Medical Considerations in Breast Cancer

Other than skin cancer, breast cancer is the most commonly occurring cancer and is the second leading cause of death in women 35 to 54 years old. The most common type is invasive ductal carcinoma which arises in the milk ducts of the breast and accounts for 80% of all cases. Invasive lobular cancer arises in the lobules of the breast and accounts for 10 to 15%. Only 5 to 10% of breast cancers occur in women with a clear genetic predisposition, while the rest are "sporadic," meaning that there is no direct family history of it. The lifetime risk of developing breast cancer is greatly increased if a woman inherits a harmful mutation in BRCA1 or BRCA2 genes. Such women have an increased risk of developing breast cancer or ovarian cancer before menopause. Often, they have multiple,

---

1. Adapted from Sperry, L. (2010). Breast cancer, depression, culture, and marital conflict. *The Family Journal: Counseling and Therapy with Couples and Families 18*, 62–65.

close family members who have been diagnosed with either of these medical conditions (American Cancer Society, 2010).

Breast cancer occurs more commonly in the left breast. Slow-growing cancers may take up to 8 years to become palpable at 1 cm. This cancer spreads by way of the lymphatic system and the bloodstream. The estimated growth of breast cancer is referred to as its "doubling time," that is, the time for malignant cells to double in number. Survival time of this cancer is based on tumor size and spread. The number of involved lymph nodes is the critical factor in predicting survival time. With appropriate therapy about 70 to 75% of women without lymph node involvement survive 10 years or more compared with 20 to 25% of those with lymph node involvement (Axford & O'Callaghan, 2004).

Common signs and symptoms include a lump or mass in the breast, breast pain, and changes in the size or symmetry of the breast. An unusual, spontaneous draining warrants medical investigation. Diagnostic tests include mammography, biopsy, ultrasonography, cone scans, computed tomography (CT) scans, and estrogen and progesterone receptors assays of tumor tissue (Axford & O'Callaghan, 2004).

Common treatments include surgery such as lumpectomy or mastectomy, radiation, chemotherapy, and adjuvant treatments like the drug Tamoxifen. Because grieving is commonly experienced with the loss of a breast, individual counseling and self-help groups may be indicated. Since couples' relationships can become strained even to the point of separation and divorce, marital or couples counseling may also be indicated (Sperry, 2009).

Individual Dynamics and Breast Cancer

Several individual dynamic factors impact the clinical course and outcome in the treatment of breast cancer. This section describes two well-researched individual dynamics: illness representation and depression as well as some treatment implications.

Illness Representations

As indicated earlier (chapter 3) illness representations provide a clinically useful window into a patient's inner world. By eliciting patients' view of their illness in terms of its identity, consequences, timeline, cure and control, and its cause, therapists can more effectively develop a therapeutic alliance as well as intervene to achieve positive therapeutic outcomes such as increased physical and psychological resilience, couple and family functioning, and compliance with medical regimen.

Illness representations in cancer tend to be sensitive predictors of treatment compliance, treatment outcomes, and well-being. For example, in a prospective study of breast cancer patients, illness representations, as measured by the Illness Perception Questionnaire (IPQ), were assessed. The patients' beliefs about the impact or consequences of their cancer symptoms and duration of their illness predicted their psychological morbidity after one year of treatment. In other words, those with chronically high distress had a year earlier indicated their negative perceptions and beliefs about their illness on the IPQ (Millar, Purushotham, McLatchie, George, & Murray, 2005).

Another prospective study assessed illness representations in cancer patients. This study looked at the role of illness beliefs and perceptions in the decision to participate in a support group for women with breast cancer. Logistic regression analysis showed that participation was predicted by the belief that cancer was caused by altered immunity, higher cancer-related distress, and lower avoidance tendencies. A noteworthy recommendation of this study is that support programs would do well to tailor their focus on resolving cancer-related distress rather than general anxiety or depression (Cameron, Schlatter, Ziginskas, Harman, & Benson, 2005).

Women with breast cancer differ in the subjective perception of their disease and their illness representations play an important role in perceived health in breast cancer. Women who view their breast cancer as a condition with serious symptoms and consequences, those who believe their illness is chronic, and those who consider their illness uncontrollable were found to report worse physical and mental health than those who believed the opposite. After statistically controlling for external variables, the cognitive illness representations regarding illness identity and consequences explained 57% of variance in physical health, whereas emotional illness representation and treatment control explained 47% of variance in mental health (Rozema, Völlink, & Lechner, 2009). Similarly, a study of illness perceptions in women with increased risk of breast cancer showed significantly higher levels of cancer specific distress than those in the comparison group (Rees, Fry, Cull, & Sutton, 2004).

Clinical Implications. Illness representations that are inaccurate and unrealistic tend to negatively impact responses to medical and psychosocial treatment. When there is a discrepancy between the medical view of causality and the patient's illness representations about causality, also known as an explanatory model, it is essential that the therapist work with the patient to achieve a mutually agreeable representation. For example, a patient who believes their depression is caused only by a chemical imbalance in their brain when the assessment shows that marital conflict and job stress are also present can be helped to view their illness as caused by both sets of factors which can increase patient receptivity to the couples therapy that initially was rejected. Therapists can utilize psychoeducation and cognitive restructuring strategies to revise such representations.

Because illness representations are intermediate beliefs they are relatively responsive to change efforts including education, cognitive replacement, and cognitive disputation.

Depression

Because emotional distress is commonplace among women diagnosed with breast cancer, a number of studies have studied the incidence of stress, anxiety, and depression among these women. A common statistic is that about one-half of all women experience sufficient distress, anxiety, or depression that it interferes with and impairs their daily lives (Hegel et al., 2006).

In some studies, clinical depression, that is, a major depressive episode, is identified in 10% of those with breast cancer (Hegel et al., 2006), while in other studies the range is 15 to 25% (Sephton et al., 2009). In other words, clinical depression, which is marked by symptoms of fatigue, sleep disturbance, appetite change, hopelessness, helplessness, worthlessness, and loss of interest in pleasurable activities is commonplace among these women.

Researchers studied the effect of a prior diagnosis of clinical depression on the diagnosis, treatment, and survival of older women with breast cancer. They found that women with a recent diagnosis of such depression are at greater risk for receiving nondefinitive treatment and experience worse survival after a diagnosis of breast cancer, and had a higher risk of death (Goodwin, Zhang, & Ostir, 2004). Definitive treatment means that their cancer would be appropriately and effectively treated and that their depression would be effectively and appropriately treated as well.

More recently, it was reported that clinical depression impairs the woman's ability to fight off infection and hastens the progression of the disease. This means that women with breast cancer and depression are at higher risk of cancer recurrence and early death due to their inability to mount the immune response needed to ward off infections. The more symptoms of depression exhibited, the less intense is their immune response and the higher their cortisol levels, an immune-suppressing hormone released at high levels during chronic stress and depression (Sephton et al., 2009). In short, the presence of depression, particularly untreated or partially treated depression, correlates with poor prognosis, including faster tumor growth, lowered immunity resulting in poor wound healing, and in lower survival rates.

Clinical Implications. Since depression often presents primarily with somatic symptoms—depression is converted and experienced as physical symptoms—in many cultures, it is not unusual for medical personnel to fail to recognize clinical depression. It can also be somatically expressed in certain personality styles such as obsessive-compulsive and narcissistic personality. Accordingly, therapists would do well to evaluate patients' individual, couple, and family relationships for subtle indicators of physical symptoms that could mask clinical depression. For example, a seemingly highly acculturated first generation Latina wife consulted with seven medical specialists over a period of 5 months for various pain and gastrointestinal symptoms. No organic cause was identified, although three different medications were prescribed before a psychotherapist suspected that these somatic complaints reflected increased marital discord and work stress and referred her to a psychiatrist for medication evaluation. After 4 weeks on an antidepressant her depression and somatic symptoms cleared.

Cultural Dynamics and Breast Cancer

Given that millions of Americans have no health insurance, it should not be surprising that access to appropriate cancer diagnosis and treatment is limited for some women, usually those with limited education, literacy, disabilities, or those whose cultural beliefs and practices pose barriers to effective Western medical treatments. Specifically, it has been shown that women may not seek immediate care for breast cancer symptoms because of cultural constraints regarding the use of family resources for their own health concerns or because family and marital relationships influence their own health behaviors (Freeman, Muth, & Kerner, 1995). For instance, a woman may forgo seeking medical care about a breast lump because of the cultural belief that it is improper for anyone other than her husband to see her unclothed. Or, a woman may refuse surgery (mastectomy) based on the cultural belief that her husband will no longer find her sexually acceptable after such surgery.

Besides race, ethnicity, and social class, religion and spirituality are additional elements of culture. Religious and spiritual factors can provide life-affirming resources in women's response to the diagnosis of breast cancer as well as to their adjustment to its arduous treatment and life adjustment. In particular, religious and spiritual resources have proved essential to women who have experienced the loss of a breast following mastectomy (Gail, Kristjansson, Charbonneau, & Florack, 2009). Often, this loss is accompanied by doubts about personal identity and self-worth. It is noteworthy that research finds that one in 10 women suffered a spiritual crisis associated with their breast cancer (Hegel et al., 2006).

Clinical Implications. Needless to say, counselors and therapists who are culturally sensitive and aware of these dynamics can provide expert consultation to medical personnel. Knowledge of the patient's illness representations, particularly about causality, can be quite useful. Referred to by medical anthropologists as explanatory models, such explanations of causality or why a patient believes he or she is experiencing a particular illness can be particularly valuable in both specifying or confirming a patient's level of acculturation and planning or modifying treatment. Presumably, they can also provide culturally sensitive and effective treatment to such individuals and couples.

Family Dynamics and Breast Cancer

Just as other chronic medical conditions can influence family dynamics and affect family functioning, so does breast cancer. There is a relationship between adjustment to breast cancer and family cohesion and functioning. Women with breast cancer who experienced a high level of adjustment to their medical condition as well as to their marriages, also reported high levels of family cohesion. Not surprisingly, low levels of adjustment reflected lower levels of family cohesion and overall family functioning (Friedman et al., 1988).

How do men experience breast cancer and its treatment in their partners? A qualitative study of men's perspectives of individual and family coping provides useful information for those providing individual and family therapy (Hilton, Crawford, & Tarko, 2000). Two main concerns were identified: the first focused on their partners' illness and care, and the second focused on the continuing need to keep family life going. Focusing on a wife's illness and care was reflected in men's efforts to understand, assist with decision making, get through treatment, and deal with the health care system. Three related themes were: *Being there,* which meant that men wanted to be physically present and emotionally supportive. They wanted to accompany their partners to appointments, access information and services, and provide care. Most felt unprepared and did not know what to do or how to behave. Men *relied on health care professionals* to give competent care, and to provide support and assistance. They wanted to be treated with respect and compassion and to have their views considered and respected. *Being informed and contributing to decision making* involved learning about cancer, assisting with and supporting their partners' decisions, and informing children, family, and friends.

The second major concern focused on the continuing need to keep family life going amidst the stress and disruption of their partner's cancer. There were six related themes. Most were challenged by attempting to keep patterns normal, as they struggled to keep family routines and activities intact, especially for the children. For family life to continue, men had to *help out and rely on others* to undertake household and child care activities. Men felt stretched and overwhelmed, particularly when helping at home was unfamiliar. They endeavored to be positive and to have positive people around them. They were strengthened by their partners' positive attitudes, although spouses often protected each other by not sharing fears and emotions. Most men helped by putting their own needs on hold. Initially, they were totally consumed by the cancer, its treatment, and keeping family life going; many automatically put their own needs as secondary to their wives' needs. Furthermore, they talked about adapting their work life to balance work and home demands. Some adapted work patterns and wished they had taken more time off, whereas others saw work as an escape. Finally, managing finances was an added stress as they attempted to deal with unexpected reduced incomes and increased expenses (Hilton et al., 2000).

Another study found similar results. It found that spouses of women with breast cancer negotiated the illness experience by becoming educated about the cancer, adapted their lifestyle to balance home and work responsibilities, were sensitive to their partners' emotional and physical needs, and tried to minimize illness effects by reducing daily stressors (Zahlis & Shands, 1991).

In the past much research on the impact of breast cancer has been directed to global family dynamics such as levels of family functioning and cohesion as well as adjustment of each partner to the illness. More recently, research has focused on more specific family and couple dynamics. This includes studies on couples' dynamics as they impact wound healing, a common complication of mastectomy. For example, there is considerable research on how stress and depression impair wound healing. Depressive symptoms consistently predict delayed wound healing following surgery (Kiecolt-Glaser, Marucha, Malarkey, Mercado, & Glaser, 1995; McGuire et al., 2006). Marital discord also predicts delayed wound healing. Specifically, research demonstrates that wound healing is slowed following marital conflicts when compared with supportive couples' interactions. It was also found that couples who demonstrated consistently higher levels of hostile behaviors across both their interactions healed at only 60% of the rate of low hostile couples (Kiecolt-Glaser et al., 2005).

Clinical Implications. There are some clinical implications of these research findings for individual and family therapy. The findings highlight the importance of viewing the family as a unit throughout the entire course of this disease with regard to coping, role change, distress, and concerns. They also highlight the complexities of the couple's relationship in dealing with this illness and its treatment while endeavoring to maintain a sense of family normality. Possible interventions range from providing emotional support in group therapy or support groups, to providing individual and family sessions on communication and dealing with conflicted feelings and distress, and providing individual psychotherapy to address men's needs and concerns related to issues such as supporting their partners and children, household management, asking for help, and accessing resources and services.

Clinical Illustration

Juanita presented at a community health clinic for evaluation and treatment of a growing mass in her breast. She was a 54-year-old married Mexican American female, and was accompanied by her husband of 29 years. Six months ago she noticed slight pain and a small lump in her left breast but said she thought it would go away and did not seek medical care because "we couldn't afford it." Mammography done following the medical exam revealed that the mass was the size of a 50 cent piece, suggesting a fast growing and probably aggressive tumor. Her medical history included a hysterectomy some 10 years ago, a 32-year history of smoking, and a family history of clinical depression. Juanita indicated that her father had been hospitalized and received electroshock treatments for depression and suicidal ideation. The biopsy report revealed infiltrating adenocarcinoma of the left breast which had spread to the lymph nodes in her armpit. She was referred to a local hospital for a mastectomy and removal of axillary lymph nodes. She was to begin radiation and chemotherapy but this was delayed for nearly 4 months because of poor wound healing. She had become increasingly depressed after the surgery, and her husband, who had faithfully accompanied Juanita to all her medical appointment before her surgery was no longer coming. Tearfully, Juanita recounted that they had fought almost constantly since the surgery and that "Jose won't even touch me anymore."

What accounted for her poor postoperative course with infections and slow wound healing, and why the marital difficulties? Juanita's physician was stymied by his patient's worsening condition and decided to seek consultation. He referred her to Sara Gonzalez, PhD, who provided psychosocial consultation to the medical staff and counseling with couples and family. She had considerable experience dealing with the treatment complications among clinic patients. In her evaluation of Juanita, Dr. Gonzalez identified Juanita's level of acculturation as low, and that her belief that she could not afford medical treatment when the lump and pain were first noted was not quite accurate in that families living at the poverty level such as Juanita's were eligible for free care at the community clinic. Rather, it appeared that her illness perceptions were operative and appeared to have interfered with effective treatment outcomes. These illness perceptions included: "having breast cancer means you are being punished by God" and "you are no longer a woman if you lose a breast." It may be that these or other cultural beliefs may have accounted for her delay in seeking medical care, even when it was available to her free of cost.

Dr. Gonzalez also learned that Juanita had experienced a low level of depression throughout most of her adult life, and that her current depression met DSM criteria for major depressive disorder. It seemed to manifest soon after her discovery of the small breast lump. Because she had considerable experience with the biopsychosociocultural aspects of cancer, Dr. Gonzalez was well acquainted with the psychological, cultural, and systemic factors involving breast cancer. She speculated that Juanita's untreated depression accounted for the rapid progression of her cancer and poor response to treatment, and that the metastases and comorbid depression complicated her relationship with her husband. Unfortunately, this systemic change is a common phenomenon in chronic medical conditions (Sperry, 2009).

After her evaluation, Dr. Gonzalez discussed treatment recommendations with Juanita's physician. She indicated that Juanita was clinically depressed and that this depression likely accounted for the rapid proliferation of the cancer and the retarded wound healing following the mastectomy. She recommended that Juanita be immediately evaluated for possible antidepressant treatment. She also recommended individual and couples counseling, noting that marital discord also could retard wound healing. She began individual counseling with Juanita to address her depression and cultural factors. It would also include some couples sessions to address the relational issues, much of which appeared to be culturally related.

Case Commentary. This case suggests that Juanita's slow and painful wound healing was related to both her untreated clinical depression and to the couple's marital concerns and discord. The good news is that proper treatment of depression actually increases the rate of wound healing, and that effectively addressing the couple's relational issues and discord might also facilitate wound healing. Marital conflict was a focal factor in her experience with cancer. While establishing causality is difficult and may be impossible at this point in time, nevertheless marital issues may well have been direct factors in infection and delayed wound healing. Marital issues also appeared to interact with and exacerbate her depression. Furthermore, cultural factors, particularly cultural beliefs about a woman's sexual desirability and acceptability after loss of a breast and her illness perceptions that her cancer was punishment from God for using birth control and she was "no longer a woman" after her mastectomy may have complicated her relationship with her husband. Fortunately, the expertise of Dr. Gonzalez was available to her.

Concluding Note

This segment has described breast cancer and various factors that impede treatment progress, particularly factors that can exacerbate the spread or rate of metastases of cancer. It reviewed some individual dynamics that impact breast cancer, particularly illness representations and depression, as well as links between breast cancer and culture, and between wound healing and depression. The influence of family dynamics, particularly marital discord was also discussed. Therapists and other mental health professionals who are aware of these factors can provide invaluable consultation to surgeons and other medical personnel. They can also provide critical and even lifesaving care, in the form of individual and couples counseling to women with this disease and their partners.

References

American Cancer Society. (2010). *Cancer facts and figures, 2010.* Atlanta, GA: Author.

Axford, J., & O'Callaghan, C. (2004). *Medicine* (2nd ed.). London: Wiley-Blackwell.

Cameron, L., Booth, R., Schlatter, M, Ziginskas, D., Harman, J., & Benson, S. (2005). Cognitive and affective determinants of decisions to attend a group psychosocial support program for women with breast cancer. *Psychosomatic Medicine, 67,* 584–589.

Freeman, H., Muth, B., & Kerner, J. (1995). Expanding access to cancer screening and clinical follow-up among the medically underserved. *Cancer Practice, 3,* 19–30.

Friedman, L., Baer, E., Nelson, D., Lane, M., Smith, F., & Dworkin, R. (1988). Women with breast cancer: Perception of family functioning and adjustment to illness. *Psychosomatic Medicine, 50,* 529–540.

Gail, T., Kristjansson, E., Charbonneau, & Florack, P. (2009). A longitudinal study of the role of spirituality in response to the diagnosis and treatment of breast cancer. *Journal of Behavioral Medicine, 32,* 174–180.

Goodwin, J., Zhang, D., & Ostir, G. (2004). Effect of depression on diagnosis, treatment, and survival of older women with breast cancer. *Journal of the American Geriatrics Society, 52,* 106–111

Hegel, M., Moore, C., Collins, E., Kearing, S., Gillock, K., Riggs, R., ... Ahles, T. (2006). Distress, psychiatric syndromes, and impairment of function in women with newly diagnosed breast cancer. *Cancer, 107,* 2924–2931.

Hilton, B., Crawford, J., & Tarko, M. (2000). Men's perspectives on individual and family coping with their wives' breast cancer and chemotherapy. *Western Journal of Nursing Research, 22,* 438–459.

Kiecolt-Glaser, J., Loving, T., Stowell, J., Malarkey, W., Lemeshow, S., Dickinson, S., & Glaser, R. (2005). Hostile marital interactions, proinflammatory cytokine production, and wound healing. *Archives of General Psychiatry, 62,* 1377–1384.

Kiecolt-Glaser, J., Marucha, P., Malarkey, W., Mercado, A., & Glaser, R. (1995). Slowing of wound healing by psychological stress. *Lancet, 346,* 1194–1196.

McGuire L., Heffner, K., Glaser, R., Needleman, B., Malarkey, W., Dickinson, S., ... Kiecolt-Glaser, J. (2006). Pain and wound healing in surgical patients. *Annals of Behavioral Medicine, 31,* 65–172.

Millar, K., Purushotham, A. D., McLatchie, E., George, W. D., & Murray, G. D. (2005). A 1-year prospective study of individual variation in distress, and illness perceptions, after treatment for breast cancer. *Journal of Psychosomatic Research, 58*(4), 335–342.

Rees, G., Fry, A., Cull, A., & Sutton, S. (2004). Illness perceptions and distress in women at increased risk of breast cancer. *Psychology & Health, 19,* 749–765.

Rozema, H., Völlink, T., & Lechner, L. (2009). The role of illness representations in coping and health of patients treated for breast cancer. *Psycho-Oncology, 18,* 849–857.

Sephton, S., Dhabhar, F., Keuroghlian, A., Giese-Davis, J., McEwen, B., Ionan, A., & Spiegel, D. (2009). Depression, cortisol, and suppressed cell-mediated immunity in metastatic breast cancer. *Brain, Behavior and Immunity, 23,* 1148–1155.

Sperry, L. (2009). *Treatment of chronic medical conditions: Cognitive-behavioral therapy strategies and integrative treatment protocols.* Washington, DC: American Psychological Association.

Zahlis, E., & Shands, M. (1991). Breast cancer: Demands of the illness on the patient's partner. *Journal of Psychosocial Oncology, 9,* 75–93.

17

CARDIAC DISEASE[1]

The term *cardiac disease* refers to medical conditions affecting the heart and its vessels. Technically it is called cardiovascular disease, a collection of diseases and conditions that can have widespread effects on patient health. It consists of two main types: diseases of the heart (cardio) and diseases of the blood vessels (vascular). Cardiac disease is the leading cause of death in adult men and women, and is a major public health concern in the United States. Psychological interventions with cardiac conditions have long been associated with successful cardiac treatment. Primarily affecting men in their middle years, most commonly in the form of myocardial infarction or heart attack, heart disease affects not just the victims but also all who are close to them. For most spouse/partners the possibility of a heart attack striking the husband is one of the most feared potential events in life. When a heart attack does occur, family life is disrupted for weeks or months, and the couple's relationship is permanently changed.

This chapter begins with a description of the various types of cardiac disease and treatment considerations, particularly illness perceptions. Then it discusses the impact on the family of individual and family dynamics regarding the experience of heart disease, particularly heart attack. Briefly reviewed are the impact on the individual and the relationship of marital discord, family cohesion, level of family functioning, roles, marital satisfaction, marital quality, and boundary issues on heart disease, particularly myocardial infarction or heart attack. A case example illustrates these points.

Heart Disease: Types and Treatment Considerations

Heart disease is estimated to affect one in three adults in the United States, and is the leading cause of death in both men and women. In 2003,

---

1. Adapted from Sperry, L. (2011). Treating patients with heart disease: The impact of individual and family dynamics. *The Family Journal: Counseling and Therapy with Couples and Families, 19,* 96–100.

nearly 500,000 deaths were attributed to heart disease (American Heart Association, 2006). On the positive side, heart attack mortality rates in the United States have been declining over the past 10 years.

Types of Heart Disease

Some of the more common heart diseases and conditions are briefly described. Coronary artery disease occurs when coronary arteries, the vessels that supply blood to heart muscle, become hardened and narrowed due to the buildup of cholesterol and other material, called plaque, on their inner walls. As the plaque increases in size, the inner surfaces of the coronary arteries get narrower and less blood can flow through them. Eventually, blood flow to the heart muscle is reduced, and, because blood carries much-needed oxygen, the heart muscle is not able to receive the amount of oxygen it needs. Reduced or cutoff blood flow and oxygen supply to the heart muscle can result in angina; that is, chest pain or discomfort that occurs when the heart receives an insufficient supply of blood. It is a symptom of coronary artery disease rather than a separate disease entity. Heart failure, commonly referred to as congestive heart failure, is a condition of ineffective heart pumping such that vital organs get insufficient blood, resulting in such signs and symptoms as shortness of breath, fluid retention, and fatigue. It results when heart failure has led to fluid buildup in the body. Finally, myocardial infarction, commonly called heart attack, happens when a blood clot develops at the site of plaque in a coronary artery and suddenly cuts off most or all blood supply to that part of the heart muscle. Cells in the heart muscle begin to die if they do not receive enough oxygen-rich blood. The result can be permanent damage to the heart muscle or death.

Treatment Considerations in Heart Disease

Patients with cardiac disease frequently have physical and psychological morbidity, and the quality of life of coronary artery disease patients is often hampered by concomitant feelings of depression, anxiety, anger, and stress. The psychological needs of cardiac patients can be addressed with a variety of treatments. Cardiac rehabilitation, including psychosocial interventions is increasingly recommended as beneficial to patients (Sotile, 2005).

Evidence increasingly supports tailored interventions such as lifestyle change, exercise therapy, psychosocial treatments, and medication. In addition to cardiac medication, psychotropic drugs such as antidepressants and anxiolytics can improve clinical outcomes for patients with cardiac disease (Rozanski, Blumenthal, Davidson, Saab, & Kubzansky, 2005). Furthermore, cardiac patients require multiple levels of treatment, and patients appear to benefit from access to a variety of clinical professionals including cardiologists, psychologists, physical therapists, and nurses. The biopsychosocial approach to cardiac rehabilitation has been studied extensively and convincing evidence exists that incorporating multidisciplinary care would prove beneficial for both patients and physicians (Sotile, 2005).

Two key clinical considerations in planning treatment interventions with cardiac patients are illness representations and cardiac rehabilitation programs. Given the predictive value of illness representation measures such as the IPQ and IPQ-R with regard to treatment compliance and success in cardiac rehabilitation programs, it is essential that such measures are routinely used with all cardiac patients.

Illness Representations.   An individual's constellations of perceptions and beliefs about a particular disease—understanding of it and its symptoms, cause, illness duration, impact or consequences, curability, and ability to control it—is referred to as illness representation. In cardiac disease, illness representations tend to be sensitive predictors of treatment compliance, treatment outcomes, and well-being. Research with cardiac patients indicates that illness representations are predictive of the course of cardiac illness, self-efficacy, participation in a cardiac rehabilitation program and return to work, and treatment compliance.

In a study of illness representation and their correlates in coronary heart disease, men attributed the cause of their heart disease more often to risk behaviors and their own attitudes and behaviors, while women believe that stress was the cause of their heart disease. Women also perceived more symptoms associated with it but reported less severe consequences. Heart disease severity was the most important illness representation. Stronger perceived competence was related to weaker illness identity, stronger control/cure, and less severe consequences (Aalto, Heijmans, Weinman, & Aro, 2005). Another study assessed illness representations and self-efficacy in patients with coronary heart disease (CHD). A longitudinal design was adopted with predictor variables and dependent variables, such as general self-efficacy, diet self-efficacy, exercise self-efficacy, and demographic and illness characteristic effects. These were measured while 300 patients were in the hospital and 9 months following discharge. Questionnaires measured four illness representation components: identity, consequences, time line, control/cure, and outcome expectation for diet and exercise, as well as self-efficacy—general, diet, and exercise self-efficacy measures. The same measures were collected 9 months later. Results showed that the relationship between illness representation components and specific self-efficacy changes over time, consequence and time line were significantly related to self-efficacy measures initially; however, symptom and control/cure were the variables that were significantly related to self-efficacy measures 9 months later. After statistically controlling for individuals' baseline self-efficacy measures, demographic, and illness characteristic effects, it was found that symptom and control/cure made significant contributions to exercise, diet, and self-efficacy, respectively, 9 months later. In short, this research found a significant relationship between illness representations and self-efficacy (Lau-Walker, 2006). A third study examined whether cardiac patients' initial perceptions of their myocardial infarction would predict subsequent attendance at a cardiac rehabilitation course, return to work, disability, and sexual dysfunction. The study found that when patients believed that their illness could be controlled or cured, it predicted their subsequent attendance at a cardiac rehabilitation. On the other hand, the belief that their illness would last a long time and have serious consequences was associated with a longer delay before returning to work. A strong illness identity was significantly related to greater sexual dysfunction at both 3 and 6 months (Petrie, Weinman, Sharpe, & Buckley, 1996). Finally, based on the premise that intentional noncompliance to prescribed treatment leads to poor clinical outcomes in heart failure patients, another study examined the relationship between patients' and spouse/partners' illness representations of the symptoms, cause, time line, consequences, and control of heart failure and the patients' compliance behavior. Congruence between patients and spouse/partners in perceptions was investigated to determine if congruence or lack of congruence affected patients' adherence behavior. The IPQ and Adherence Estimation Questionnaire were used to determine illness representations and adherence estimation in a sample of 60 older adult heart failure patients and their spouse/partners. Patients' and spouse/partners' perceptions of symptoms and spouse/partners' perceptions of the time line for heart failure were significantly related to patients' adherence behavior. The addition of the spouse/partners' illness representations to the patients' illness representations explained 52% of the variance in patients' adherence behavior. A significant linear relationship was not found between the amount of congruence between patients and spouse/partners and patients' adherence behavior. However, patient adherence increased when patients and partners were congruent in perceptions of control of heart failure (Fox, 2001).

Cardiac Rehabilitation. Cardiac rehabilitation programs have an important part to play in treatment for certain patients. These programs assist patients and their families to better understand and make a commitment to treatment regimens, make major changes in health behaviors, modify illness perceptions and health beliefs, and lower cardiac risk factors. Cardiac rehabilitation programs are a significant component of management and treatment for many cardiac patients. The ability of patients to access and actively participate in such programs can greatly influence the individuals' quality of life. In some cases, lack of access to rehabilitation has been shown to negatively influence patient morbidity and mortality (Sotile, 2005). There are several CBT strategies which are applicable to the process of cardiac rehabilitation. Some of these are unique to rehabilitation, such as the process of risk factor modification, while others are mainstays of health-focused counseling and psychotherapy (Bennett & Carroll, 1994).

Individual Dynamics in Heart Disease

Several comorbidities are associated with CVD, including stress, anxiety, depression, and anger which are common in cardiac patients and have been shown to negatively influence recovery from heart disease (Rozanski et al., 2005; Sotile, 2005). In addition, psychosocial risk factors such as high levels of hostility, social isolation, and chronic marital and family conflict can adversely affect patient adherence to treatment (Rozanski et al., 2005; Sotile, 2005).

Family and Couple Dynamics in Heart Disease

It has long been suspected that heart disease runs in families. A study of more than 130,000 families has confirmed this. It found that families having one or more members with heart disease represented only 14% of the general population but accounted for 70% of premature heart attacks and 86% of early strokes (Chow, Pell, Walker, O'Dowd, Dominiczak, & Pell, 2007). It is most likely that genetics, illness perceptions, and health behaviors, as well as family dynamics account for these findings. This section focuses on the impact of family dynamics on heart disease, particularly heart attack.

A study involving 300 middle-aged married couples provided some interesting findings about the physical effects of marital discord. Couples in which no heart disease was previously diagnosed were prompted to engage in an argument that was rated for levels of hostility (i.e., tendency to experience anger, and antagonism—argumentative, mistrusting, and controlling or cold interpersonal behavior). Two days later, the couples had chest scans to assess coronary artery calcification. Interestingly, antagonism but not anger was an independent predictor of coronary artery calcification. An additional finding was that women who were rated as hostile were more likely to have coronary disease and an increased chance of heart attack, while for men it is antagonism and controlling behavior in arguments that increases heart risk (Smith et al., 2007). In short, it appears that older couples should take care over the manner in which they argue if they want to avoid heart attacks.

There are other family dynamics that have been studied with regard to heart disease. These include family cohesion, social involvement, level of family functioning, roles, marital satisfaction, quality of the marital relationship, and boundary issues. For example, Quinn (1999) found that family relationships outweighed other social factors in terms of their importance for maintaining cardiovascular health, recovering from cardiac events, and preventing heart disease. Previously, it was reported that both family cohesion and active involvement with family, friends, and religious or social organizations were important coping resources in family adjustment to the crisis of a heart attack (Dhooper, 1983). Typically, family members attempt to maintain their previous level of family functioning in the face of a serious health event such as a heart attack. However, roles within the family frequently change to meet the needs of family members and the demands of the medical condition. In reacting to a heart attack, couples are likely to adjust their patterns of interacting with friends or renegotiate patterns of interaction in their own relationship (Hilscher, Bartley, & Zarski, 2005).

Heart disease, particularly following a heart attack in one partner, inevitably "threatens family homeostasis and psychosocial effects ripple through the family and back again, as family members attempt to adjust to their situation" (Hilscher et al., 2005, p. 223). It inevitably redefines the marital relationship. Research suggests that the response of couples to the disease varies. Some research indicates that after a myocardial infarction or bypass surgery there is an increase in marital satisfaction (Revenson, 1994). Other studies have documented high levels of anxiety and depression (Coyne, Ellard, & Smith, 1990; Suls, Green, Rose, Lounsberry, & Gordon, 1997). In a study of 189 congestive heart failure patients, Coyne et al. (1990) found that marital quality predicted 4-year survival rates for both male and female patients as accurately as the New York Heart Association classification scale (a highly regarded predictor of patient mortality). Other researchers identified the quality of the marital relationship as a critical factor affecting family members' health among patients suffering from heart disease (Kriegsman, Penninx, & van Eijk, 1994; Rohrbaugh et al., 2002). For couples experiencing heart disease, relationship quality can be effectively enhanced by nurturing and caring, by being more gentle and forgiving, and by attending to intimacy needs (Sotile, 2004).

The partner of the heart disease patient is frequently challenged to cope both as a primary provider of support and as a family member who needs support in coping with the patient's medical condition (Revenson, 1994). The partner's coping response can be adaptive or nonadaptive. An example of a nonadaptive coping response is overprotectiveness, which can manifest as efforts to shield the patient from perceived burdens such as physical demands, household chores, decision making, or financial responsibility; overprotectiveness is basically a boundary issue. Fearing that the patient is not fully capable, the overprotective partner or family member attempts to protect the patient. If the boundary is too rigid, the partner or family member may not permit others to help in the recovery process (Hilscher, Bartley, & Zarski, 2005). Overprotectiveness may be an effort to manage the near loss and continued threat of loss of the significant other (Fiske, Coyne, & Smith, 1991), but it may also diminish the patient's sense of self-efficacy. Research results are not unequivocal. One study with couples in which one partner had suffered a heart attack suggested that overprotectiveness is only destructive if coupled with hostility (Fiske et al., 1991). Another study of postmyocardial infarction patients and spouses that examined protective buffering (i.e., hiding concerns from the spouse) found increased psychological distress for both patients and spouses when the other engaged in protective buffering (Suls et al., 1997).

Integrative Treatment of Heart Disease

Effective treatment of heart disease involves an integration of medical interventions with psychoeducational and psychosocial interventions, including family counseling. Often such integrated treatment can be provided in a comprehensive cardiac rehabilitation program. Because of the significant psychological component, counseling or referral for individual therapy and family counseling are commonly intervention choices today (Sperry, 2006, 2009).

Case Illustration

Jim R. is a 52-year old married Caucasian accountant who experienced a heart attack while running to catch a commuter train. He was hospitalized and received treatment in an intensive coronary care unit. Part of his discharge plan included referral to the medical center's cardiac rehabilitation program. The program's staff consisted of three physicians and two master's level mental health counselors with training in cardiac rehab. Jim mentioned to the counselor who was conducting the initial evaluation interview that he didn't think he needed any psychological help but that he was concerned about sexual functioning. When asked about this, Jim indicated that he was afraid that sexual activity might cause another heart attack. Since all participants and their spouses in the outpatient program take the IPQ-R prior to their evaluation interview, the counselor was able to query Jim further about his illness representations. Because of Jim's beliefs that his heart disease would not be easily cured or controlled, and that it would be a long time before he could probably return to work, it seemed likely that compliance issues were likely in terms of program attendance, lifestyle modification, and medication use. Sally, Jim's wife, had similar beliefs about Jim's curability and return to work. The results of 10 years of clinic data indicated that family counseling was indicated when patients and partners showed this pattern. Accordingly, twice weekly couples sessions were incorporated into Jim's program schedule. Since their own child was grown and had been living on her own for some years in a distant city there were no plans to involve her in sessions.

During these conjoint sessions with Jim and Sally the counselor utilized CBT to review and modify these treatment hindering illness beliefs. During the course of these sessions, issues pertaining to symptom control, return to work, compliance with medication and lifestyle changes, as well as sexual performance and activity were discussed. Jim's attendance was above average as was his participation in exercise, meditation-based stress management, and other program modalities. He reported no problems with sexual performance, moods, or energy level. Accordingly, he was able to return to work in 8 weeks rather than in the 10 months he had originally predicted it would take.

Case Commentary

This case example illustrates how a counselor can utilize individual and couples therapeutic interventions to increase illness acceptance, modify illness perceptions, and reduce relational discord, while increasing health and well-being.

Concluding Note

Heart disease in its various forms is a chronic medical condition which can significantly impact individual patients and their families. Because significant psychosocial features and sequelae are commonly noted, especially following a heart attack, individual and family interventions are commonly indicated as part of a comprehensive and integrative treatment. Since, family counselors and other mental health professionals can potentially provide these individual and family interventions, such professionals can expand their scope of practice by becoming more knowledgeable and competent in providing such services.

References

Aalto, A., Heijmans, M., Weinman, J., & Aro, A. (2005). Illness perceptions in coronary heart disease: Sociodemographic, illness-related, and psychosocial correlates. *Journal of Psychosomatic Research, 58*, 393–402.

American Heart Association. (2006). Heart disease and stroke statistics. *2006 Update.* New York, NY: Author.

Bennett, P., & Carroll, D. (1994). Cognitive-behavioral interventions in cardiac rehabilitation. *Journal of Psychosomatic Research, 38*, 169–182.

Chow, C., Pell, A., Walker, A., O' Dowd, C., Dominiczak, A., & Pell, J. (2007). Families of patients with premature coronary heart disease: an obvious but neglected target for primary prevention. *British Medical Journal, 335*, 481–485.

Coyne, J., Ellard, J., & Smith, D. (1990). Social support, interdependence, and the dilemmas of helping. In B. Sarason, I. Sarason, & G. Pierce (Eds.), *Social support: An interactional view* (pp. 129–149). New York, NY: Wiley.

Dhooper, S. (1983). Coronary heart disease and family functioning. *Journal of Social Service Research, 7,* 19–38.

Fiske, V., Coyne, J., & Smith, D. A. (1991). Couples coping with myocardial infarction: An emprical reconsideration of the role of overprotectiveness. *Journal of Family Psychology, 5,* 4–20.

Fox, O. (2001). Congruence of illness representation between older adult heart failure patients and their spouses or partners and its relationship to adherence behavior. *Dissertation Abstracts International: Section B: The Sciences and Engineering, 62*(6-B), 2664.

Hilscher, R., Bartley, A., & Zarski, J. (2005). A heart does not beat alone: Coronary heart disease through a family systems lens. *Families Systems & Health, 23,* 220–235.

Kriegsman, D. M. W., Penninx, B. W. J. H., & van Eijk, J. T. M. (1994). Chronic disease in the elderly and its impact on the family. *Family Systems Medicine, 12,* 249–267.

Lau-Walker, M. (2006). Predicting self-efficacy using illness perception components: A patient survey. *British Journal of Health Psychology, 11,* 643–661.

Petrie. K., Weinman, J., Sharpe, N., & Buckley, J. (1996). Role of patients' view of their illness in predicting return to work and functioning after myocardial infarction: Longitudinal study. *British Medical Journal, 312,* 1191–1194.

Quinn, M. H. (1999). Family relationships and cardiovascular health: A review with implications for family psychology. *Family Psychologist, 15,* 10–13.

Revenson, T. A. (1994). Social support and marital coping with chronic illness. *Annals of Behavioral Medicine, 16,* 122–130.

Rohrbaugh, M., Cranford, J., Shoham, V., Nicklas, J., Sonnega, J., & Coyne, J. (2002). Couples coping with congestive heart failure: Role and gender differences in psychological distress. *Journal of Family Psychology, 16,* 3–13.

Rozanski, A., Blumenthal, J. A., Davidson, K. W., Saab P. G., & Kubzansky, L. (2005). The epidemiology, pathophysiology, and management of psychosocial risk factors in cardiac practice: The emerging field of behavioral cardiology. *Journal of the American College of Cardiology, 45,* 637–651.

Sotile, W. (2004). *Thriving with heart disease.* New York, NY: Free Press.

Sotile, W. (2005). Biopsychosocial care of heart patients: Are we practicing what we preach? *Families, Systems & Health, 23,* 400–403.

Smith, T., Uchino, B., Berg, C., Florsheim, P., Pearce, G., Hawkins, M., Hopkins, P., & Yoon, H. (2007). Hostile personality traits and coronary artery calcification in middle-aged and older married couples: Different effects for self-reports versus spouse ratings. *Psychosomatic Medicine, 69,* 441–448

Sperry, L. (2006). *Psychological treatment of chronic illness.* Washington, DC: American Psychological Association.

Sperry, L. (2009). *Treatment of chronic medical conditions. Cognitive behavioral therapy strategies and integrative protocols.* Washington, DC: American Psychological Association.

Suls, J., Green, P., Rose, G., Lounsbury, P., & Gordon, E. (1997). Hiding worries from one's spouse: Associations between coping via protective buffering and distress in male postmyocardial infarction patients and their wives. *Journal of Behavioral Medicine, 20,* 333–349.

18

CHRONIC FATIGUE SYNDROME[1]

Chronic fatigue syndrome (CFS) is a clinically defined condition characterized by severe disabling fatigue and a combination of symptoms that prominently features self-reported impairments in concentration and short-term memory, sleep disturbances, and musculoskeletal pain. Although it has only recently been recognized as a medical condition, CFS is an increasingly common chronic disease. Because there is no specific laboratory test or clinical signs for CFS, accurate prevalence data is not available. However, the Centers for Disease Control and Prevention (CDC; 2002) estimates that as many as 500,000 people in the United States have CFS or a CFS-like condition. It has also been observed that CFS is diagnosed two to four times more often in women than in men. It is a condition that affects not only patients but their families (Sperry, 2006).

This chapter begins with a brief description of the medical aspects of CFS. It then describes various family dynamics, including the family life cycle, associated with CFS. Case material illustrates various clinical issues associated with CSF throughout the six stages of the family life cycle.

Medical Aspects of Chronic Fatigue Syndrome

Diagnostic Considerations

Chronic fatigue syndrome remains somewhat of a controversial medical condition. Because its diagnosis is typically made only after other medical and psychiatric causes of chronic fatiguing illness have been ruled out, it is referred to as a diagnosis by exclusion. Even though there are no pathognomonic (i.e., characteristic and definitive) signs of this disorder or

---

1. Adapted from Sperry, L. (2011). Recognizing family dynamics in the treatment of chronic fatigue syndrome. *The Family Journal: Counseling and Therapy for Couples and Families, 20,* 79–85.

diagnostic tests currently available, the following definition was developed by a national task force and published in the prestigious *Annals of Internal Medicine* and is accepted by many in the medical community (Fukuda et al., 1994).

CFS is defined by the presence of the following: (1) clinically evaluated, unexplained persistent or relapsing chronic fatigue that is of new or definite onset (has not been lifelong); is not the result of ongoing exertion; is not substantially alleviated by rest; and results in substantial reduction in previous levels of occupational, educational, social, or personal activities; and (2) the concurrent occurrence of four or more of the following symptoms, all of which must have persisted or recurred during six or more consecutive months of illness and must not have predated the fatigue: self-reported impairment in short-term memory or concentration severe enough to cause substantial reduction in previous levels of occupational, educational, social, or personal activities; sore throat; tender cervical or auxiliary lymph nodes; muscle pain; multijoint pain without joint swelling or redness; headaches of a new type, pattern, or severity; nonrefreshing sleep; and postexertional malaise lasting more than 24 hours (Fukuda et al., 1994).

There is yet to be consensus on the risk factors and causes for CFS. Although CFS was originally thought to be triggered by the Epstein-Barr virus, the cause of mononucleosis, and other viral conditions such as herpes and polio, CFS has been shown to be noncontiguous. There is growing speculation that the actual cause is a combination of a weakened immune system and the presence of a virus, and one or more of the following risk factors: chronic candidacies; a history of recurrent use of antibiotics or nonsteroidal anti-inflammatory drugs (NSAIDS; such as Tylenol, Motrin, and Celebrex); chronic infections such as sinusitis or prostatitis; chemical exposure or sensitivity to cigarette smoke, perfume or paint fumes, or other chemicals; leaky gut syndrome; a diet high in sugar and caffeine.

For many sufferers, CFS begins after a minor illness, such as a cold, the flu, or during a period of high stress. Unlike flu symptoms, which usually go away in a few days or weeks, CFS symptoms continue on and off for more than 6 months. As noted above, reported symptoms include: headache, tender lymph nodes, fatigue and weakness, muscle and joint aches, and inability to concentrate.

The clinical course of CFS varies from person to person. For most, CFS symptoms reach a certain level and become stable early in the course of illness and thereafter come and go. Some individuals get better completely, but it is not clear how frequently this happens. Emotional support and counseling can help the individual and significant others cope with the uncertain outlook and the waxing and waning of symptoms and energy level of this illness.

General Treatment Considerations

Once the diagnosis of CFS is established a behavioral health treatment plan is developed. If a child or adolescent is involved it is essential that a treatment plan is negotiated with the family; it is not optional. It is assumed that the behavioral health professionals should work collaboratively with the patient's physician. If the patient is a child or adolescent, the behavioral health professional consults with the pediatrician, as well as liaising with school personnel on the best way of reintegrating the young person back into the classroom and with his or her circle of friends. As with all chronic illnesses, the clinician and the family need to elicit their illness perceptions and arrive at a common understanding of the illness, one hopes a biopsychosocial view, which can then be used as a basis for planning interventions. In CFS, this may mean some work with the parents to explain that a purely physical understanding of the illness is insufficient. The behavioral health clinician does well to foster realistic optimism and challenge nihilism. Children understand straightforward analogies to explain things such as muscle wasting during rest (for example, wasting while a broken leg is splinted).

Medical treatment may include a trial of an antiviral drug such Zovirax. Antidepressants sometimes help to improve sleep and relieve mild, general pain. Some individuals benefit from other drugs for acute anxiety or for dizziness and extreme tenderness in the skin.

Common to most self-management protocols are several health behaviors that appear to be useful in symptom reduction and even resolution of the condition. These include: a balanced diet; adequate rest; regular exercise that does not cause more fatigue; limiting stress; pacing oneself physically, emotionally, and intellectually; and emotional and spiritual health recommendations. A balanced, whole foods diet is important; that is, one that emphasizes quality protein and complex carbohydrates such as organic vegetables, whole grains, beans, fish, eggs, and poultry. Sugar, caffeine, dairy products, alcohol, aspartame, and refined carbohydrates such as white flour and white rice are to be avoided. Walking and mild aerobic exercise along with mild stretching is the preferred exercise regimen. Since psychological factors can be prominent, particularly depression, a number of mental and emotional health techniques may be indicated: stress reduction methods such as controlled breathing and biofeedback. Others include massage and bodywork therapies, journaling, planned retreats and vacations, and creative activities such as art and music. Since CFS involves a depletion of life force energy, it can be thought of as a spiritual condition. Some spiritual disciplines or techniques, such as prayer, meditation, gratitude and acceptance, and forgiveness might serve to strengthen the individual's immune system (Sperry, 2006).

Family Dynamics in Chronic Fatigue Syndrome

The clinical value of the family systems perspective becomes evident when considering specific family dynamics. For example, an afflicted family member's explanatory model (beliefs regarding one's illness) and the social environment both contribute to the severity of the condition (Vercoulen et al., 1994). Of particular note is that unresolved relational issues and loss tend to remain dormant in a marriage and suddenly emerge when triggered by a medical condition in the current nuclear family. Penn (1983) indicates that coalitions that emerge in the context of a chronic medical condition can be isomorphic of those existing in each partner's family of origin.

The family systems perspective is helpful in identifying the family dynamics associated with CFS. This theoretical model was first applied to CFS by Goodwin (1997, 2000). A useful family system dynamic for understanding chronic medical conditions such as CFS is the family life cycle. Chapter 2 provides a detailed discussion of family style and family life stages. The following is a capsule summary of the six family stages along with a case illustration.

1. Leaving Home

The challenge facing young adults in this stage is simultaneous involvement with both their parents and their peers. Adapting to family challenges may impede their normal development with persons their own age. Achieving a level of independence is not complete until the young adult begins to live away from home and establish intimate relationships outside the family. A diagnosis of CFS in this phase could lead to several behavioral shifts. The young adult's development and independence from the family might be delayed because of a lack of initiative with others, such as when a girlfriend or boyfriend leaves them because of the illness, parental overprotection, or because of difficulties finding a job.

Case Example. Cynthia was 20 years old when she was diagnosed with CFS. Although she had worked as a waitress for several restaurants, she had difficulty maintaining a job due to periods of extreme fatigue. She was an only child, and, even though her parents insisted that she be employed, they also believed that they had to protect her because of her illness. Despite being unemployed because of her symptoms and fearing that she wasn't following the trajectory of a career and living on her own like her friends, she was able to achieve some personal independence by broadening her social network and initiating a special friendship with a young man.

2. *Forming a Stable Couple Relationship*

In this phase in which a committed couple relationship is established, the partners must establish several pacts. These include defining boundaries with their respective families and other social systems (e.g., friends and coworkers), and clarifying rules including communications patterns. The diagnosis of CFS in this phase can be devastating for a couple that is not fully consolidated.

Case Example.   Some 2 years later Cynthia, who was introduced in the case example above, married Robert. The two had met over a year ago. Robert's mother suffers from lupus, so he has some familiarity with what it is like to live in a family with a chronic medical condition. However, because his father and older sister were, and remain, the primary caretakers for his mother, he has no firsthand experience with that role. Their first months together were increasingly stressful for the couple. While it was agreed that Cynthia would not work outside the home, Robert expected her to do housekeeping, prepare meals, and be available to him sexually. These expectations were experienced by her as "demands" which only increased her stress and exacerbated her symptoms. Three or more days a week she would be in bed when Robert arrived home from a demanding job. The house would not be cleaned, dinner was not ready, and after they argued sexually intimacy was out of the question. Both agreed to couples counseling. In the first sessions, expectations, rules, and boundaries were discussed and revised. Robert also agreed to attend a support group for partners of CFS patients.

3. *Birth of Children*

In this stage, when the committed couple bears children they must find new ways to relate to each other. Not only do the rules change, a new family subsystem, the parental subsystem is formed. Childbirth necessitates more distancing of the couple from their families of origin, while at the same time involving proximity because the two families are joined by this event, as grandparents, aunts, and uncles are created.

Case Example.   Jenna was 22 when she was diagnosed with CFS. Now at the age of 27 she is considering having a baby with her partner. Her father's three heart attacks and her CFS led her to delay this decision. Also, the birth of her sister's second child rekindled her desire to become a mother herself. But, she did not have sufficient strength to do it alone and she sometimes felt insecure with her partner and particularly with her in-laws, who doubted both the validity of her medical condition and her level of impairment. When she became confident enough to better handle stress in her life and to ask for help from her partner, several changes occurred. First, her overprotective attitude toward her father decreased, she began to drive a car, her social network expanded, and she and her partner became more committed. As a result, she felt more confident in her quest to become pregnant.

4. Living with Adolescents

In the fourth stage, the children have become adolescents, the couple's initial difficulties have resolved with time, their vision of life has matured, and stable relationships have been forged with their families of origin and with each other.

Case Example.   Jeff was 38 years and had spent nearly 20 years working as a mechanic until he had to leave his job because of CFS and a back injury. Although he qualified for disability, he grieved the loss of gainful employment and because his wife Laurie now had to assume all family responsibilities. He was particularly concerned about their 16-year-old daughter who was living at home and was expecting a child with her boyfriend Jack, who had recently been deployed to Afghanistan with his marine battalion. Jason and Laurie had discouraged their daughter from dating Jack because he was 5 years older. In her rebellion she acted out sexually and become pregnant. The stress of anticipating an infant in the household only exacerbated Jeff's condition. In family counseling, he learned to lower his expectations of himself and his daughter, avoid isolation by extending his social network, and relinquish the role of provider and head of the household to his wife. Not surprisingly, these circumstances and roles had previously exacerbated his fatigue.

5. Launching Children

Families can experience a crisis when their children leave home. Couples can face a turbulent period that progressively abates after their children have gone and the couple creates a new relationship with corresponding new rules and boundaries. They can resolve remaining conflicts and allow their grown children to have partners and professions, while as a couple they prepare for the transition to the role of grandparents. This entails learning how to be good grandparents and create new rules so that they can participate in the life of their children and be able to function on their own at home.

Case Example.   Jerry, age 49, has been married to Jill for 27 years. Over the past 3 years Jerry has become increasingly disabled by CFS and Type

2 diabetes. Their only child, Justin, had uneventfully left home when he graduated from a local college 5 years ago and soon afterwards married. Since then Jerry and Jill have had a stable marriage in which both maintained many outside, independent interests. In short, they had moved smoothly through the transition to a more centrifugal phase of the family's life cycle. However, as Jerry's chronic medical conditions worsened, he was forced to stop working and went on disability. This effectively reversed the normal process of family disengagement. Jill took a second job that necessitated her quitting her hobbies and civic involvements. Justin and his wife moved into the neighborhood to assist with the care of his father and the family home. Jerry felt himself to be a burden to everyone. The essential goal of family counseling centered on reversing some of the family system's centripetal overreaction back to a more realistic balance. For Jerry, this meant a reworking of his life structure to accommodate his real limitations while maximizing a return to his basically independent style. For Jill and their son, this meant developing realistic expectations for Jerry and reestablishing key aspects of their autonomy within a family system dealing with a chronic medical condition.

6. Retirement and Old Age

Withdrawal from active life can mean that the couple is face-to-face, 24 hours a day, a fact that can create friction. One problem that may arise in this stage is excessive protection of one member by the other, thereby enhancing a debilitating somatic syndrome, such as CFS.

Case Example. Some 12 years later Jerry, who was introduced in the case example above, continued on disability but now he and Jill were living in a retirement community. After 30 years Jill retired with a full pension and the couple decided that it was too difficult to maintain their household by themselves. Some 6 months before, their son's job was transferred to another city. Up until the point when he and his wife moved, Justin had taken care of bills and managed all repairs of his parents' house. The decision to move to a retirement community with an assisted living unit was simple: Jerry's health had continued to decline, especially diabetic complications including neuropathy and blindness in one eye. Jill's retirement meant less stress on her and their marriage, more time for caregiving, and more quality time with Jerry. This included involvement in various activities available in their new community. No longer concerned about sufficient income and house repairs, both were able to enjoy their older years together. They now had two grandchildren and were able to visit them regularly since they were within 2 hours driving distance.

Developmental and Biopsychosocial Consideration

Family factors become relevant with children because of the impact that family members have on their expectations and explanatory models. Parents may become more caring, more child-centered, and less confrontational. Interactions may center on illness. Role changes occur within the family system and these may inadvertently contribute to maintenance of illness. There seems to be a point at the beginning of illness when parents search for information, but there comes a time when they choose a path and a set of beliefs. Some parents choose a biopsychosocial treatment approach, while others choose to remove their children from any treatment. Some even remove their CFS child or adolescent from school. Needless to say, choices can impact prognosis. Despite the fact that there is substantial evidence that physical illnesses have psychological consequences, and psychological illnesses have physical consequences, many adopt an exclusively biological explanatory model of CFS. Families who adopt this explanatory model often resent efforts to address psychological considerations, believing CFS to be an untreatable physical condition. My clinical experience is that young persons who come from families with such views may have the worst prognosis, in comparison to those who hold a biopsychosocial explanatory model. It should be noted that family dynamics are part of the "social" in the biopsychosocial model.

Developmental-School Considerations. Young persons with CFS are likely to miss a lot of school. Despite the fact that many children and adolescents have home tutors they usually only cover limited amounts of time and curriculum, so they are likely to miss out educationally and they can miss out on the developmental tasks of childhood and adolescence. This can become a vicious cycle: the more they miss, the more frightened they become, and the more they miss because of their fear. It is not uncommon for confident, outgoing gregarious young persons at the outset of illness, to become terrified of being around friends a year later. They also tend to miss school even after recovery from CFS. Those who attempt to maintain very high educational or athletic standards may find return to school even more difficult. CFS symptoms, such as poor concentration and problems with low mood and social withdrawal, are also factors in the vicious cycle which can prevent return to school.

Biopsychosocial Considerations. Children with CFS often become anxious, depressed, or angry. This may be in response to CFS or may have developed before it. Significant life events such as loss and bereavement have been reported in some young persons prior to the development of CFS. In my clinical experience, young persons with CFS are more likely to have problems with low mood, social withdrawal, and isolation, and it seems that they have more mood disturbance than those who have suffered CFS from childhood.

Family-Focused Interventions

Although cognitive behavioral therapy (CBT) is the most commonly used intervention in behavioral health settings, it is typically provided in an individual treatment context. When it comes to treating chronic medical conditions in children, adolescents, or adults, a family systems approach can provide an integrated vision of various levels influencing the medical condition, both at its onset and during its development. Even though CBT delivered in an individual context has been demonstrated to be effective in improving the symptoms of CFS (Price, Mitchell, Tidy, & Hunot, 2008), a family-focused intervention has been shown to be even more effective.

In treating CFS in adolescents, a family-focused CBT intervention was compared with an individually focused CBT intervention consisting largely of psychoeducation. The study involved 63 adolescents (43 girls and 20 boys) who were randomly assigned to either treatment delivered over 6 months. School attendance was the main outcome, which was assessed at the end of treatment and at 3, 6, and 12 months follow-up. While gains were achieved by both interventions, those who received family-focused CBT returned to school more quickly and were attending school for longer than those who received psychoeducation (Chaldera, Dearya, Husaina, & Walwyna, 2010).

Because of its effectiveness, a detailed description of this family-focused intervention follows. The intervention consisted of 13 CBT biweekly sessions. It emphasized building rapport with all family members and establishing a collaborative relationship with the family. Six treatment targets were involved. First, it encouraged the participant to achieve a balance between activity and rest. Second, it gradually increased the participant's activities including home, social, and school life. Then, it established a consistent sleep routine. Next, it addressed the participant's interfering beliefs such as fear regarding the benefits of activity or exercise, overly high self-expectations, and all-or-nothing thinking. Fifth, it encouraged family members to express their own views about the illness and achieved a mutually agreed upon direction for moving forward. Finally, it addressed relapse prevention and established a tailored relapse prevention plan (Chaldera et al., 2010).

The parent who provided the majority of the care, usually the mother, was supported during the transition period as the adolescents became more independent. Homework assignments were negotiated with participants at each session and a treatment guide was given to the family. Specific concerns of the parents and siblings were elicited and addressed. As improvement often coincided with the adolescent maturing and differentiating from the family, these factors were addressed in treatment. In addition, therapists functioned as brokers in disputes between adolescent and the parents (Chaldera et al., 2010).

Concluding Note

This chapter has reviewed relevant diagnostic and treatment considerations for CFS that can be of value to behavioral health professionals. It has emphasized how the stage of the family life cycle can provide a useful lens through which to assess specific family dynamics and focus treatment.

References

Centers for Disease Control and Prevention. (2002). *Chronic fatigue syndrome.* Retrieved from http://www.cdc.gov/cfs/index.html (updated May 16, 2012)

Chaldera, T., Dearya, V., Husaina, K., & Walwyna, R. (2010). Family-focused cognitive behaviour therapy versus psycho-education for chronic fatigue syndrome in 11- to 18-year-olds: A randomized controlled treatment trial. *Psychological Medicine, 40*(8), 1269–1279.

Fukuda, K., Straus, S., Hickie, I., Sharpe, M., Dobbins, J., & Komaroff, A. (1994). The chronic fatigues syndrome: A comprehensive approach to its definition and study. *Annals of Internal Medicine, 121,* 953–959.

Goodwin, S. S. (1997). The marital relationship and health in women with chronic fatigue and immune dysfunction syndrome: Views of wives and husbands. *Nursing Research, 46,* 138–146.

Goodwin, S. S. (2000). Peoples' perceptions of wives' CFS symptoms, symptom change, and impact on the marital relationship. *Issues in Mental Health Nursing, 21,* 347–363.

Penn, P. (1983). Coalitions and binding interactions in families with chronic illness. *Family Systems Medicine, 1,* 16–25.

Price, J., Mitchell, E., Tidy, E., & Hunot, V. (2008). Cognitive behaviour therapy for chronic fatigue syndrome in adults (review). *Cochrane Database of Systematic Reviews.* doi: 10.1002/14651858.

Sperry, L. (2006). *Psychological treatment of chronic illness.* Washington, DC: American Psychological Association.

Vercoulen, J., Swanink, C., Fennis, J., Galama, J., Van der Meer, J., & Bleijenberg, G. (1994). Dimensional assessment of chronic fatigue syndrome. *Journal of Psychosomatic Research, 38,* 383–392.

19

DIABETES[1]

Diabetes mellitus, commonly referred to as diabetes, is a syndrome characterized by hyperglycemia (i.e., high levels of glucose or sugar in the blood), that results in varying degrees of impairment in insulin secretion or insulin action or both. There a two types of diabetes: Type 1 and Type 2. Both are usually diagnosed in asymptomatic individuals during a routine medical exam with blood and urine screening tests. Generally speaking, Type 1 is more severe than Type 2 diabetes. Since the onset of Type 1 diabetes is usually in early life, long-term nonadherence with diet and insulin control can result in serious consequences such as retinopathy, nephropathy, neuropathy, and cardiovascular disease. Diabetes is the leading cause of blindness, nontraumatic lower limb amputation, physiological erectile dysfunction, and end-stage renal disease. Furthermore, nonadherence with a Type 2 treatment regimen may also lead to end-stage organ damage, yet can be less severe if its onset is later in life (American Diabetes Association, 2007). Psychosocial factors and psychiatric comorbidities are commonly associated with diabetes. Among these is psychopathology in patients, in their families, or both that influence adherence to treatment. Because of the limitations of the medical management approach in dealing with this issue, psychological interventions, including health-focused counseling and family therapy, have become a standard of care in the United States (Gonder-Frederick, Cox, & Ritterband, 2002).

This chapter begins with some basic background on diabetes as a chronic medical condition that is often associated with psychiatric morbidity. Unfortunately, medical personnel face significant challenges with treatment nonadherence and poor treatment outcomes in diabetic patients and their families who manifest borderline pathology. Fortunately, counselors and family therapists knowledgeable about diabetes as a disease process as

---

1. Adapted from Sperry, L. (2010). Treating diabetes with severe personality-disordered individuals and families. *The Family Journal: Counseling and Therapy with Couples and Families, 18,* 432–442.

well as borderline pathology and its treatment can provide consultation to medical personnel on such "difficult cases" or therapy to patients and their families. This chapter provides an introduction to diabetes and borderline dynamics in patients and family members.

Diabetes: Background Information

This section provides background information on diabetes. Addressed are: prevalence, cultural factors, psychiatric comorbidities, and family dynamics.

Prevalence

There are some 20.8 million children and adults in the United States who have diabetes. This represents 7% of the population. While an estimated 14.6 million have been diagnosed, 6.2 million people—nearly one-third—are unaware that they have the disease (American Diabetes Association, 2007). Approximately 90% have Type 2 diabetes which has been associated with obesity in adults, and more recently even with obesity in adolescents and children. Accordingly, diabetes represents an increasing health concern in the United States particularly since its prevalence is related to obesity and sedentary lifestyles among Americans (American Diabetes Association, 2007).

Cultural Factors

Those of African, Latin American, Asian, or Aboriginal ethnic ancestry have an increased risk of developing Type 2 diabetes. Risk levels for these groups are between two and six times higher than they are for those of Caucasian origin. As a group, minorities have a much higher risk for Type 2 and Type 1 than Caucasians. African Americans are 1.7 times more likely to have diabetes than Caucasians, and twice as likely to experience diabetes-related blindness, amputation, and kidney disease. Hispanic Americans have two to four times the incidence of Type 2 diabetes of Caucasians (Feifer & Tansman, 1999). Furthermore, African American youth have poorer glycemic control than white youth. Finally, lower socioeconomic status is also associated with poor metabolic control and recurrent hospitalization (Gonder-Frederick et al., 2002).

Psychological Comorbidities

Anxiety and depression are the most common comorbidities among adult diabetics, while depression and eating disorders are common among adolescent diabetics (Snoek & Skinner, 2002). Anxiety disorders are more prevalent in diabetics who have poor insulin control, and clinical depression is noted in 15 to 20% of diabetic individuals. Anxiety disorders commonly complicate treatment adherence (Redman, 2004). Depression is a significant risk factor for all age groups (Gonder-Frederick et al., 2002) and appears to precede the development of diabetes (Williams, Clouse, & Lustman, 2006). Depression is correlated with negative health behaviors such as smoking, alcohol and other drug abuse, and dysregulation in appetite and eating (Williams et al., 2006). Additionally, depression is associated with poor self-management and metabolic control, high relapse rates, increased complications, and decreased quality of life (Gonder-Frederick et al., 2002). The prevalence of eating disorders is 62% among diabetic adolescents while only 22% among nondiabetic adolescents (Rydall, Rodin, Olmstead, Devenyi, & Daneman, 1997). Type 1 female adolescents may attempt to control their weight by adjusting their insulin levels, as do Type 1 male adolescent wrestlers (Hoffman, 2001). Such insulin adjustment is dangerous and can result in long-term diabetic complications (Hoffman, 2001). Since both weight loss and weight gain can affect glycemic control, close monitoring of glucose levels and disordered eating and depression are essential.

Family Dynamics

Family dynamics can play a significant role in the onset, course, and treatment of diabetes as demonstrated by research on diabetes and family conflict. For example, adolescent diabetics from families with high conflict are likely to have had their diabetes triggered by it and tend to have lower glycemic control, while those from families with low conflict and high cohesion tend to have better glycemic control. In families with less cohesion and greater conflict, children and adolescents are more likely to experience recurrent episodes of ketoacidosis, very low blood glucose levels, and severe hypoglycemia. Family conflict can also trigger or exacerbate disordered eating behavior in adolescents (Gonder-Frederick et al., 2002). Often this is due to insulin omission, which has been associated with recurrent diabetic ketoacidosis (Howells et al., 2002).

Personality Disorders and Borderline Pathology

When diabetic patients are described as "difficult to treat" it is not uncommon for personality disorder dynamics to be operative. It may be that the patient and one or more family members meet criteria for a personality disorder. Occasionally, one or more family members may at first appear to be reasonably functioning since they may work or attend school, but on closer examination their work or school performance and functionality may be rated as minimal to average at best, as is their performance

177

and functionality with activities in the home. Too often the entire family shares a common pathology. It is extremely rare for one family member to be personality disordered and considerably impaired while all other family members are high functioning, assuming that the impaired individual is actively involved with his or her family. Among the most difficult to treat are patients and families with borderline dynamics. Unfortunately, such patients and their families are an increasing challenge in health care settings.

This section begins with a brief description of personality disorders followed by general information on borderline pathology in families and basic treatment strategies.

Personality Disorders

Personality disorders are commonly defined as enduring patterns of perceiving, relating, and thinking which are inflexible, maladaptive, and lead to clinically significant distress or impairment (Sperry, 2003). These disorders can be distinguished by level of severity. For example, Millon (1999) considered the borderline personality disorder, the paranoid personality disorder, and the schizotypal personality disorder as the severe personality disorders. Borderline pathology is commonly observed in many difficult to treat medical patients and their families.

Borderline Pathology in Families

Borderline families are basically families in which chaos is the leitmotif. Chaos has an interesting cyclical pattern in these families. In other words, the family is always in chaos with "rigid-to-chaos" fluctuations (Hampson & Beavers, 2004). To the less discerning observer it seems overt and intense (chaos) for a given period of time and then appears to recede and is gone. The reality is that it never goes away. The more discerning observer will note that it continues in a subtle and attenuated (rigid) form in the background. Another characteristic of these families is that they are unable to nurture one another. Instead of nurturing their children, parents find it easier to be demanding, intrusive, abusive, or neglectful. At some level they recognize that their children and their spouse need nurturance but not having the experience of being nurtured, they expect others, such as therapists, health care workers, school personnel, or social agencies to provide it. As a result, the borderline family learns that satisfaction must be sought outside the family. These families have been described as "open in their conflicts but deny warmth, fear, and human needs. They are much more visible to the community when in trouble than when functioning reasonably well" (Beavers & Hampson, 1990, p. 174). When an older adolescent or young adult is diagnosed with a borderline personality disorder with a GAF of 50 or lower, it is rare not to find that the family of origin is a borderline family or that the extended family is also borderline.

There are some psychiatric conditions that are characteristically observed in the borderline family. Most common are the externalizing disorders such as conduct disorder and substance abuse and substance dependent disorders. Cyclical disorders are also quite common and reflect their rigid-to-chaos fluctuations (Hampson & Beavers, 2004). Borderline personality disorder is common among family members, especially mothers of children meeting diagnostic criteria. Bipolar I and, particularly, Bipolar II disorder are common comorbidities. Cyclothymic disorder and schizoaffective disorder may also accompany the Axis II disorder.

Treatment Targets and Interventions for Borderline Pathology in Families

In order to succeed in therapy, families with borderline pathology do well to work with counselors and therapists who have the capacity to help them in a number of ways. Effective therapists for these families are those who can maintain effective control, provide and teach limit setting, assist them in organizing simple actions and activities, strengthen subsystem and generational boundaries, and assist them in taking risks in the face of neediness and emotional pain.

It is essential that therapists endeavoring to work with such families recognize that they neither trust therapists nor do they trust words. Because of their trust deficits these families have difficulty with all authority figures to varying degrees, including physicians and therapists. Because they distrust words they will not be responsive to detailed inquiries, such as the elicitation of extensive clinical history taking. Their typical response to early childhood queries is: "I don't remember anything back then." If the therapist attempts to pursue the matter they might say: "I told you, I don't remember anything." And, if they are particularly reactive and impulsive at the moment, they may say something like: "Don't you understand English" as they walk out the door. In short, they are not likely to respond to "talk therapies" that are "there-and then" focused, but can be reasonably respond to action-oriented therapies" that are "here-and-now" focused.

Primary treatment targets with borderline families include establishing healthy boundaries and increasing coherence; that is, meaningful connections among family members, and reducing chaotic and self-injurious behavior, if indicated. Boundary issues abound in the borderline family. While family members may verbally deny their need for attachment, their nonverbal behavior shows clinging behavior. Children may leave home angry and upset but later return with no expression of warmth or regret. Similarly, a significant other will separate only to return back to their partner as if there was no breakup (Beavers & Hampson, 1990). This pattern of separation-reunion, "can't live with, and can't live without" is characteristic of couples in borderline families.

The need for coherence in these families is achieved by increasing effective behavioral controls. Positive reframing is a basic and effective therapeutic intervention in this regard. Intense conflict, hostile outburst, and personal attacks can be reframed as the expression of caring and concern. Such reframes may at first be confusing to the family but they are effective in reducing impulsive and hurtful behaviors.

Limit setting is another basic therapeutic intervention for increasing coherence. When a family arrives halfway through a scheduled session, a conscientious therapist might be relieved that at least the family arrived, and proceed to give them a full hour of treatment even though it creates problems for the next scheduled session. Such a clinical decision reinforces the family belief that authority figures are fools and cannot set or maintain reasonable limits out of fear of creating havoc. As a result, intimidation and irresponsibility is rewarded and the family learns that it is more useful and effective than thoughtfulness and responsible behavior. Accordingly, instead of accepting the family's chaotic or intimidating behaviors, the therapist would do better to order or insist that family leaders, usually the parents, maintain order. As limit setting is addressed, unclear generational and subsystem boundaries will be manifest. Helping parents set limits is a critical step for families in developing coherence (Beavers & Hampson, 1990).

Borderline Dynamics in Diabetic Patients and their Families

The previous section described personality disorders and borderline dynamics and pathology in general. In contrast, this section focuses specifically on borderline pathology in diabetic patients and their families.

Borderline Dynamics in Diabetic Patients

Individuals with borderline pathology are characterized by lability and instability which is evident, in one form or other, in all medical encounters. However, it is during the course of chronic illness that the pathology of the borderline personality pattern is most evident. Initially, the social behavior of these patients may seem engaging or charming, but as relationships become more intense and complicated, treatment becomes confounded or diverted by the borderline patient's tendency to fragment relationships, splitting and help seeking behaviors, and alternating displays of dependency and rage. Their acute sensitivity to the vulnerabilities of others, including physicians and nurses, inevitably seems to draws them into conflict. Since they are consumed with relational issues and personal identity conflicts, disease detection is an afterthought for them. After a chronic disease is diagnosed, even if their illness representation is accurate, it tends to be highly emotionally charged and liable to distortion by subsequent relational changes. Adhering to treatment regimens is predictably erratic for these patients and is often characterized by nonadherence as they act out in protest any relational conflicts or dissatisfactions (Sperry, 2006).

Even though patients with borderline personalities may possess adequate social skills and demeanor when they are in nondistressing circumstances, distress, particularly relational stress, negatively impacts them as evident by their inability to tolerate frustrations, sustain relationships, and maintain a coherent, consistent course of action. Because a chronic illness tends to increase their dependence on others, they need others even more so to meet their basic needs, such as money if they are unable to work, for transportation if they cannot drive, for shopping if they are bedridden, as well as other disease-specific activities. These are examples of problem-focused coping which is disrupted by illness episodes that keep them from performing these activities themselves. All these demands and consequences accumulate, increasing their stress burden in addition to the reduced level of energy and the negative feelings associated with a chronic illness. They can be particularly problematic for borderline patients, given their erratic, capricious style of interpersonal relating. It should not be too surprising that often helpers cower at the thought of having to deal with this family member.

Like other chronic illnesses that requires self-monitoring, self-discipline, and consistency, borderline patients, as well as their health providers, face a constant challenge in dealing with diabetes (Harper, 2004). Lability and overmodulated affects are reflected in endocrine surges, and thus maintaining stable blood sugar levels is a major challenge for these patients. This instability is complicated by impulsive dietary indiscretion, substance abuse, and nicotine and caffeine use—which greatly constricts small blood vessels—as well as inattention or neglect of insulin regulation due to emotional interpersonal conflicts. Being accountable for such health behaviors, such as stable blood sugars, requires psychological requisites lacking in most borderline personalities. These include a cohesive sense of self and the capacity to modulate affects. Even in psychologically mature diabetics, maintaining a resolve to resist "forbidden foods" is a difficult and significant accomplishment, often taken for granted by physicians and other health care providers.

Even though borderline patients may accept the responsibility to be accountable for maintaining stable blood sugar levels in order to prevent long-range complications, emotionally they find actualizing this promise extraordinarily difficult. Even if they are initially successful in implementing a diet and blood sugar monitoring plan, maintaining it without relapse or departing from the schedule tends to be their downfall. While adverse physical consequences of poor control may have a transient sober-ing effect on these individuals at the time the indiscretions occur, these are not likely to serve as effective determinants of future health-related behav-iors. Since the borderline's lability and instability are usually triggered by interpersonal issues, monitoring the relational aspect of their lives clearly must become an essential component of their treatment management. Self-neglect during a relationship conflict can precipitate a diabetic crisis, such as a coma. This usually occurs because borderline patients transiently decompensate and forget to take their insulin or deliberately stop taking insulin to elicit guilt or remorse from their partner or family. Similarly, if they binge eat or drink excessively, their sugar levels can become unstable and result in a crisis. Knowing that these scenarios are possible and pre-dicting the likelihood that they will occur probably suggests the need for psychological intervention (Sperry, 2006). For instance, if the diabetic patient's relationships are tumultuous and fragile, individual psychother-apy probably should be regarded as an essential component of their treat-ment plan.

Borderline Dynamics in Diabetic Families

Since each family member is impacted by the actions of others, a new marriage, birth of a child, separation or divorce, adolescent turbulence, job loss, and, chronic illness can produce conflict and difficulty. While the healthiest family can withstand and adapt to such stressors, personality-disordered families react poorly. When borderline pathology is present in one or more family members, reverberations are experienced throughout the family unit (Kresiman & Kreisman, 2004). This is particularly evi-dent in adolescent relationships. "The adolescent's developmental quest for identity mimics the borderline individual's struggle. It is a constant mix of reaching for intimate connections and retreating from them. The crucial distinction is that the normal adolescent will eventually evolve into a more mature adult, whereas the borderline individual does not approach adulthood with a clearly defined sense of self" (Kresiman & Kreisman, 2004, p. 121).

Parents with borderline personality dynamics, like their own par-ents, often lack healthy role models for effective parenting. As a result it becomes "difficult for children to trust and form close attachments with parents, who themselves are struggling with issues of identity, autonomy, and impulsivity. Single parents with borderline characteristics are even more handicapped, because they may lack many social skills" (Kresiman & Kreisman, 2004, p. 123).

DIABETES

Treatment Interventions for Diabetic Patients and Families Borderline Pathology

Treatment targets and treatment interventions for families with borderline pathology were described in the treatment intervention segment of the preceding section. A basic strategy for working with diabetic families with borderline pathology is to proceed to achieve some measure of success with the general treatment targets before addressing the treatment targets specific to diabetes. These general treatment targets for borderline pathology in families include: establishing healthy boundaries, increasing coherence, and reducing chaotic and injurious behavior. Only then does it make sense to address the treatment targets specific to diabetes patients and their families with borderline pathology: treatment adherence with diet, exercise, blood monitoring, medication, and so on. For it is only when chaos is reduced, adequate boundaries are established, and a reasonable degree of coherence is achieved that it is reasonable to switch the treatment focus to specific diabetes targets.

Concluding Note

It has been noted that when patients with diabetes are identified as "difficult to treat" it is quite likely that patients, and often their families, meet criteria for a severe personality disorder. When this disorder involves borderline pathology, treatment nonadherence and poor response to medical treatment are commonly observed. Since medical personnel are not trained to deal effectively with diabetics and their families with borderline pathology, counselors and family therapists with knowledge and experience in working with such pathology can provide invaluable clinical experience. It has been argued that individual and family therapy must first focus on general treatment targets for borderline pathology before endeavoring to achieve treatment targets specific to diabetes such as increasing treatment adherence with diet, exercise, blood monitoring, or medication.

References

American Diabetes Association. (2007). *Annual review of diabetes.* New York, NY: Author.

Beavers, W., & Hampson, R. (1990). *Successful families: Assessment and intervention.* New York, NY: Norton.

Feifer, C., & Tansman, M. (1999). Promoting psychology in diabetes primary care. *Professional Psychology: Research and Practice, 30*(1), 14–21.

Gonder-Frederick, L. A., Cox, D. J., & Ritterband, L. M. (2002). Diabetes and behavioral medicine. *Journal of Consulting and Clinical Psychology, 70*(3), 611–625.

Hampson, R., & Beavers, W. (2004). Observational assessment of couples and families. In L. Sperry (Ed.), *Assessment of couples and families: Contemporary and cutting-edge strategies* (pp. 91–116). New York, NY: Routledge.

Harper, R. (2004). *Personality-guided therapy in behavioral medicine.* Washington, DC: American Psychological Association.

Hoffman, R. P. (2001). Eating disorders in adolescents with type 1 diabetes. *Postgraduate Medicine, 109*(4), 67–74.

Howells, L., Wilson, A. C., Skinner, T. C., Newton, R., Morris, A. D., & Greene, S. A. (2002). A randomized control trial of the effect of negotiated telephone support on glycaemic control in young people with Type 1 diabetes. *Diabetic Medicine, 19,* 643–648.

Kresiman, J., & Kreisman, J. (2004). Marital and family treatment of borderline personality disorder. In M. MacFarlane (Ed.), *Family treatment of personality disorders: Advances in clinical practice* (pp. 117–148). New York, NY: Haworth Press

Millon, T. (1999). *Personality guided therapy.* New York: NY: Wiley.

Redman, B. K. (2004). *Patient self-management of chronic disease: The health care provider's challenge.* Sudbury, MA: Jones & Bartlett.

Rydall, A. C., Rodin, G. M., Olmstead, M. P., Devenyi, R. G., & Daneman, D. (1997). Disordered eating behavior and microvascular complications in young women with insulin-dependent diabetes mellitus. *New England Journal of Medicine, 336,* 1849–1854.

Snoek, F. J., & Skinner, T. C. (2002). Psychological counseling in problematic diabetes: Does it help? *Diabetic Medicine, 19*(4), 265–273.

Sperry, L. (2003). *Handbook of diagnosis and treatment of DSM-IV-TR personality disorders* (2nd ed.). New York, NY: Brunner/Mazel.

Sperry, L. (2006). *Psychological treatment of chronic illness: The biopsychosocial therapy approach.* Washington, DC: APA Books.

Sperry, L. (2009). *Treatment of chronic medical conditions: Cognitive-behavioral therapy strategies and integrative treatment protocols.* Washington, DC: APA Books.

Williams, M. M., Clouse, R. E., & Lustman, P. (2006). Treating depression to prevent diabetes and its complications: Understanding depression as a medical risk factor. *Clinical Diabetes, 24*(2), 79–86.

20

SYSTEMIC LUPUS ERYTHEMATOSUS[1]

Systemic lupus erythematosus (SLE), sometimes referred to as lupus, is an autoimmune disease in which antibodies attack healthy tissue. Affected individuals typically experience such symptoms as joint and muscle pain, skin rash, fatigue, mouth ulcers, hair loss, and weight loss (Moses, Wiggers, Nicholas, & Cockburn, 2005). SLE can affect any body system including the skin, joints, kidney, heart, lungs, nervous system, blood, and other organs or systems (Giffords, 2003). Pain and fatigue are some of the most difficult and dispiriting symptoms that SLE patients endure (Sohng, 2003).

As a chronic medical condition, SLE is characterized by an uncertain prognosis, an uncertain course, and is significantly impacted by and significantly impacts individual and family dynamics. Accordingly, a biopsychosocial perspective provides a unique insight into this disease as well as integrative treatments that can reduce its physical, psychological, and family and interpersonal effects (Sperry, 2006). This chapter describes SLE in terms of its biopsychosocial features, with an emphasis on individual, couple, and family dynamics. Since psychological interventions are central to effective integrative treatment, these dynamics can be addressed in individual and couples counseling. A case example illustrates these points.

Medical Aspects of SLE

Besides SLE, there are three other types of lupus erythematosus. The first is discoid lupus erythematosus, a chronic skin disorder in which a red, raised rash appears on the face, scalp, or elsewhere. The second type is subacute cutaneous lupus erythematosus, a milder disease characterized

---

1. Adapted from Sperry, L. (2011). Systemic lupus erythematosus: The impact of individual, couple, and family dynamics. *The Family Journal: Counseling and Therapy with Couples and Families,* *19,* 328–332.

by skin lesions that appear on parts of the body exposed to sun. The third is drug-induced lupus which is caused by medications and which presents with symptoms similar to SLE. Approximately 1.5 million Americans experience some type of lupus erythematosus, of which 70% or 1 million suffer from SLE (Giffords, 2003). This chapter addresses SLE only.

In addition to being the most common, SLE is the most devastating disease and challenging illness of the four types. It is also a perplexing disease in that the course and symptom can vary greatly from one patient to another. Symptoms can range from mild to severe and may come and go over time, and for many, SLE is characterized by periods of exacerbation of symptoms, called flares, and periods of remission. Nevertheless, for some the experience of SLE is that of mild disease with little variation. For others, it is a more severe disease with little variation (Sperry, 2009). Yet, for others it is a progressively worsening disease that waxes and wanes.

There are, however, some common symptoms which characterize this condition: painful or swollen joints (arthritis), unexplained fever, and extreme fatigue, a characteristic red skin rash across the nose and cheeks, the so-called butterfly (malar) rash; chest pain upon deep breathing; unusual loss of hair; pale or purple fingers or toes from cold or stress (i.e., Raynaud's phenomenon); sensitivity to the sun; swelling in legs or around eyes; mouth ulcers; swollen glands; and extreme fatigue. Other symptoms include chest pain, hair loss, anemia, and mouth ulcers. Some patients experience headaches, dizziness, depression, confusion, or seizures. New symptoms may continue to appear years after the initial diagnosis, and different symptoms can occur at different times (Sperry, 2009).

SLE is a complex disease, and its cause is unknown. There has been much speculation about causes, triggers, and exacerbants. It is likely that a combination of genetic, environmental, and possibly hormonal factors work together to cause the disease. No specific "SLE gene" has yet to be identified, but studies suggest that several different genes may be involved in determining an individual's vulnerability and likelihood for developing the disease, as well as which tissues and organs will be affected, and the severity of disease. Some have suggested that certain toxins may be causal. Cigarette smoke exposes a vulnerable individual to upwards of 400 toxins and, according to one meta-analysis, may be causally linked to SLE (Costenbader et al., 2004). Furthermore, certain factors are believed to trigger SLE. These include: stress, sunlight, certain drugs, and viruses. It is likely that a number of factors are involved in the expression of the disease.

A distinctive feature of this medical condition is that the diagnosis process is often difficult and lengthy. In other words, establishing a formal diagnosis of SLE may not be made for quite some time after symptoms are first brought to a physician. In the past a diagnosis of SLE might take from

5 to 7 years. More recently, the time frame has shortened, largely because of advances in diagnostic assessment. Today, the average time period for a diagnosis of SLE ranges from 1 to 3 years (Giffords, 2003). Needless to say, this delay can be frustrating and distressing for both patients and family members.

Gender and Cultural Factors

For reasons not fully understood, 9 out of 10 people with SLE are women. While SLE can occur at any time throughout the lifecycle, its incidence during the childbearing years is 10 to 15 times higher. Premenopausal women with lupus appear to be at increased risk of other diseases such as diabetes mellitus, familial hypercholesterolemia, and polycystic ovary syndrome (Manzi et al., 1997). Women with lupus ages 35 to 44 were over 50 times more likely to have a myocardial infarction than women without lupus and there also may be increased risk of angina (Manzi et al., 1997), which is likely due to both treatment and disease factors. The significant factors appeared to be older age at lupus diagnosis, longer lupus disease duration, longer corticosteroid use, hypercholesterolemia, and postmeno- pausal status. While SLE may affect white women, it is two to three times more common in African American, Latina, Asian, and Native American women (Giffords, 2003). Genetic factors may influence the frequency of occurrence, with Asian ethnicities more commonly affected (Ebert, Chap- man, & Shoenfeld, 2005). Interestingly, SLE can run in families, but the risk is rather low.

Prognosis

At present, there is no cure for SLE. However, it can be effectively treated and managed, and most individuals with the disease can lead active, healthy lives. Most SLE patients (78%) reported that they are coping well with their illness. Pain (65%), lifestyle changes (61%), and emotional problems associated with the illness (50%) are the most difficult factors for coping with SLE. With appropriate medical care and self-management 80 to 90% of those with it can expect to live a normal life span (Sperry, 2009). Considering the morbidity and mortality of SLE, some patients adapt and manage quite well considering the lessened quality of life often associated with having a painful and potentially fatal disease.

Individual Dynamics in SLE

Individual dynamics in SLE include medical and psychiatric comorbidi- ties as well as illness representations. Premenopausal women with lupus appear to be at increased risk of other diseases such as: diabetes mellitus, familial hypercholesterolemia, and polycystic ovary syndrome (Manzi et al., 1997). Women with lupus may also be at increased risk of myocardial infarction and angina (Manzi et al., 1997). Manzi et al. (1997) found that women with lupus who were 35 to 44 years of age were over 50 times more likely to have a myocardial infarction than women without lupus. This is likely due to both treatment and disease factors. The significant factors appeared to be older age at lupus diagnosis, longer lupus disease duration, longer corticosteroid use, hypercholesterolemia, and postmenopausal status. Psychological distress is common in SLE patients and anxiety and depression are common in this population (Walker et al., 2000; Moses et al., 2005). Other comorbidities include lupus psychosis and headache. While half of SLE patients studied experienced emotional problems as a result of SLE, some 15 to 60% developed depression. Nevertheless, anxiety appears to be a greater concern for SLE patients than is depression (Segui et al., 2000).

Illness Representations

The term *illness representation* refers to an individual's constellations of perceptions and beliefs about a particular disease; his or her understanding of it and its symptoms, cause, time or illness duration, impact or consequences, curability, and ability to control it. Illness representations in SLE tend to be sensitive predictors of treatment compliance, treatment outcomes, and well-being. Recent research demonstrates three clinically relevant considerations. First, beliefs about ability to control SLE are key to effective treatment compliance. Second, illness representations change over time. And, third, clinicians can effectively work with patients to modify their beliefs about control of SLE (Sperry, 2009).

Goodman and colleagues (Goodman, Morrissey, Graham, & Bossingham, 2005a) identified the illness representations of SLE patients using a semistructured interview informed by the self-regulatory model (Leventhal, Diefenbach, & Leventhal, 1992). Noteworthy was that beliefs about ability to control one's SLE are important in treatment compliance and clinical outcomes. They also found that over time illness representations did in fact change for various reasons. The implications of these findings is that clinicians should be prepared for the likelihood of changes in the illness representations over the course of their patients' illness, as this could be helpful in informing interventions for such patients (Goodman et al., 2005a). Another study by Goodman and colleagues (2005b) addressed treatment interfering with illness representations. They particularly focused on patients' beliefs about their inability to control their SLE condition and symptoms, and they developed an intervention for changing such beliefs.

Couple and Family Dynamics in SLE

As with other chronic illnesses, marital discord, separation, and divorce are not uncommon in SLE. Because of the protracted time lag between symptom expression and SLE diagnosis, family dynamics—particularly marital conflict—are commonly associated with this disorder. Karasz and Ouellette (1995) studied women with lupus and reported that disease severity is linked to psychological distress when there is a strain on valued social roles. They suggest that clinicians find ways to help SLE patients maintain their valued roles, especially with regard to family and work. Another study found that the social support needs of some SLE patients were not being adequately met by family members (Moses et al., 2005). The employment capacity of SLE patients varies, but the lack of employment or underemployment and subsequent financial stressors on SLE patients can exacerbate a couple's relational concerns (Moses et al., 2005).

Individual, Couples, and Family
Treatment Considerations in SLE

The treatment of SLE is typically a collaborative effort between the patient and several types of health care clinicians: family physicians or internists, rheumatologists, clinical immunologists, nephrologists, hematologists, dermatologists, neurologists, as well as nurses, psychologists, mental health counselors, and social workers (Sperry, 2009). The range and effectiveness of treatments for SLE have increased dramatically, giving clinicians more choices in managing the disease. It is important for the patient to work closely with clinicians and take an active role in self-managing the disease.

Because the variability of SLE course and severity is greater than any other chronic illness, SLE requires a tailored treatment approach. Since SLE patients are not a homogenous group, these patients benefit from targeted strategies that account for their individual psychosocial and behavioral responses to pain. Disease severity appears to be a useful focus for targeting treatment to patients (Moses et al., 2005). Measures that are helpful in planning tailored treatment include psychosocial and behavioral adaptation assessments which provide data on distress due to pain, relationship difficulties, and limitations on activity (Greco, Rudy, & Manzi, 2003). Treatments to be tailored include coping skills training, cognitive restructuring, increasing self-esteem, breathing and relaxation exercises, social problem solving, communication-skills training, and individual, group, and family therapy (Rinaldi et al., 2006). Specific treatment consideration includes illness representations, family dynamics and social support, quality of life, and diagnosis.

A recently reported randomized control study of 122 SLE patients and their partners, provided patients in the treatment group with a 1-hour intervention about self-efficacy, couples communication about lupus, social support, and problem solving followed by monthly phone follow-up for 6 months. The control group received an attention placebo, a 45-minute video about lupus, and monthly phone calls. It was reported that the treatment group scored higher in couple communication, self-efficacy, and mental health status, as well as lower fatigue scores. Although there was no effect on disease progression this study suggests that this couples intervention has considerable therapeutic value (Karlson et al., 2004). The take home message for couples and family counselors is that psychoeducation involving problem solving and communication skills can be a useful adjunctive intervention with couples dealing with SLE.

Case Illustration

Wendy and Bob J. had been married some 7 years and experienced relational difficulties for the past 2 years. That coincided with Wendy's diagnosis and the beginning of her treatment for SLE. It is noteworthy that her diagnosis was made during the course of fertility treatments she had been undergoing for some 3 years. The couple's hopes and plans for a family seemed to all but disappear as her illness was diagnosed and appeared to take center stage in their lives. Even though her doctors told her that she had a milder form of the disease, Wendy intermittently experienced severe joint pain and headaches, along with chronic fatigue. Most of the time she had little energy to do even routine chores, and it soon became clear that continuing with her professional work was becoming all but impossible. On the advice of her physician, she had resigned her elementary school teaching position a year and a half ago. She could still do basic things such as preparing meals and light cleanup but she could not do much more. Nevertheless, there were days when she felt energetic enough to think she was actually getting better and would set out to take on tasks she had easily accomplished in the past. Inevitably, she would overdo it and exacerbate her condition.

Although relational discord occurred occasionally before the diagnosis, it predictably had increased as Wendy's symptoms worsened and were exacerbated by various demands in the home and in the relationship. Although Wendy had largely accepted her illness, Bob had not. On the one hand, he accepted the doctor's assessment that SLE would limit Wendy's functioning, but on the other hand, he expected that she would continue to do many things for him that he had become accustomed to in the past. Her submissive style and lack of assertive communication only seemed to compound matters.

The couple was referred by Wendy's physician for couples counseling to a counselor with training and experience in health-focused psychotherapy and couples counseling. The counselor quickly recognized that Wendy's illness not only impaired her functioning but also magnified the influence of her personal style of submissiveness on relational dynamics which predictably had negatively impacted their functioning as a couple. Her illness representations were elicited by means of the Illness Perception Questionnaire-Revised (Moss-Morris et al., 2002). She gave highest ratings to the following personal items: that her illness didn't make any sense to her, that her efforts would have no effect on the outcome of her illness, and that there was nothing she could do to help her condition. Her ratings were equally high for the following relational items: that SLE caused difficulty for those close to her, and that her illness strongly affected the way others viewed her. In short, she experienced SLE as very disempowering to herself and her marriage. It also became clear that Bob had little understanding of the psychosocial and relational impact of SLE. Like Wendy he experienced it as disempowering to their marriage.

The counselor also noted that Wendy had only partially accepted her illness and that she seemed to be continually looping between the chronic illness phases of crisis and stabilization without ever progressing to the phases of resolution and integration. When queried about her depression, she reported some vegetative symptoms such as insomnia and decreased appetite but attributed these to her medications. She denied suicidal ideation but, with some embarrassment, revealed that she never really took the antidepressant because of what she had heard in the media about sexual side effects. She did admit that she pushed herself hard at work "to remain competitive" but was concerned that she couldn't handle stress like she had when she was in her 20s.

Three therapeutic goals were mutually set. The first goal was to use conjoint sessions to increase the couple's understanding of SLE as a chronic, progressive illness. Individual sessions were also indicated to therapeutically process Wendy's negative illness perceptions and increase acceptance of her illness. The second goal was to better understand their personal and interpersonal dynamics and the interplay and impact of SLE on them as individuals and as a couple. The third goal was to modify their relational pattern vis-à-vis the challenge of the chronic illness they both faced.

The case demonstrates that a chronic illness like SLE can and does impact individual and couple functioning while also magnifying the influence of the individual dynamics of one or both spouses. In this instance, Wendy's submissive and nonassertive style amplified the effects of her chronic illness, which together served to increase relational discord. Wendy's disempowering illness perceptions and lack of illness acceptance further complicated matters. Couples counseling facilitated an exploration of the thoughts, behaviors, feelings, and expectations of each spouse in a nonthreatening manner. Furthermore, the strategy "surfaced" the unrealistic expectations that each spouse had for the other in a way that engendered little or no resistance. It is also noteworthy that Bob's recognition of his unrealistic expectations of Wendy would likely reduce his resistance to accepting her illness, something that has heretofore fueled their relational discord.

Concluding Note

SLE is a chronic medical condition which can significantly impact individual patients and their families. Like other chronic medical conditions, SLE has significant psychosocial features and sequellae, which are far more prevalent than behavioral and psychiatric disorders combined. Therefore, it is incumbent on family counselors and other mental health professionals to become more knowledgeable and better equipped to effectively deal with these chronic medical conditions because it is the rare counseling client who does not have at least one comorbid chronic medical condition. The case example illustrates how a counselor can utilize individual and couples therapeutic interventions to increase illness acceptance, modify illness perceptions, and reduce relational discord, while increasing health and well-being.

References

Costenbader, K., Kim, D., Peerzada, J., Lockman, S., Nobles-Knight, D., Petri, M., & Karlson, E. (2004). Cigarette smoking and the risk of systemic lupus erythematosus: A meta-analysis. *Arthritis & Rheumatism, 50*(3), 849–857.

Ebert, T., Chapman, J., & Shoenfeld, Y. (2005). Anti-ribosomal P-protein and its role in psychiatric manifestations of systemic lupus erythematosus: Myth or reality? *Lupus, 14*, 571–575.

Giffords, E. (2003). Understanding and managing systemic lupus erythematosus (SLE). *Journal of Social Work in Health Care, 37*, 57–72.

Goodman, D., Morrissey, S., Graham, S., & Bossingham, D. (2005a). Illness representations of systemic lupus erythematosus. *Qualitative Health Research, 15*, 606–619.

Goodman, D., Morrissey, S., Graham, S., & Bossingham, D. (2005b). The application of cognitive-behaviour therapy in altering illness representations of systemic lupus erythematosus. *Behaviour Change, 22*, 156–171.

Greco, C., Rudy, T., & Manzi, S. (2003). Adaptation to chronic pain in systemic lupus erythematosus: Applicability of the multidimensional pain inventory. *Pain, 4*, 39–50.

Karasz, A., & Ouellette, S. (1995). Role strain and psychological well-being in women with systemic lupus erythematosus. *Women & Health, 23*(3), 41–49.

Karlson, E., Liang, M., Eaton, H., Huang, J., Fitzgerald, L., Rogers, M., & Daltroy, L. (2004). A randomized clinical trial of a psychoeducational intervention to improve outcomes in systemic lupus erythematosus. *Arthritis & Rheumatism, 50*(6) 1832–1841

Leventhal, H., Diefenbach, M., & Leventhal, E. (1992). Illness cognition: Using common sense to understand treatment adherence and affect cognition interactions. *Cognitive Therapy and Research, 16*, 143–163.

Manzi, S., Meilahn, E., Rairie, J., Conte, C., Medsger, T., Jansen-McWilliams, L., … Kuller, L. (1997). Age specific incidence rates of myocardial infarction and angina in women with systemic lupus erythematosus: Comparison with the Framingham Study. *American Journal of Epidemiology, 145*(5), 408–415.

Moses, N., Wiggers, J., Nicholas, C., & Cockburn, J. (2005). Prevalence and correlates of perceived unmet needs of people with systemic lupus erythematosus. *Patient Education and Counseling, 57,* 30–38.

Moss-Morris, R., Weinman, J., Petrie, K. J., Horne, R., Cameron, L. D., & Buick, D. (2002). The Revised Illness Perception Questionnaire (IPQ-R). *Psychology and Health, 17,* 1–16.

Rinaldi, S., Ghisi, M., Iaccarino, L, Zampieri, S., Girardello, A., Piercarlo, S., ... Doria, A. (2006). Influence of coping skills on health-related quality of life in patients with systemic lupus erythematosus. *Arthritis & Rheumatism, 55,* 427–433.

Segui, J., Ramos-Casals, M., Garcia-Carrasco, M., de Flores, T., Cerver, R., Valdes, M., ... Ingelmo, M. (2000). Psychiatric and psychological disorders in patients with systemic lupus erythematosus: A longitudinal study of active and inactive stages of the disease. *Lupus, 9,* 584–588.

Sohng, K.-Y. (2003). Effects of a self-management course for patients with systemic lupus erythematosus. *Journal of Advanced Nursing, 42*(5), 479–486.

Sperry, L. (2006). *Psychological treatment of chronic illness: A biopsychosocial therapy approach.* Washington, DC: American Psychological Association.

Sperry, L. (2009). *Treatment of chronic medical conditions.* Washington, DC: American Psychological Association.

Walker, S., Smarr, K., Parker, J., Weidensaul, D., Nelson, W., & McMurray, R. (2000). Mood states and disease activity in patients with systemic lupus erythematosus treated with bromocriptine. *Lupus, 9,* 527–533.

Part III

INTEGRATED BEHAVIORAL HEALTH

Competence and Training

21

COMPETENCE[1]

Competence is an increasingly common term in professional parlance these days, irrespective of whether the profession is law, medicine, management, psychology, or counseling. Competence is increasingly discussed in the clinical sphere, the ethical sphere, and particularly, the cultural sphere. Professionals are increasingly expected to provide services that are clinically, ethically, and culturally competent. Whether the professional counselor provides services to individuals, couples, or families, competent practice is expected. This is particularly indicated when medical conditions are the focus of counseling or consultation. Accordingly, clinicians would do well to consider the implications of clinical, ethical, and cultural competence in their work. This chapter describes these areas of competence and their components and illustrates them with case material. It should be noted that this chapter focuses on overall competence and not specific competencies. For example, developing an effective case conceptualization or establishing an effective therapeutic relationship are both specific competencies that reflect overall clinical competence.

This chapter begins with descriptions and definitions of clinical, ethical, and cultural competence, as well as their requisite components. Next, it discusses the interrelatedness of the three. Then, a case example is provided that illustrates clinical, ethical, and cultural competence in counseling and consulting with individuals and families, particularly when a medical condition is present.

Clinical, Ethical, and Cultural Competence: Descriptions and Definitions

This section briefly describes and defines clinical, ethical, and cultural competence, in the process distinguishing the components of each

---

1. Adapted from Sperry, L. (2011). Culturally, clinically, and ethically competent practice with individual and families dealing with medical conditions. *The Family Journal: Counseling and Therapy for Couples and Families, 19*, 212–216.

competence: knowledge, awareness, and sensitivity. A case example illustrates clinical, ethical, and cultural competence.

Clinical Competence

The components of clinical competence include clinical knowledge, clinical awareness, and clinical sensitivity. Briefly, clinical knowledge is acquaintance with the clinical facts of a medical, psychological, or relational condition as well as general diagnostic and treatment considerations. Clinical awareness builds on clinical knowledge and involves the capacity to recognize a clinical problem or issue in a specific client situation. Clinical sensitivity is an extension of clinical awareness and involves the capacity to anticipate likely consequences of the clinical condition in a specific situation and to respond empathically. Clinical competence is essentially an extension of clinical sensitivity. As such, it involves the capacity to provide appropriate and effective action in a given situation.

Effective professional practice, including counseling practice, involves much more than clinical knowledge and clinical awareness; it requires clinical sensitivity and clinical competence. While clinical knowledge is theory-based and categorized by clinical signs and symptoms, clinical sensitivity and competence involves a response to the signs and symptoms as well as the human vulnerability manifest in the client experiencing those signs and symptoms (Nortvedt, 2001).

Consider the following situation. An elderly Asian female patient had undergone thoracic surgery the day before and had complained of considerable pain that evening. Upon entering the patient's room the next morning, the surgeon was instantly struck by the uneasiness expressed in the patient's face and body. She looked exhausted and uncomfortable, with facial grimaces, but said nothing. Yet, she attempted, with considerable difficulty, to bow her head in recognition of the surgeon's social status. Before the surgeon said anything and before he queried the patient or did a brief physical exam, he is immediately worried about the patient's status, particularly the likelihood of a progressing pneumothorax (i.e., a collapsing lung). Facial expressions speak volumes. The patient's expression of distress and discomfort immediately signaled several clinically relevant questions about the previous surgery and the focus of the subsequent physical exam that would follow. Empathically, the surgeon responded to the patient's distress and cultural demeanor by soft speech and a gentle touch of her hand in anticipation that the pneumothorax might have to be quickly reversed.

In this example, clinical sensitivity is sensitivity regarding the patient, her illness, and her culture. This sensitivity reflects clinical knowledge and awareness of the patient's condition as well as cultural factors. The clinician's knowledge about the patient's illness and subsequent therapeutic interventions will be significantly influenced by the realities of a patient's condition and situation and the surgeon's clinical competence. This is because the patient's vulnerability, including her pain, suffering, and discomfort, are value-laden. It has been said that "sensitivity to the moral realities of a patient's clinical condition might reveal important and medically significant changes in the patient's clinical condition" (Nortvedt, 2001, p. 26).

Ethical Competence

The components of ethical competency include ethical knowledge, ethical awareness, and ethical sensitivity. Briefly, ethical knowledge is acquaintance with ethical principles, codes, and guidelines. Ethical awareness builds on ethical knowledge and the capacity to recognize an ethical consideration or issue in a specific client situation (Sperry, 2007). Ethical sensitivity is an extension of ethical awareness and involves the capacity to anticipate likely consequences of a particular ethical consideration and to respond empathically (Sperry, 2010a). Ethical competence is essentially an extension of ethical sensitivity. As such, it involves the capacity to provide appropriate and effective action in a given situation.

As with clinical competence, the ethically competent professional can anticipate possible scenarios and consequences, and respond both empathically and in a clinically competent manner (Rest, 1994). Unfortunately, survey data suggests that a sizeable percentage of trainees and experienced mental health professionals fail to exhibit ethical sensitivity, much less high levels of it (Fleck-Hendersen, 1995). By extrapolation, it could be concluded that ethical competence is similarly deficient in these individuals.

Cultural Competence

The components of cultural competence include cultural knowledge, cultural awareness, and cultural sensitivity. Briefly, cultural knowledge is acquaintance with facts about ethnicity, social class, acculturation, religion, gender, and age (Sue & Sue, 2003). Cultural awareness builds on cultural knowledge plus the capacity to recognize a cultural problem or issue in a specific client situation. Cultural sensitivity is an extension of cultural awareness and involves the capacity to anticipate likely consequences of a particular cultural problem or issue and to respond empathically (Sperry, 2010a). Cultural competence is essentially an extension of cultural sensitivity (Goh, 2005). It is the capacity to translate the counselor's cultural sensitivity into action that results in an effective therapeutic relationship and treatment process which in turn result in positive treatment outcomes (Paniagua, 2005). In short, it is the capacity to provide appropriate and effective action in a given situation.

Table 21.1 Clinical, Ethical, and Cultural Competency: Components and Definitions

Components	Definitions
Clinical Knowledge	Acquaintance with clinical facts of a condition
Clinical Awareness	Clinical knowledge (+) recognize it in a specific client situation
Clinical Sensitivity	Clinical awareness (+) anticipate consequences and respond appropriately
Clinical Competence	Clinical sensitivity (+) take appropriate and effective clinical action
Ethical Knowledge	Acquaintance with ethical principles, codes, and guidelines
Ethical Awareness	Ethical knowledge (+) recognize it in a specific client situation
Ethical Sensitivity	Ethical awareness (+) anticipate consequences and respond appropriately
Ethical Competence	Ethical sensitivity (+) take appropriate and effective ethical action
Cultural Knowledge	Acquaintance with facts about ethnicity, acculturation, social class, etc.
Cultural Awareness	Cultural knowledge (+) recognize it in a specific client situation
Cultural Sensitivity	Cultural awareness (+) anticipate consequences and respond appropriately
Cultural Competence	Cultural sensitivity (+) take appropriate and effective action

Table 21.1 summarizes this discussion with brief definitions of clinical, ethical, and cultural competence.

The Interrelatedness of Clinical, Ethical, and Cultural Competence

Most research and publications on clinical competence, ethical competence, and cultural competence considers these three as separate entities. This section suggests that they are, in fact, interrelated.

Clinical competence and expertise or mastery is an important area of counseling practice as well as counseling research (Jennings, Goh, Skovholt, Hanson, & Banerjee-Stevens, 2003; Skovholt & Jennings, 2005). Achieving clinical competency has been described as a process that involves mastery in the three related domains—cognitive, emotional, and relational—that are vital to the success or failure of therapists and counselors (Jennings, Hanson, Skovholt, & Grier, 2005).

Training culturally competent counselors is essential for effective counseling practice (Sue & Sue, 2003). This sentiment is reflected in the standards of the Council for the Accreditation of Counseling and Related Educational Programs (CACREP; 2009). A key requirement is that CACREP accredited programs provide students with training and knowledge in working with culturally diverse clients. There is increasing recognition that developing clinical competency or expertise should occur in the context of striving for cultural competence. While both clinical and cultural competency have too often been investigated rather independently of each other, they have been shown to be closely interrelated (Goh, 2005). An interesting description of the closeness of their interrelatedness is: "The presence of multicultural competence is *synonymous* [emphasis added] with general counseling competence" (Coleman, 1998, p. 153).

Just as clinical competency is too often considered as separate from cultural competency, clinical and cultural competency are too often separated from ethical competency. But viewed from a larger perspective, culturally competent counseling can and should occur in the context of ethically competent practice (Arredondo & Toporek, 2004). As noted earlier, basic to ethical competence is the principle that the counselor's primary responsibility is to respect diversity and promote the client's welfare. This principle serves as a superordinate criterion for all decisions involving cultural and clinical matters. In short, clinical, cultural, and ethical competence are closely interrelated and highly effective practice requires that they be demonstrated simultaneously (Sperry, 2011).

In short, there is an intimate interrelationship between clinical, ethical, and cultural competence. Accordingly, competence in one area without competence in the other two can be problematic. Clinical competence is a necessary condition for effective professional practice, but it is seldom a sufficient condition, and that is because ethical and cultural competence are also necessary conditions. The following example illustrates this interrelatedness.

An emergency room physician concludes that a blood transfusion is needed to stabilize a 16-year-old patient injured in a motorcycle accident who is becoming "shocky" because of blood loss. The patient, who had been present to person, place, and time, is now drifting in and out of consciousness. In talking with the patient's family the physician learns that both the patient and family are Christian Scientists. While he had originally considered seeking the family's written consent for a blood transfusion, he anticipates that the family might object to a blood transfusion on religious grounds. A blood transfusion is the gold standard for treatment of shock caused by blood loss, but because there is a likelihood that it is incompatible with the patient's cultural (i.e., religious) beliefs, he proceeds tentatively. Instead of attempting to "force" the transfusion, which would reflect cultural and ethical incompetence, he tells the family that while a blood transfusion is the treatment of choice, there is another option. The family opts for the alternative treatment strategy which is the administration of a volume expander (i.e., a blood substitute). This clinical action was effective and was well received by the family because it was culturally responsive. In addition to demonstrating cultural competence, the physician's clinical action also reflected clinical and ethical competence.

Implications for Counseling and Consulting with Individuals and Families

That clinical competence, ethical competence, and cultural competence are interrelated has implications and applications in counseling practice, particularly for counseling and consulting with individuals and families, and when working with individuals and families that are experiencing a medical condition.

Case Example. The following illustration is based on a case example appearing in an issue of *The Family Journal* (Sperry, 2010b). A brief summary of the case is followed by a commentary on the clinical, cultural, and ethical competence demonstrated by the counselor who consulted on the case.

Juanita H. is a 54-year-old married, first generation Mexican American female diagnosed with metastatic breast cancer. Following a mastectomy and removal of lymph nodes, she was to begin radiation and chemotherapy but this was delayed for nearly 4 months because of poor wound healing. She had become increasingly depressed after the surgery, and her husband, who had faithfully accompanied Juanita to all her medical appointment before her surgery was no longer coming. Tearfully, Juanita recounted that they had fought almost constantly since the surgery and that "Jose won't even touch me anymore." Juanita's physician was stymied by his patient's worsening condition and could not explain her poor postoperative course of infections and slow wound healing. He also was not able to appreciate cultural factors or the marital difficulties. Frustrated, he decided to seek consultation from Serafina Garcia, PhD, who is licensed as both a mental health counselor and as a marital and family therapist. She had considerable experience working with clients wherein cultural factors and marital issues exacerbated their medical conditions.

In their initial consultation, Dr. Garcia identified Juanita's level of acculturation as low, and that her belief that she could not afford medical treatment was not accurate, which presumably delayed the onset of medical treatment and allowed the fast growing cancer to metastasize. Rather, her illness perceptions were operative and "interfered "with effective treatment outcomes. These illness perceptions included: "having breast cancer means you are being punished by God" and "You are no longer a woman if you lose a breast." She also found that Juanita had experienced a low level of depression throughout most of her adult life, but it was exacerbated soon after Juanita's discovery of the small breast lump.

After the evaluation, Dr. Garcia discussed treatment recommendations with Juanita's physician. She indicated that Juanita was clinically depressed, but was probably not easily identified by other health professionals accustomed to prototypic DSM-IV presentations. Instead, Juanita experienced primarily somatic symptoms not uncommon in immigrants from Mexico. This untreated depression together with untreated marital conflict most likely accounted for the rapid proliferation of the cancer and the retarded wound healing. Accordingly, immediate evaluation for possible antidepressant treatment was recommended. Also recommended was individual and couples counseling because marital discord can also retard wound healing. Dr. Garcia offered to provide this treatment to address depressive and relational issues, both of which appeared to be culturally influenced.

Case Commentary

Dr. Garcia's consultation resulted in a biopsychosociocultural formulation that was considerably broader and more clinically useful than the physician's biomedical formulation that excluded essential cultural, couple, and family dynamics. Without such a comprehensive formulation, it is unlikely that another counselor-consultant would have achieved the same degree of clinical, cultural, and ethical sensitivity and competence as Dr. Garcia. In short, this case suggests that a comprehensive case formulation is a prerequisite for a high degree of clinical, cultural, and ethical sensitivity and competence.

Dr. Garcia's clinical competence is evident in her sensitive clinical evaluation of Juanita's medical-psychological status, illness perceptions, underlying depression, couple and family dynamics, and the influence of factors interfering with wound healing. It was not simply clinical knowledge or awareness that facilitated this expanded diagnostic and clinical formulation. Rather, it was also Dr. Garcia's capacity to identify likely consequences and respond with sufficient empathy to achieve an effective therapeutic alliance so that Juanita could more fully collaborate in the evaluation.

Dr. Garcia was also able to demonstrate cultural competence by quickly identifying Juanita's level of acculturation, the cultural presentation of Juanita's depression, and the cultural dynamics reflected in her illness perceptions, family dynamics, and marital discord. In addition, Dr. Garcia was able to offer a culturally sensitive treatment plan and provide culturally sensitive counseling that was tailored to Juanita's personal needs, and cultural and family circumstances.

Furthermore, Dr. Garcia was able to demonstrate ethical sensitivity in both respecting Juanita's ethnicity, acculturation, and social class, but also by promoting her welfare (Principle A.1.a of the ACA Ethics Code). By providing a consultation and also counseling that were both clinically sensitive and competent, as well as ethically sensitive, Dr. Garcia demonstrated ethical competence.

Concluding Note

While counseling theory and research typically considers clinical competence, ethical competence, and cultural competence as separate entities, counseling practice suggests that the three are intimately related. There is increasing awareness of the importance of the theoretical and practical value of these domains of competence, but obstacles persist in more fully implementing this awareness in counseling practice. A main obstacle is a lack of consensus on terminology with regard to distinctions and definitions. This article offers consistency in the definitions of clinical, ethical, and cultural competence and their components: knowledge, awareness, and sensitivity. These definitions and distinctions have been set forth in hopes of fostering dialogue which is an essential prerequisite for achieving consensus on these distinctions and definitions.

References

Arredondo, P., & Toporek, R. L. (2004). Multicultural counseling competencies = ethical practice. *Journal of Mental Health Counseling, 26,* 44–55.

Coleman, H. (1998). General and multicultural counseling competency: Apples and oranges? *Journal of Multicultural Counseling and Development, 26,* 147–156.

Council for the Accreditation of Counseling and Related Educational Programs. (2009). *The 2009 standards.* Alexandria, VA: Author.

Fleck-Hendersen, A. (1995). Ethical sensitivity: A theoretical and empirical study. *Dissertation Abstracts International, 56,* 2862B.

Goh, M. (2005). Cultural competence and master therapists: An inextricable relationship. *Journal of Mental Health Counseling, 27,* 71–81.

Jennings, L., Goh, M., Skovholt, T. M., Hanson, M., & Banerjee-Stevens, D. (2003). Multiple factors in the development of expert counselors and therapists. *Journal of Career Development, 30,* 59–72.

Jennings, L., Hanson, M., Skovholt, T., & Grier, T. (2005). Searching for mastery. *Journal of Mental Health Counseling, 27,* 19–31.

Nortvedt, P. (2001). Clinical sensitivity: The inseparability of ethical perceptiveness and clinical knowledge. *Scholarly Inquiry for Nursing Practice: An International Journal, 15,* 25–43.

Paniagua, F. (2005). *Assessing and treating cultural diverse clients: A practical guide.* Thousand Oaks, CA: Sage.

Rest, J. (1994). Background: Theory and research. In J. Rest & D. Narcvaez (Eds.), *Moral development in the professions: Psychology and applied ethics* (pp. 1–26). Hillsdale, NJ: Erlbaum.

Skovholt, T., & Jennings, L. (2005). Mastery and expertise in counseling. *Journal of Mental Health Counseling, 27,* 13–18.

Sperry, L. (2007). *The ethical and professional practice of counseling and psychotherapy.* Boston, MA: Allyn & Bacon.

Sperry, L. (2010a). Ethical sensitivity in Christian healthcare practice. *Journal of Christian Healing, 26,* 29–34.

Sperry, L. (2010b). Breast cancer, depression, culture, and marital conflict. *The Family Journal, 18,* 62–65.

Sperry, L. (2011). Culturally, clinically, and ethically competence practice with individual and families dealing with medical conditions. *The Family Journal: Counseling and Therapy for Couples and Families, 19,* 212–216.

Sue, D. W., & Sue, D. (2003). *Counseling the culturally diverse: Theory and practice* (4th ed.). New York, NY: John Wiley.

22

COMPETENCY-BASED TRAINING[1]

A paradigm shift is occurring in the training of health and mental health professionals today. It involves a shift in orientation from input-based to output- or outcomes-based instruction. Typically, counselor training programs that employ input-based or traditional instructional methods focus on mastery of knowledge through lectures, directed reading, discussion, and minimum client contact. Here learning is typically evaluated by examinations, term papers, and other written assignments (J. Miller, 2010). This contrasts with outcomes-based instruction with its focus on mastery of competencies through simulated counseling activities, coaching, client feedback, and reflection. Here learning is more likely to be evaluated with a demonstration of learned skills, rubrics, portfolios, and other forms of objective structured assessments. Furthermore, whereas input-based instruction is guided by core curriculum standards, outcomes-based instruction is guided by core competency standards (Sperry, 2010).

In the current era of accountability in health and mental health care, outcomes-based and competency-based learning is quickly becoming the norm for training competent professionals. This is not to imply that the input-based learning is no longer considered important and useful, but rather that it will assume a more limited role in the education and training of professional counselors. It is likely that certain required courses in graduate counseling programs, such as Legal and Ethical Issues in Counseling, Life Span Development, and Research Methods, will continue to be taught with largely input-based instructional methods. In contrast, clinically oriented courses, particularly prepracticum, practicum, and internship courses will be largely outcomes-based and competency-based training experiences.

---

1. Adapted from Sperry, L. (2012). Training counselors to work competently with individuals and families with health and mental health issues. *The Family Journal: Counseling and Therapy with Couples and Families, 20,* 196–199.

This chapter provides a detailed description of input-based instruction, followed by a detailed description of outcome-based instruction. Then, it illustrates how two courses required of mental health and family counseling students are taught from an input-based model and from an outcome-based model where health issues are involved. First, these two models of instruction and evaluation are compared and contrasted.

Contrasting Views of Instruction and Evaluations

A useful way of comparing and contrasting these two models of instruction is with G. Miller's (1990) pyramid and conceptualization of clinical competence. There are four progressive levels of competence in the pyramid. The first level, "knows," is the base of the pyramid and represents factual knowledge gained by reading and studying didactic materials. The second level, "knows how," represents the ability to use knowledge in a particular context. The third level, "shows how," reflects the trainee's capacity to appropriately interview and provide counseling intervention in a simulated or practice situation. The fourth level, "does," is the top of the pyramid and represents actual counseling practice in a real life setting (Van der Vleuten, 2000).

G. Miller's pyramid is also useful in comparing and contrasting the assessment and evaluation methods utilized in both instructional models. Input-based or traditional methods of assessment such as written tests and oral examinations can be quite useful in assessing "knows" and "knows how," but such indirect measures are too limited in assessing the higher levels of competence. Assessing counseling competence at the "shows how" and "does" levels is central in the outcome-based or competency model, but more direct and sophisticated methods of evaluation are required. For example, direct observations of counselor-trainees interviewing clients and providing counseling interventions is more appropriate and effective in evaluating the "shows how" level of competence, whereas assessment of the "does" level would involve evaluating an intern's overall counseling competence in live or videotaped supervision. In both instances, rubric-based evaluation can provide immediate and objective feedback. For counselor education programs, the challenge is to develop training strategies and assessment methods, particularly rubrics, to address the "shows how" level of competency.

Table 22.1 characterizes both the input-based and the outcomes-based training models in terms of goals, criterion, course delivery, and evaluation method. The following two sections describe and illustrate these models in considerable detail.

Table 22.1 Types of Instruction in the Education of Professional Counselors

Type	Input-Based and Knowledge-Based Instruction	Outcomes-Based and Competency-Based Instruction
Goal	To meet curricular objectives	To achieve core competencies
Criterion	Core curriculum and requirement-based	Competency-based
Course delivery	1. Lecture 2. Class discussion 3. Term paper or written assignments 4. Midterm and final examinations	1. Directed learning 2. Counseling simulations with feedback 3. Assigned simulated activities 4. Deliberate practice 5. Self-reflection 6. Continuous monitoring and evaluation
Evaluation	Input-based evaluation	Outcomes-based evaluation

Input-Based Instruction

Input-based instruction is the traditional mode of instruction characteristic of most graduate education, including counselor education, and continues for an extended period of time. Its basic goal is to meet course objectives in a core curriculum. As such it focuses primarily on the acquisition of knowledge and understanding which is the primary criterion, and secondarily on skill-acquisition. It is also a standards-based form of instruction. In the training of professional counselors a standards-based program prepares students for meeting the requirements of licensure or certification. This means a student is expected to achieve passing grades in designated courses. This is followed by meeting requirements for supervised experience and passing state or national licensing or certification exams. Licensure or certification is achieved after all these standards and specific requirements are met. In this model, the license or certificate holders are presumed to have achieved a minimal level of competence in a given professional specialty based on completion of specified requirements. Accordingly, they are deemed capable of the independent practice of a counseling specialty, which means direct supervision is no longer required. In recent years this assumption has been challenged.

The delivery of such input-oriented instruction presumes that a given input of knowledge and understanding is necessary to achieve competency. Accordingly, the primary mode of instruction is the direct delivery of instruction through a lecture format. The lecture format might consist of a formal delivered presentation alone or aided by overhead or PowerPoint slides. It could be video assisted or include a demonstration. Instructors who can deliver lecture material in an interesting and entertaining

208

manner are typically given high ratings by students. Class discussion is considered important in grounding the lecture material in the students' experience. Assigned activities such as required readings, term papers, and other written assignments are intended to complement and extend the instructor delivered material. Examinations, whether written or oral, are intended to assess knowledge acquisition. Input-based evaluation is given an air of respectability when course grades are quantifiable in terms of total points from exams, papers, and other assigned activities.

Illustration of Input-Based Training and Instruction

Following are examples of how two required counselor education courses are commonly taught from the perspective of an input-based model of instruction.

Psychopathology in Counseling. Basic to the delivery of this course are lectures, videos, and course readings on the parameters of psychopathology. The use and particularly the limitations of the medical model on which *DSM-IV-TR* is based are discussed. Considerable discussion occurs in many counselor education programs emphasizing the strengths-based focus of the counseling profession. This course typically focuses on the principal diagnostic categories: anxiety disorders, mood disorders, psychotic disorders, substance abuse disorders, eating disorders, and the personality disorders. The limitations are discussed. In training counselors to become sensitive to a client's health issues, students are taught the value of coding Axis III (medical conditions) of the *DSM*. The role of diagnosis and treatment options for counselors is discussed. Videotape that demonstrates the diagnostic features of these disorders are shown and discussed in general terms. A term paper on an approved topic involving a specific diagnostic condition is a major requirement. Students are expected to pass a midterm and final exam on diagnostic conditions. For all practical purposes the delivery of this course basically repeats the abnormal psychology course that many counseling students took as undergraduates.

Family Counseling. This course is lecture and discussion based. Lectures are enhanced with videotapes of various approaches and required readings. Family counseling is situated in relation to individual counseling, and its history and origins are articulated. Couples counseling as a type of family counseling is discussed and illustrated. The basic terminology and systems theory are explained and family dynamics and the family life cycle are described. An overview of family therapy approaches is provided with an emphasis on Adlerian, structural, strategic, object relations, cognitive behavioral, narrative, and solution-focused. In training counselors to become sensitive to the role and impact of health issues on family dynamics and functioning, appropriate case material is introduced and discussed. Videotapes of these various approaches are viewed in class followed by general discussion. A term paper on an approved topic is a major requirement. Successful completion of the course typically requires students to pass a knowledge-focused examination(s).

Outcomes-Based Instruction

Outcomes-based instruction, also called competency-based learning, is increasingly common in graduate programs as regional accrediting bodies and specialty accreditation standards have begun to require it. In this instruction model the goal is for students to achieve a level of sufficiency in both knowledge of counseling theory and in counseling skills and practice. The criterion for completing a graduate program is not simply knowledge acquisition as in the input-oriented model, but also a measurable level of competence in counseling practice at or above the minimal level of competence. It has been noted that the current competency movement is influencing licensure and certification boards to require applicants to demonstrate competence in counseling practice in addition to knowledge of counseling theory.

The delivery of outcomes-based instruction differs from input-oriented instruction. The difference ranges by degrees depending on the course. For instance, greater differences will be noted in prepracticum, practicum, and internship courses than in more didactic courses. The designation *directed learning* represents the main difference. Directed learning may include focused lectures, but it includes simulated activities that involve assessment of the learner's performance evaluation.

For example, in teaching the process of writing case conceptualizations the instructor may begin by defining and describing case conceptualizations and presenting examples of adequate and inadequate conceptualizations. This is followed by guidelines for developing an adequate conceptualization. Then graded case material (easy to more complex) is provided for which students follow the guidelines and draft a case conceptualization. Then the instructor reviews the student's draft and provides immediate feedback. In a prepracticum course, simulated counseling encounters can effectively promote the learning of specific counseling practice competencies. In dyads with one student in the counselor role and the other in the client role, the "client" presents with a scripted problem which is then processed by the "counselor" for 10 minutes. If the "counselor" gets stuck or off track the instructor provides immediate feedback evaluation in the form of coaching, and if no coaching is indicated, the instructor provides immediate feedback guided by a rubric which assesses the "counselor's" performance on observable criteria.

Other forms of delivery include assigned simulated activities which occur between class meetings. These may include case conceptualization exercises, diagnostic evaluation interviews, and simulated counseling encounters. Since research shows that deliberate practice and self-reflection significantly increase counseling practice competencies, these activities may be assigned. For example, practicum and internship students can be assigned to keep a journal in which they reflect on how they handled or could have handled given counseling challenges. From an outcomes-oriented perspective practicum and internship experiences offer trainees multiple opportunities to receive ongoing feedback of their counseling performance from supervisors, and from clients utilizing ultrabrief rating scales such as the Outcomes Rating Scale and Session Rating Scale (S. Miller, Duncan, Brown, Sorrell, & Chalk, 2006).

Illustration of Outcomes-Based Training and Instruction

Following are examples of how two required counselor education courses are commonly taught from the perspective of an outcomes-oriented, competency based model of instruction.

Psychopathology in Counseling. In addition to providing an overview of the anxiety disorders, mood disorders, psychotic disorders, substance abuse disorders, eating disorders, and the personality disorders, this course requires students to achieve a minimal level of sufficiency in conducting diagnostic evaluations, writing an initial evaluation report, and providing counseling interventions for specific diagnostic conditions. A basic directed learning strategy for achieving competence in assessing and diagnosing psychopathology is the use of selected videotapes that demonstrate effective diagnostic interviewing for specific diagnostic conditions. Before the video clip is shown, the diagnostic criteria for that condition are presented. While viewing the video students are asked to carefully observe how the diagnostic interview is conducted, to assess *DSM* criteria, and rule in and rule out other diagnostic considerations. Class discussion after the video focuses on identifying specific criteria elicited in the interview. Assigned simulated activities require students to achieve sufficiency in accurately utilizing the *DSM* and diagnosing 10 clinical cases. Specific written and verbal feedback reinforce this competency. Students are also expected to conduct two complete diagnostic evaluations and prepare an initial evaluation report following a protocol of 11 sections including presenting problem, mental status exam, case conceptualization including a cultural formulation, five axes *DSM* diagnoses, and a detailed treatment formulation and plan. These reports are rubric evaluated with specific feedback. The third competency involves implementing a counseling intervention for a specified diagnostic condition. Previously, transcriptions of earlier sessions of a simulated case have been enacted in class. Students then provide a transcription of a follow-up session which is rubric-evaluated. A final written examination involves two cases in which students evaluate case material and diagnose Axis I, II, and IV. Students also engage in self-reflection on their learning experience and log it. Since individual psychopathology is expressed within a family context, students are oriented to the Global Assessment of Relationship Functioning (GARF) scale by means of short video clips of the five ranges of family functioning and associated Axis I disorders. Like GAF, GARF can also be included in Axis V, and students are expected to do so.

Family Counseling.   In addition to providing an overview of the origins of family counseling and systems theory, this course requires students to achieve a minimal level of sufficiency in conducting family assessments and initiating family interventions. Assessment of family functioning and resilience is emphasized by means of the genogram, measures of family functioning, particularly family resilience, and the Beavers Interactional Scales. Trigger tapes are utilized to teach the use of a rating scale for family functioning, and case material is utilized to teach the correct use of the genogram. Family interventions are introduced with videotapes of the family therapy approaches: Adlerian, structural, strategic, object relations, cognitive behavioral, narrative, and solution-focused. Assigned simulated activities require students to assess four families using these methods and developing an assessment report with a systemic case conceptualization and treatment plan. Written reports of the family assessment are rubric-evaluated as is the brief class presentation of one of these assessments. Students also learn a method of coaching parents through simulation exercises. Then they utilize this method to coach two sets of the parents they have previously assessed. The cases are then written up and submitted along with the transcriptions of that coaching. The instructor then evaluates this material with the aid of rubrics which provide focused feedback to the student. Students present one of the reports and the transcription to the class.

Concluding Note

The shift from input-based to outcomes-based instruction is underway and will continue to gain momentum. Paradigm shifts are like that: new ways inevitably replace traditional and time-honored ways of doing things. Colleagues who have read the above descriptions of these two forms of course delivery report their surprise at how different course delivery and evaluation was for the two forms of instruction. Not surprisingly, because this shift involves significant changes in how courses are planned, delivered, and evaluated, these changes can be expected to engender discomfort, fear, and suspicion among some counselor educators and supervisors. Grieving the passing of the old ways of training counselors is to be expected. At the same time, the expectation is that there will be noticeable positive changes in student competence and confidence as they complete outcomes-based training and enter practice as licensed counselors or therapists.

References

Miller, G. (1990). The assessment of clinical skills/competence/performance. *Academic Medicine, 65*(9), 63–67.

Miller, J. (2010). Competency-based training: Using the objective structured clinical exercise (OSCE) in marriage and family therapy. *Journal of Marital and Family Therapy, 36,* 320–332.

Miller, S., Duncan, B., Brown, J., Sorrell, R., & Chalk, M. (2006). Using outcomes to inform and improve treatment outcomes: The partners for change outcomes management system. *Journal of Brief Therapy, 5,* 5–23.

Sperry, L. (2010). *Core competencies in counseling and psychotherapy: Becoming a highly competent and effective therapist.* New York, NY: Routledge

Van der Vleuten, C. (2000). Validity of final examinations in undergraduate medical training. *British Medical Journal, 321,* 1217–1219.

INDEX